EMERSON

The Wisest American

ALSO BY
Phillips Russell

BENJAMIN FRANKLIN
THE FIRST CIVILIZED
AMERICAN

JOHN PAUL JONES
MAN OF ACTION

RED TIGER
ADVENTURES IN
YUCATAN & MEXICO

EMERSON

THE WISEST AMERICAN

by Phillips Russell

New York
BRENTANO'S·PUBLISHERS
Mcmxxix

To

L. P. R.

CONTENTS

PORTRAITS

Ralph Waldo Emerson

PART ONE
Doubting Youth

Chapter One

I

IT happened to be Emerson's fifty-ninth birthday, part of which he spent pottering around the barnyard with his son Edward. Before he returned to the house, he decided to put the calf into its stall. The calf, a big heifer, resisted with that calm obstinacy which has often filled otherwise kindly owners of animals with vindictive red thoughts. The son grasped an ear, the father pushed diligently from behind, and together they tried to propel the animal into the barn. Emerson hated being heated like this; he often complained that outdoor activities drugged a scholar and unfitted him for his proper tasks; but he was not the man to forsake an undertaking once begun, and again he put his weight behind the animal. The heifer remained firm, rolling the whites of her eyes and breathing out through her moist nostrils a milky but stubborn odor.

Emerson paused and gazed upon the animal in bewilderment. The situation was unprecedented. He had read the philosophy of Plato and Plotinus, the science of Newton and Bacon, the poetry of Hafiz and Herbert, the teachings of Buddha and Confucius, the histories of Plutarch and the Sieur de Joinville, the memoirs of Goethe and Napoleon; only recently he had been through the *Études de la Nature* of Saint-Pierre; but none of them had said anything about

❖ 3 ❖

an effective and harmonious method of pushing a female calf into a barn. Emerson had no physical strength and sometimes lamented that he lacked that commanding presence which awes with an eye, a word; but one merit he possessed in abundance — persistence.

He therefore gave an encouraging signal to Edward, and once more they fell upon the animal. The heifer planted her splay feet and remained as before. The pale face of the sage reddened and perspiring beads gathered upon his high white forehead. And then an Irish servant girl came by. With an amused glance she thrust a finger into the animal's mouth, and the calf, seduced by this maternal imitation, at once followed her into the barn. Edward looked at his father and grinned; but Emerson was already absorbed in thought, his eyes fixed musingly upon the ground. He returned to the house and, after cleansing his hands of their hairy, bovine smell, recorded the incident in his journal, adding this telling declaration:

" I like people who can do things."

II

All his life Emerson admired, with an eye that kindled as it watched, people who could perform the needed, external actions of daily life. He read of crashing deeds with excitement, and the lives of the men of action filled him with exaltation. If they performed ably, he even found excuses for their crimes and deviltries. One of his heroes was Napoleon Bonaparte; more often than any other this name appears in Emerson's works, with the single exception of Shakespeare's, and one of the most lyric sketches in *Representative Men* deals with the Corsican, his love for whom Emerson tried to dissemble, at the end, by calling him " an impostor and a rogue."

In reading of deeds that he himself could not perform Emerson found what he regarded as one of heaven's own gifts — compensation. He could do so few practical, manual things himself. He could not multiply seven times nine with certainty. To face the packing of a trunk unnerved him, and his occasional spurts of outdoor labor, which he liked to think of as contributing to some great Whole, often left him exhausted and grievously unfitted him for writing such essays as *Farming*. He sometimes scorned himself for his love of bookish solitude, and drove himself out into the open, where with a spade he made a great show of establishing direct contact with the healing earth. But his elder son, little Waldo, " deep-eyed boy," was not deceived by these ostentatious labors. " Look out, father," he would say. " You'll dig your leg."

III

Near the house in Summer Street, Boston, where Emerson was born only three years after the opening of the nineteenth century, was the grassy Common. Around it lay pastures, wide fields, orchards, and a pond; the harbor front, with its odorous wharves, was not far away; but Emerson, " a spiritual-looking boy in blue nankeen," was not permitted to enjoy these enticements, which exist as if especially created for boyhood. He could take the cow to pasture, but he must come straight home again. He slid down none of the hills gloriously iced with frozen snow; he never had a sled. With the rough boys of the Round Point, who came through Summer Street on their way to riotous games upon the Common, he was not permitted to speak. In their battles with the freshly laundered West Enders he took no part. There is no record of his ever having been smitten healthfully upon the nose or received the bracing tonic of a black eye. When he played, he played indoors. An uncle said to him one day: " How is it, Ralph, that all the boys dislike you and quarrel with you, while the grown people are fond of you? "

From all the roughage which Nature seemingly intends shall be included in the diet of men as well as animals, young Emerson was kept apart. During his entire boyhood a barrier, frail but firm, stood between him and the gritty edges of quotidian life. It was composed of skirts, and they belonged to his aunt, his mother, and her friends. And what these pious women did for him, they did in the name of love. They were not only pious women: in their day they were wise, too; but wiser than they was the rhyming of Mother Goose, who knew that little boys, even Emersons, are made of snaps and snails, and puppy dogs' tails. It would have been better for their charge if they had read more of Mother Goose and less of theology.

Years afterward Emerson mourned his lack of " that part of education which is conducted in the nursery and the playground, in fights and frolics, in business and politics." Even in his maturity he sometimes looked with wistfulness upon the more robust avenues of living, wishing he could be more the sweating participant and less the cool-browed spectator; but at other moments when his eye, of a serene and ocean blue, fell upon the ranker growths of life, he turned his glance elsewhere and was glad that within his frail being his secret self had been safely locked. At that inner door the world sometimes raged and clawed, shouting abuse or ridicule, but when he heard its voice at all, it was as if from a distance. No blast, no jar, ever ruffled more than the surface of that pool, the soul of Emerson.

No one could ever recall having seen him run, even in his childhood. No one ever dared to slap him on the back. In conversation he was fond of a certain "levity," but he rarely opened his mouth to laugh. He smiled easily and often, but a laugh found itself checked by the barrier of his closed teeth, so that it seemed to force itself out of his contained countenance through his nose, the "high, predaceous nose" of the Emersons. He was incapable of stepping out of his character. Even Thoreau could not picture Emerson trundling a barrow through the streets. He was the child of an immaculate conception. Vices, weaknesses, he had none, save one which he called "my cardinal vice of intellectual dissipation — sinful strolling from book to book." He confessed to Thomas Carlyle: "I sit and read and write with very little system, and as far as regards composition, with the most fragmentary result: paragraphs incomprehensible, each sentence an infinitely repellent particle."

This confession reveals one of the sources of Emerson's strength: he knew, almost to the final ell, his limitations. "God," as he explained it, "has given me the seeing eye, but not the working hand." And it would be true, if paradoxical, to say that he enlarged his boundaries by remaining strictly within them.

Chapter Two

I

ONE day, shortly before the close of the eighteenth century, a certain Massachusetts young man, intent upon a career, resolved to remain single. In his journal he wrote large his determination never to " name marriage " to any woman. The rest can be surmised. In June, 1796, he " rode out with Miss R. H., and talked with her on the subject of matrimony." In the following October he married her.

" We are poor and cold," he wrote, " and have little meal, and little wood, and little meat, but thank God, courage enough."

These courageous young people were William Emerson and Ruth Haskins. They had children rapidly; the fourth was Ralph Waldo Emerson.

" Men," wrote this child subsequently, " are what their mothers made them "; and so to comprehend the man Emerson, we must begin with the woman who gave him birth, and much besides. She gave him many of her own features (" a man," wrote the child again, " finds room in his face for all his ancestors ") — the tall brow, the shapely head, the firm chin, and the somewhat pronounced nose, to which were added the " high, predaceous " elements native to the Emersons. It was she, too, perhaps, from whom he learned a love of solitude; we find her writing to a friend, " My partiality for retirement and rural scenes is great; and my aversion is great to the useless ceremony, parade, and pomp that almost necessarily are attached to a town life."

This was the mother whom her son called " whitest of women." She was an introspective woman, retiring every morning to her chamber for prayer and meditation, where none dared disturb her. She also kept a journal for the purpose of " writing down minutely " her " dealings with God." She was industrious, keeping in a convenient drawer a roll of knitting which she drew out whenever visitors called, that time might not be wasted in talk alone. She had self-control, which at a later time might have been called repression; one night, when she was at an advanced age, she fell and broke her hip, but she would not call for help, waiting until the servant came at the usual hour the next morning. She had both grace and sweetness of disposition, but with them went a certain interior coldness that prevented her children from showing her spontaneous affection. " She was a good disciplinarian," wrote one of her intimates, " firm and decided in the government of her children. The law of obedience must be fulfilled. . . ."

Of her five sons, she had least hopes of little Ralph Waldo. He revealed no marked gifts; he lacked concentration in his studies; his attention wandered easily; and one trait in particular filled her with foreboding: as an infant he sucked his thumb. She made him a mitten which she tied on his hand with firmness.

II

As a child, the mother of Emerson had been molded by certain influences which, no doubt, through her penetrated to her own children. Her mother, Hannah Upham, is described as calm and amiable, and full of good works, which she performed with a certain stateliness. All her life she persisted in attending the Congregational Church, although her husband, John Haskins, preferred, as became one of royalist leanings, the Episcopal or Church of England. A key to John Haskins is found in his nickname, "Honest John." He retained a bluff vigor derived from his two years at sea, and a gift for pungent sayings which his neighbors loved to quote. He began life as a cooper, making barrels for New England's rum traders. After marriage and the arrival of sixteen children, he became a distiller; for, though the Puritan age frowned upon many indulgences, alcohol was not among them. The Puritan needed it for that heat without which sin could not be successfully attacked.

The Haskins children were permitted to select their own church, giving their reasons in writing. They divided about equally between their father's and mother's. Ruth chose the Episcopal Church. On Sunday mornings the sixteen children could be seen issuing from the Haskins home in a long line, headed by their parents. In military formation they marched to a certain corner, but there they marked time and divided into two columns, the mother leading one to the Park Street Church, while tramp, tramp, off marched the other to Trinity behind their stately father.

An anecdote of John Haskins has come down which enables us to behold the maternal grandfather of Emerson as in the flesh. One day while the family was at dinner, a fire broke out in a nearby building. The children sprang up with a joyful noise.

"One moment," called the father. With uplifted hand, he pronounced the blessing customary at the end of each meal: "The Lord be praised for all his mercies."

Pause, and gradual opening of eyes.

"Now, boys, run!"

III

The husband of Ruth Haskins and the father of Emerson was the Reverend William Emerson, who for almost all his forty-two years suffered from doing things for which he had no genuine liking. From teaching school, he entered the ministry at the age of twenty-three. He did not wish to, but "yielded on hearing Dr. Ripley [his mother's second husband] pray that his mother's strong desire that he should be a minister might be fulfilled." He was bland and handsome, and by nature a hearty man, loving music and good company; but in his diary he felt compelled to reproach himself for spending too much time in singing and playing the bass viol. He craved congenial society and sometimes resorted to the desperate expedient of inviting as many as twelve fellow-preachers to breakfast. But afterwards he would condemn himself for undue "accessibility" and "levity," and bow humbly before the rebuke of his sister, Mary Moody Emerson, when she said, "The present world is too real to you." It was the constant checks he placed upon his own harmless impulses that perhaps caused him to transfer his repressions to his children. He was at times unnaturally severe with them; he once terrorized little Ralph Waldo by forcing him to bathe in open salt water before he had become accustomed to it, and on his small sons he inflicted intellectual drills altogether beyond their infantile years. Once, when absent from home, he wrote to his wife:

"William [aged five] will recite to you, as he does to me, if you have leisure to hear him, a sentence of English grammar before breakfast — though I think, if only one can be attended to, Ralph [aged three] should be that one. . . . I hope John Clarke can repeat passages from Addison, Shakespeare, Milton, Pope, etc." John Clarke was just seven years old.

Whether due to this premature forcing, or to an unhealthfully confined, indoor life, or to some inherited constitutional defect, there was something seriously lacking in the stamina of the Emerson children. John Clarke, the oldest, died when a lad. Mary Caroline, the youngest, died in her third year. Edward Bliss, whose reason wavered in his early twenties, and Charles Chauncey, who suffered from melancholia, were too frail to live beyond their young manhood, while Robert Bulkeley suffered from a mental deficiency which kept him isolated on a farm for life. Of six sons, William and Ralph Waldo alone survived to a rational manhood. William was gifted with a strength of body and an impassivity of mind which averted precocity and enabled him to escape from over-stimulation early in life. How did the timid little Ralph Waldo manage to live until men were proud to call him master?

IV

Although never combative, he contained an element which, under stress, remained firmly resistant. Perhaps this was due to the example of that ancestor who, in certain respects, was chief of them all — the Reverend Peter Bulkeley, the Bedfordshire non-conformist who, on being silenced by Archbishop Laud for refusing as rector of Odell to carry out certain ceremonies of the Church of England, firmly took himself, in 1635, to Massachusetts, and there formed a farming colony at Musketaquid, which he significantly renamed Concord, although concord did not extend to the rebellious Anne Hutchinson, whom the synod of which he was moderator drove out to Rhode Island. He was Concord's first minister, its leading scholar, and its father, prophet, and counsellor. He was the author of a Puritan treatise called the *Gospel Covenant,* and of occasional poetry in Latin. His granddaughter, Elizabeth, was married to the Reverend Joseph Emerson, son of Thomas Emerson, the Ipswich baker who had come from England.

Clusters of peaceful ministers appear along the descending line until we reach the Reverend William Emerson, grandfather of Ralph Waldo, who, though a lyric poet in his hours, was restrained with difficulty from personally bludgeoning the British in the Battle of Concord Bridge, which he witnessed from his own home, afterwards famed as the Old Manse. With fire still in his eye, he joined the Colonial Army as chaplain at Ticonderoga (where the patriot soldiers " vied with each other in profanity, drunkenness, and every vice "), fell ill, and died on the way home, at the age of thirty-three. His wife, Phoebe Bliss, was a minister's daughter.

So, standing behind Ralph Waldo's cradle might have been descried the shades of eight generations of ministers or other bookish men, introspective and dreaming of another and better world, and married to devout, indoor women. We know that even in Emerson's time it was rare to behold respectable women out-of-doors, because, on once seeing a hatless group outside his own house, he observed they looked as if they were going to a fire.

With the blood of those pious men and women was mingled that of others a trifle more worldly. In character, however, Emerson's ancestors were doubtless much alike — staid, steady, and God-fearing, in that Calvinistic fashion prevalent up to at least 1851, when Herman Melville wrote to Nathaniel Hawthorne:

" The reason the mass of men fear God, and *at bottom dislike* [1] Him, is because they rather distrust his heart, and fancy Him all brain like a watch."

Hawthorne's comment is not on record, but he might have replied that the Americans of that day, beneath the psalm-singing and the shouting, disliked and distrusted God because they had accepted Him ready-made from John Calvin. There was no one to tell them that Calvin had created God in his own image. They had to wait for Emerson; but even Emerson never dared to say that in so many words. He merely notified them that Calvin's God was dead.

[1] The italics are Melville's.

Chapter Three

I

NO star arose in the east, nor did other portent occur, when the little Emerson was born. His father was too busy to be at hand to greet him, and in his diary he mentions his third son's arrival quite casually as among the " also " incidents of May 25, 1803:

" Mr. Puffer preached his Election Sermon to great acceptance. This day also, whilst I was at dinner at Governor Strong's my son Ralph Waldo was born. Mrs. E. well. Club at Mr. Adams's."

The Reverend William Emerson, who previously had been minister in the village of Harvard, twelve miles from Concord, where his yearly salary had been $333.30, was then minister of the First Church (Old Brick) at Boston, where he received fourteen dollars a week, the use of the parish dwelling-house on Summer Street, corner of Chauncey, and twenty cords of wood. He soon benefitted by an increase in salary, wrote and published several theological and historical papers, took charge of the *Monthly Anthology*, (the precursor of the *North American Review*), formed the Anthology Club, instigated the club's collection of books which grew into the Boston Athenaeum Library, and was otherwise expanding in grateful activities, when he was seized with a marasmus, aggravated by a tuberculous tendency, and died at the age of forty-two, when Ralph Waldo was eight years old.

Mrs. Emerson found herself confronting existence with six children, all under the age of ten. The only wealth left behind by her husband was in that alone which he cared to accumulate: books. The First Church voted her $500 annually for seven years; but even with this assistance and that of friends it was necessary to impose on herself and her brood a frugality which left its lean mark on the impressionable Ralph, both in physique and imagination. In his maturity he sometimes longed for wealth, not for itself, but for " the independence of manner and conversation it would bestow, and which I eagerly covet and seldom quite attain, in some companies never."

Ralph and William had to wear the same overcoat by turns. Their mother took in boarders and required the boys to help her with the housework. In a letter to his Aunt Mary, written when he was ten years old, Ralph described exactly how he had spent a typical day. On April 9, 1813, he rose at 5:55 A.M., helped his older brother make the fire, and set the table for prayers. About 6:15 he called his mother, and, while she was dressing, rehearsed with his brothers a spelling lesson. Breakfast was finished about 7:15, and from then till 8:00 he could play or read. He confessed he was " rather inclined to the former." He then went to the Latin School and translated Virgil until 11:00. Thence he went to a private school where he wrote and ciphered until 1:00. He was more than once a truant here, and suffered consequent imprisonment on bread and water. One hour was allowed for lunch at home. Afterwards he returned to the Latin School for grammar study. On returning home, he ran errands for his mother and brought in the firewood, after which he could play. After supper he recited a hymn or Bible chapter, and took turns with his brothers reading aloud from Rollin's *History*. At 8:00 he said his prayers and went to bed. Covered to his chin in the icy room, he sometimes tried to read Plato's *Dialogues,* and for long afterwards associated Plato with the smell of wool.

Ralph Waldo was neither a particularly apt nor a diligent pupil. He often dreaded " tomorrow's merciless lesson," and mitigated the rigors of the Latin School by surreptitiously reading between lessons a smuggled novel. These stolen moments were sweet, and he afterwards regarded them as well spent; they balanced a diet composed too exclusively of intellectual bran and gravel. He also wrote comic or mock-heroic verses, perhaps to offset the solemn declamations required at school.

During his boyhood he betrayed at inappropriate moments a nervous tendency to giggle — no doubt a symptom of Nature's efforts to relax too taut a tension. This tendency toward " levity " pursued him into adult days, and it was his efforts to subdue it which perhaps caused him to dread being made to laugh. One of his reasons for cutting himself off from Margaret Fuller was that she made him laugh too boisterously. Emerson could not bear being thrown off his equilibrium; it had been too hardly won.

II

This austere regime threw the young Emersons almost entirely upon themselves for companionship and diversion.

They were the world. At its four corners stood a brother. Through the windows between these posts they looked out upon a world with eyes provided for them by books. Even in their frolics in barn or woodshed, they did not waste their time upon the mere exercise of muscles, but kindled each other with scraps of poetry and song, imitations of the orators of the day, or criticism of the latest sermon. In a letter to Edward, then at boarding-school, Ralph wrote that his mother suggested he borrow *Charles VII* or some other history, to " amuse " him during vacation. Ralph added that at school he himself had begun *Telemachus* in French, and at home was reading Priestley's *Lectures on History*.

Despite the weight of their tasks at home and school, we have Emerson's word for it that the four brothers were neither unhappy nor conscious of tax or privation. Looking back on the home picture, he wrote in later years: " What is the hoop that holds them stanch? It is the iron band of poverty, of necessity, of austerity, which, excluding them from the sensual enjoyments which make other boys too early old, has directed their activity into safe and right channels, and made them, despite themselves, reverers of the grand, the beautiful, and the good."

The operation was successful except that the patients either died or suffered enfeebled health. On the other hand, out of the sacrifice emerged a Ralph Waldo Emerson. Whether this was because of the process or in spite of it, there is no means of knowing.

Mrs. Emerson was not entirely alone in the upbringing and governance of her boys. She was assisted at times by two women, one of whom was her friend, Sarah Alden Bradford, later Mrs. Samuel Ripley. This was a gifted woman, proficient in Greek and mathematics, who, from the time of the Reverend William Emerson's death, supervised Ralph's education, advising him as to books and lessons, and corresponding with him as an equal. Long after her marriage and his own, she remained his friend and adviser.

Of all the women who surrounded the budding Emerson, however, the most powerful formative influence was that which emanated, as from a blast furnace, from the person of his aunt, Mary Moody Emerson. In Emerson's Journals the names of his father and mother appear but seldom. That of his Aunt Mary appears repeatedly, and in such terms as unmistakably to indicate that to this volcanic woman he largely owed the shape and direction of his boyish mind. He regarded her with an affection in which were elements of terror and awe. Ralph Waldo Emerson was physically the child of William Emerson and Ruth Haskins. But he was the spiritual child of the unmarried Mary Moody Emerson. Born with a Napoleonic soul in a frail feminine body, and assigned to a pent, frustrated life by the conditions around her, she sought fulfillment and a measure of assuagement through the men of her blood, but none responded until the docile and amiable Ralph Waldo came within her orbit. Upon him she fixed a baleful, glittering eye, and summoned him to be great. She dared him to fail to be great. He *must* be great. And Ralph, smiling and obedient, began to climb toward those peaks to which she pointed. At first he ascended haltingly and with many pauses, but at length with gathering confidence, reporting at intervals to Aunt Mary where she stood at the foot of the ladder, pistol in hand.

Chapter Four

I

THE natural history of aunts awaits a compiler. The maiden aunt of promising children may be, and often has been, greater than the mother; yet her labors, gleaming hopes, and obscure sacrifices, her solitary broodings and vicarious ambitions, have seldom received attention from the historian or the biographer. As a molder and shaper of the unpromising material of nephews and nieces, she has been allowed to live, toil, and die unpraised. The early American aunt alone deserves volumes; but of only one of these lonely figures have we an adequate portrait in prose. Among the aunts of her country, Mary Moody Emerson deserves high rank.

An incident, which at the time made laughter run around the decorous circles of Concord, has been recorded so as to give us an outline of her redoubtable temperament. She was receiving a formal call from the mother of Henry David Thoreau, upon whom, as a young and original writer, Emerson's aunt had bestowed an interest and attention which Mrs. Thoreau wished to acknowledge. Mrs. Thoreau was seventy years old, lively, and an inveterate gossip. This being an unusual occasion, she had adorned herself with a formidable headdress. It was a cap from which streamed long yellow ribbons, matched by bonnet-ribbons of even greater length.

Miss Emerson greeted her, seated visitor and self, and then closed her eyes as Mrs. Thoreau launched volubly into her favorite subject, " My son Henry."

" Mrs. Thoreau," said Miss Emerson at last, " you may have noticed, that while we were speaking of your admirable son I kept my eyes shut."

" Yes, madam," answered Mrs. Thoreau, " I noticed it."

" It was because," explained Miss Emerson, " I did not wish to look upon those ribbons of yours. I don't like to see a person of your time of life and serious character guilty of such levity in her dress."

II

" Her wit," Ralph Waldo Emerson once wrote of his aunt, " is the wild horse of the desert. . . . She reminds one in these days of an old aristocrat, say Queen Elizabeth shaking the Duchess of —— on her deathbed, or of Sarah of Marlborough as she walks with her stick to the oyster-shop." And again: " She tramples on the common humanities all day, and they rise as ghosts and torment her at night."

Emerson's Aunt Mary suffered from what today we would call severe complexes. She used to send Elizabeth Hoar, Emerson's friend and confidante, around the shops to discover for her a bonnet that did not look just like other people's, while she severely criticized Elizabeth's mother for wearing a bonnet that " conformed."

Dress to Emerson's Aunt Mary was more than a protection against cold; it was a symbol and a sign. Years before her death she made herself a shroud, and then, " thinking it a pity to let it lie idle," wore it as a nightgown. Finding it of durable material, she then cloaked herself in it during horseback rides over solitary hills. Finally, she made it a definite article of her wardrobe and declined to travel without " this dear and indispensable contingency."

She was sometimes accused of being odd by intention, but this she denied. She wrote in her diary for August, 1847: " My oddities were never designed — effect of an uncalculating constitution at first, then through isolation; and as to dress, from duty. To be singular of choice, without singular talents and virtues, is as ridiculous as ungrateful."

Secretly yearning to be admired, and avid of conversation, she confessed to her journal: " It is so universal with all classes to avoid contact with me that I blame none. The fact has generally increased piety and self-love." She went on to record this pathetic admission: " As a traveller enters some fine palace and finds all the doors closed, and he only allowed the use of some avenues and passages, so have I wandered from the cradle over the apartments of social affections, or the cabinets of natural or moral philosophy, the recesses of ancient and modern lore. All say — Forebear to enter the pales of the initiated by birth, wealth, talents, and patronage. I submit with delight, for it is the echo of a decree from above; and from the highway hedges where I get lodging, and from the rays which burst forth when the crowd are entering these noble saloons, whilst I stand in the doors, I get a pleasing vision which is an earnest of the interminable skies where the mansions are prepared for the poor."

III

Mary Emerson's tragedy was the tragedy of the woman of her time and place — to have a mind which found no companionship, an energy which doubled back upon itself for lack of a normal outlet, an ability deprived of a channel broad enough to flow through freely. The able woman has always found it difficult to discover room to stand in. In the America of the early nineteenth century there was not even a niche. If she was to realize herself, it must be through some man. Let her marry! She did, indeed, once consider marriage, but the man in the case did not convince her, and none other offered. And so, through a long life she wandered desolately from one home to another, where in the one she was nurse to the sick or infantile, in the other a pent-up boarder, until at last she became the possessor of a little Maine farm situated in an immense solitude. By nature she was torrentially energetic, and she was restricted to carding wool and baking bread; by temperament she was romantic — she had a burning admiration for Byron — and the men she knew were mostly cool, Calvinistic preachers; by upbringing she was a student of philosophy, science, and the classics, and she spent years as attendant to an insane aunt.

As a girl she was brought up with elderly people. Her mother had married again and had new children to look after. Companions of her own age she had none. She rarely saw her brothers and sisters. Their home was at Concord while hers was at Malden, first at her grandmother's and then at an aunt's. This aunt had a shiftless husband, and one of Mary's duties was to watch at windows for the approach of sheriffs and debt-collectors. On occasion she injected color into a monotonous existence by visits to the families of her nieces and nephews. Particularly did they claim her services in times of illness or disaster. When not toiling, chiefly for others, she was reading. Her great-nephew once listed the authors with which she was familiar: Milton, Young, Akenside, Samuel Clarke, Jonathan Edwards, Plato, Plotinus, Marcus Antoninus, Stewart, Coleridge, Cousin, Herder, Locke, Madame de Stael, Channing, Mackintosh, Byron, " and always the Bible." She roamed through all the current philosophies and kept abreast of the sciences. She liked to entice haughty young neo-intellectuals into a lulling conversation and fall upon them with bludgeons and battle-axes: " Descartes and his vortices, Leibnitz and his monads, Spinoza and his *Unica Substantia*."

" I like that apathy," she used to say, " which is a triumph to overset." Emerson said: " Her wit was so fertile and only used to strike, that she never used it for display, any more than a wasp would parade his sting."

Of all the Concord young men she most liked young Thoreau. This was her way of attracting the hermit into her orbit:

" Will my young friend visit me tomorrow as early as he can? . . . I wish for your writings, hoping they will give me a clearer clue to your faith, its nature, its destination, and object. . . . To enter the interior of a peculiar organization of mind is desirable to all who think and read in intermittent solitude."

The author of *Walden,* who permitted himself to be friend toward few women, must have responded, for he called her

" the wittiest and most vivacious woman that I know." Why?
" She gives her companion occasion to utter his best thought."
Thoreau was reading her one of his prose pieces one day
when she suddenly turned upon him suspiciously:

" Is that god spelt with a little g? "

IV

She was the particular dread of ministers, for, as often as
not, a few moments' conversation would reveal that she knew
more than they. In her later years circumstances often compelled her to migrate from town to town. Finding that in
few places was she, in her single state, welcome as an inmate,
she was " likely to steer first to the minister's house and pray
his wife to take a boarder." She was apt to overwhelm new
friends with her velocity, " for she knew she should disgust
them soon, and resolved to have their best hours."

Prosy talk she could not endure, and he who could not
send the conversational ball back over the net soon knew
that, for her, he had ceased to exist. If a visitor tired her she
asked that she be read to, and if a companion tried to wax
pretentious in conversation she was capable of asking suddenly, " How's your cat? " At other times her loneliness
drove her to seek society at any price.

" I walked yesterday five or more miles," she writes in
her journal, " lost to mental or heart existence, through
fatigue — just fit for the society I went into, all mildness and
the most commonplace virtue. . . . A mediocrity does seem
to me more distant from eminent virtue than the extremes of
station, though after all it must depend on the nature of

the heart. A mediocre mind will be deranged in either extreme of wealth or poverty, praise or censure, society or solitude. The feverish lust of notice perhaps in all these cases would injure the heart of common refinement and virtue."

The word " feverish " appears often in her diaries, glowing like a restless coal in the midst of grey-cloaked, barely restrained words. " Had I prospered in life, what a proud, excited being I might have been. Loving to shine, flattered and flattering, anxious, and wrapped in others, frail, feverish as myself."

Emerson wrote that her life marked " the precise time when the power of the old creed yielded to the influence of modern science and humanity." Brought up in the straitest sect of the Calvinists, she yet could not resist the fascinations of geology as outlined in *Moses's Cosmogony* and what was then the new and startling economics of Adam Smith in his *Wealth of Nations*. Her vigorous intellect was incessantly clashing with her not less vigorous emotions, and between the two she knew little peace. Often did she tell herself in her diary that she was satisfied to contemplate the rural scene in solitude and to see in nature a transparency behind which sat the majestic Deity into whose being she craved to be wholly absorbed. But she protested too much. She could not submit to a spiritual God without occasional fierce tugs at the material ties which bound her. She confessed to her efforts, at Malden, " to wake up the soul amid the dreary scenes of monotonous Sabbaths, when Nature looked like a pulpit," and on her Maine farm she wrote:

" Ah! as I walked out this afternoon, so sad was wearied Nature that I felt her whisper to me, ' Even these leaves you used to think my better emblems have lost their charm on me too, and I weary of my pilgrimage — tired that I must again be clothed in the grandeurs of winter, and anon be bedizened in flowers and cascades. Oh, if there be a power superior to me — and that there is, my own dread fetters proclaim — when will He let my lights go out, my tides cease to be an eternal ebb? Oh for transformation! I am not infinite, nor have I power or will, but bound and imprisoned, the tool of mind, even of the beings I feed and adorn.' "

V

Deprived of a natural channel for her blazing energies, she bent their rays fiercely upon her nephews. After the death of young Ralph Waldo Emerson's father, she came to Concord to assist the widow. " Scorn trifles," she used to say to Ralph. The stars or nothing. Over him she held the rigors in which she herself had been brought up. Of her grandfather, the Reverend Joseph Emerson, she wrote: " If it had not been for my grandmother, my father (William Emerson) would have been killed, perhaps, by confinement, for his father thought he ought never to leave his lessons. The children sat upon a settle, with lessons or catechism, the biggest at one end, the next in size at the other, and the little one in the middle. For outdoor relaxation there was the farm work; but even that was grudged."

It was in accordance with this stern tradition that little Ralph Emerson was never allowed to have a sled. He could only hang on the gate and watch other boys go by on their way to their games on the Common, and be jeered as they discovered his blue nankeen clothes.

But even after Ralph Waldo had begun to be famous and had encompassed some of " the great circling truths," she was still not satisfied. She often criticized him severely, just as she used to tell his father, " The present world is too real to you." At times she refused to receive her favorite nephew at all and would not even permit him to call on her. However, he, who well knew his aunt's foibles, was not offended.

" She is no statute-book of practical commandments," he wrote, " nor orderly digest of any system of philosophy, divine or human, but a Bible, miscellaneous in its parts, but one in spirit, wherein are sentences of condemnation, promises, and covenants of love that make foolish the wisdom of the world with the power of God."

She was no ogre, however, and outwardly had none of the grimness associated with disapproving aunts. " She was a little, fair, blue-eyed woman," wrote Elizabeth Hoar, " her face never wrinkled, and with a delicate pink color when past eighty (she was eighty-nine when she left this world) — a blue flash in her eyes like the gleam of steel — yellow hair, which, however, was cut close and covered up with a black band and a mob-cap."

VI

Her solitude lasted for twenty years. She gradually became reconciled to it, meantime trying to subdue her ardent energies by contemplating the tranquillity of Nature and by musing upon the extent of the Infinite.

" Oh, to dream more deeply! " she wrote in her journal. " To lose external objects a little more! Yet the hold on them is so slight that duty is lost sight of, perhaps, at times. Sadness is better than walking, talking, acting somnambulism. Yes, this entire solitude with the Being who makes the powers of life! Even Fame, which lives in other states of Virtue, palls. Usefulness, if it requires action, seems less like existence than the desire of being absorbed in God, retaining consciousness."

Firmly she clung to the belief, despite her Calvinism, that it was possible for the believer to unite himself with God, without the intervention of any Savior, even Jesus. " Honors, pleasures, labors, I always refuse, compared to this divine partaking of existence; — but how rare, how dependent on the organs through which the soul operates! "

The monotony of existence, to one so energetic as she, became agonizing. She even welcomed pain and sickness as " fine medicine." She became the Saint Theresa of Maine. " Constantly offer myself," she wrote, " to continue the obscurest and loneliest thing ever heard of, with one proviso — His agency." Finally, in an anguish of loneliness, she prayed for death. The diaries of her advancing years are filled with references to death and the worm. She had her bed made in the form of a coffin, and when the tower of a church adjoining the house cast a shadow shaped like a casket, she was delighted. " O Time! Thou loiterer! " she cried.

In July, 1826, she wrote, " I pray to die, though happier myriads and mine own companions press nearer to the throne," but by 1833 her ambition even in this respect remained unfulfilled: " I have given up, the last year or two, the hope of dying. In the lowest ebb of health nothing is ominous; diet and exercise restore. . . . I enter my dear sixty the last of this month." Two years later she mentioned a " tedious indisposition; hoped, as it took a new form, it would open the cool, sweet grave." She talked of the grave so much that her friends gradually became callous to her desire for death, and at length found comedy in it. Her nephew promised to inscribe her epitaph: " Here lies the Angel of Death," and her intimates, finding her comfortably dressed in a new shroud, would say, " I wish you joy of the worm."

When at last she did die, the event had — we are told by Ralph Waldo Emerson himself — " a comic tinge." Her body, which had been for so long tired of life, was taken to Concord for burial. It seemed incredible that death, which for more than a score of years had eluded Mary Moody Emerson's persistent grasp, had at last come forward and given her her desire. There was no sorrow anywhere, even among the gentle ladies of Concord. On the contrary, as they gathered at the edges of her grave, they averted their eyes from each other, lest, remembering the departed's greatest and most oft-discussed obsession, they should be betrayed into a smile. And they knew Emerson's Aunt Mary would not have minded. A funeral at which there had been peals, not of mournful bells, but of silver laughter, would have been approved by her eccentric fancy as altogether seemly.

Chapter Five

I

IT has been observed that wherever an organism is long exposed in any part to an undue stimulus or irritation, it at length develops for itself a shield. Thus the eagle has grown a membrane over its eye that enables it to look into the sun, the horse develops a callosity where the harness rubs, and the oyster excretes a shell which entirely encloses its feeble body.

When Emerson was still in his early teens a physician who had just examined him exclaimed, " Boy, you've got no stamina." The doctor referred, of course, to his physical vitality. This was no news to Emerson; and his inner self had already begun to seek a shield for the deficiency. With powerful forces both of heredity and environment focussed upon him, with steely wills now pushing, now pulling him, with energetic influences trying through him to gain their ends regardless of his own, he knew in his secret self that he must have that protection if he was to win, or even to survive. And slowly his psyche began to build around itself the needed structure. Impalpable at first, it at length became a tissue, a veil, which, however translucent and bendable, provided protection; and then, as accretion continued through his adolescence and young manhood, it became a shell behind which the interior Emerson at last was safe.

II

When Emerson was only fourteen years old, he entered Harvard College, over which the Unitarians had won command. There were some preliminary tremors on the part of his mother, both on account of the low state of the family funds and her fears regarding his possible unreadiness, for he was weak in mathematics and Greek. His appointment as president's freshman, or messenger, however, which procured him free lodging, abated the first fear, and the ease with which he passed the entrance examination banished the second.

"To tell the truth," Ralph confided in a letter to his brother William, " I do not think it necessary to understand Mathematics and Greek thoroughly to be a good and useful, or even a great man. . . . Mathematics I hate."

Later the economic strain was further eased by small grants of money from bequests to the college and by his appointment as waiter at Junior Hall, where for two terms he served meals to his fellows. For this labor he received three-fourths of his meals free. None of these economic aids, however, quite removed what he afterwards described as his " goading, soul-sickening sense of extreme poverty."

His brother William was already a senior at Harvard, and he no doubt did what he could to introduce Ralph to companions of his own age, but from the first the younger lad showed no taste for the gregariousness of student life. Even had he done so, the situation of his room, immediately beneath the president's study, and his position as messenger, which necessarily allied him with the enemy, the faculty, would have cut him off from the free flow of companionship. Hence in his lonely room the boy set about the creation of his own world. He found few attractions in his studies, for Harvard " courses " at that time consisted of little beyond recitations based on memory and mechanically prepared for and delivered. The college as a whole no doubt deserved the gibe ascribed to Thoreau in the course of a conversation with Emerson years later. Emerson was inclined to say a good word for colleges on the ground that they taught most of the branches of knowledge.

" Yes," said Thoreau, " all the branches and none of the roots."

III

In his very first term Emerson learned that if he was to obtain an education — in the sense of the Latin derivation, *a leading-out* — he must get it himself; for the Harvard system, like that of most schools of the period, was only a driving-in. " One of the benefits of a college education," he wrote, " is to show the boy its little avail." And so, while the other boys were busy with their loafing, their sports, pranks, talk, and convivialities, Emerson was busy with himself and his books — not the books of his classes but of his own unsystematic selection. Afterwards he did not regret his solitude, which he was always ready to glorify as a thing which " is to genius the stern friend, the cold, obscure shelter where moult the wings which will bear it farther than suns and stars." Then, too, " The high advantage of university life is often the mere mechanical one . . . of a separate chamber and fire, which parents will allow the boy without hesitation at Cambridge, but do not think needful at home."

At another time he also observed: " Books are good only so far as a boy is ready for them. . . . Archery, cricket, gun and fishing rod, horse and boat, are all educators, liberalizers; and so are dancing, dress, and the street talk."

But Emerson, from his infancy up, had had the help of none of these educators; and so, while other lads played, hunted, danced, and mixed in street talk, he sat in his room and read and wrote, wrote and read. For exercise he made entries in his journal and for diversion he read, as became an earnest young Puritan, Milton. He also delighted in Shakespeare, Plato, and Montaigne. As a counterweight he took doses from Mosheim's *Church History*, Erskine's *Sermons*, and Bishop Berkeley's *Philosophy*. Thus strengthened, he roamed farther afield and entered upon this random list which, when seventeen years old, he recorded as " Books to be Sought ":

Wordsworth's *Recluse; Quarterly Review*, September, 1819, Liber VIII of Buchanan's *Scotland* — Wallace; Spenser's *View of the State of Ireland;* Camden's *Annals of Queen Elizabeth;* Kennet's *Life and Characters of Greek Poets;* Hody, *De Illustribus Graecis;* Middleton's *Cicero;* Burton's *Melancholy;* Barrow's *Sermons;* Hobbe's *Leviathan;* Joinville's *Life of St. Louis;* Froissart's *History of England;* Chaucer's Works; Bayle's Dictionnaire; Corinne; Massinger's Plays; Fletcher's Plays; Bentley's *Phalaris;* Peter's *Letters; Letters from Eastern States; Waverly;* Cogan on the Passions; Sir Charles Grandison.

As if consciously shaping himself for the career of an

orator, he practised expression by making copious entries in his journal, and collected resounding words and phrases which at the time seemed to him to be deeply poetical. Among these jewels of rhetoric were the following:

till its dye was doubled on the crimson cross
rescuing and crowning virtue
booked in alphabet
star-crossed
sycophant smile
spikenard
panoply
halidom

The results of this practice appeared in tentative essays which glittered with the paste gems of sentiment, regarded in that day as " beautiful language." For example, this is the beginning of an entry for April 2, 1820:

" Spring has returned and has begun to unfold her beautiful array, to throw herself on wild-flower couches, to walk abroad on the hills and summon her songsters to do her sweet homage . . ."

The flowers of oratorical rhetoric were admired no less by Harvard boys than by their parents, and the chief matinee idol of the faculty was Edward Everett, professor of Greek Literature. To prepare himself for the chair, Everett had visited Europe. From there he had returned laden with metaphors, curios, and similes, which he flung to his audiences as if they were violets. On the platform he did not so much speak as prance. He had gifts as an actor which he spread lavishly before his entranced students. Emerson admired him extravagantly until he discovered that his carefully posed idol had feet of clay which vainly tried to look like Daniel Webster's.

It may have been the eloquence of Everett, however, which tilted the imagination of the impressionable Ralph definitely in the direction of Greek studies. At the age of sixteen the lad recorded this serious resolution: " To make myself acquainted with the Greek language and antiquities and history with long and serious attention and study."

He had encountered a fork in the road and he had chosen the path which was, for him, the only one suited to his nature. The cast of the American mind had been molded by England; it was practical, organizing, and a little hard — in short, Roman. But Ralph thus signified that he meant to be as Greek as was possible to a young New Englander of Puritan ancestry.

IV

For most of the time the boy was content with his solitary labors, but there were moments when he experienced what he described as a " terrible void." Young blood was revolting against this elderly reclusion, and his constant self-searching was affecting his nerves; but he feared that his languors and restless vacuums indicated he was a born laggard, destined to fail miserably in life's race, beneath the eyes of his Aunt Mary. Instead of slinging his books into a corner and going out to join his fellows in their diversions, his recipe was more books. He advised himself:

1. To read over the chapter mottoes in Scott's novels, or to read particularly *The Bride of Lammermoor*. This ro-

mance remained one of his favorites throughout life, though Emerson had an aversion for what he called "dismal stories."

2. To con the home-scenes in Cowper's *Task*.

3. To study old tragedies such as Ben Jonson's, Otway's, or Congreve's.

He added pathetically: "In short, anything of that kind which leads as far as possible from the usual trains of thought."

He could read drama in book form as much as he pleased, but to have attended a theatrical performance of any kind would have brought upon him the ten-dollar fine imposed for such offences by the college authorities.

V

It was not until his second year that Emerson touched the rim of student life. The sophomores went on strike against some faculty ruling, and Emerson actually had the hardihood to join the rebellion and remain at home until the affair had been settled. But in this year his unnatural mode of life exacted a penalty; he suffered from a languorous malady which he could only call "apathy," and was troubled by a pain in the chest — both being signs that the slender spire of his vitality was even thinner than usual. He was permitted to occupy a room more healthfully placed, and here in his junior year he made a further advance into the circle of experience. He joined a club called the Conventicle, wrote rhymes and songs for the members, and partook lightly of their Malaga wine. "You send your child to the schoolmaster," wrote Emerson later, " but it is the school-boys who educate him."

His roommate was the very last person whom one would expect to have found associated with Emerson. This was John Gailliard Keith Gourdin, a careless young blade from Charleston, South Carolina. To Emerson, life was real and very earnest; to Gourdin it was something much more care-less and leisurely. Like the sons of other Southern planters who had been sent to Harvard for " finishing," Gourdin, although no dullard in books, paid far more attention to his clothes and his pleasures than to his classes. From his swallow-tailed coat, " tapered to an arrow-point angle," to his " delicate calf-skin boots," as Oliver Wendell Holmes once described his kind, Gourdin represented almost every-thing that a born Puritan like Emerson most distrusted and disliked. Gourdin was of partial French ancestry — a bit of a Latin; and Emerson could never quite like anything living that was Latin. His dudish roommate was also representative of an alien social class — slave-holding, money-careless, work-evading, and rather external in mode of life. If Emer-son liked Gourdin in any respect, it was probably with an ef-fort. His writings do not mention his roommate except to record the fact that Gourdin was threatened with expulsion from the Pythologian, a discussion and debating club organ-ized in their own room, for repeated failure to attend meet-ings. With Robert Gourdin, his roommate's older brother, and Motte and Barnwell, other students from South Carolina, Emerson was friendly, but John Gourdin probably remained in his recollection as that " Southern fop," which he later used in his writings for odious comparison.

VI

In his instinctive efforts to educate himself — lead himself out of his monastic cell and gain contact with living minds — Emerson joined an enterprise which almost instantly disclosed exciting vistas of thought. It was a student circle which subscribed to the more important British magazines and reviews. Through these mediums he became acquainted with the fact that thought was not dead and embalmed in college libraries, but was living, continuous, and contemporaneous. They introduced him to the men who became his four first heroes among living writers — Carlyle, Coleridge, Landor, and Wordsworth. It was through Coleridge and Carlyle that he felt the first whiffs of the breeze that was blowing across England and even tossing the dry leaves on American shores. This breeze was stirred up by the new German philosophy. Now for the first time he read the teachings of Schelling, Kant, Fichte, Goethe, and Jacobi. It was true, after all, that ideas had not been folded up with the grave-clothes of Plato and Aristotle. He tasted the new offerings gingerly and then with rising interest. A similar infection gradually spread through the Boston and sub-Boston intelligentsia, and in time the Absolute and the Relative were as familiar in certain homes as seaweed ornaments on the parlor mantel.

Kant and Schelling, especially, provided the diet to which young Ralph, already fascinated by the poetic philosophy of Plato and the mystical teachings of those " grandees of thought," the Neo-Platonists, was bound to relish. Kant's doctrines were the product of a reaction from the eighteenth century materialistic philosophy of the English Locke and the Scottish Hume, who held that the one source of knowledge was experience gained by the employment of the senses. Kant led the counter-attack for the idealists. He maintained that the senses give us only the appearance of things, and that true knowledge results from the union of mind and matter, or subject and object. After him came the romantic Schelling who went a step further and declared that subject and object become one in the Absolute.

The Germans supplied to the New England intellectuals not only new ideas but new words. Among them was the historic term " transcendental," which was destined not only to influence Emerson's thinking, but to carry away that of some of his closest friends into far flights through the empyrean. Kant applied the term to that mode of cognition which lies outside of and above all experience; and in 1800 Schelling gave further publicity to the word by naming one of his pamphlets " Transcendental Idealism."

These new German teachers confirmed in Emerson what he had already sifted from Plato and Plato's mystic expounders: that anterior to all things was an Ineffable Oneness, to know which was impossible within the limits of the intellect; and that at the core of all things, beneath their apparent difference in structure, lay an unbreakable unity.

VII

All this time Emerson was preparing himself for that office for which his family and relatives had designed him

EMERSON AS A YOUNG MAN

— the ministry; but, like his father, he had no enthusiasm for it, and he afterwards confessed that he had sometimes had hopes that some country college would call him to the chair of rhetoric. At another time he told his aunt: " In my daydreams I do often hunger and thirst to be a painter." An urge to draw lay in the ends of his fingers, and while idling over his notebooks his pen would subconsciously shape crude sketches and designs on the margin. He made an excellent water-color — an indoor product, of course — of his bare room in Hollis Hall, and in his diary he wrote down directions for engraving on glass. But in general his ambitions as to a career were vague and diffuse, and in an effort to resolve his uncertainties he resorted one day to the *Virgilianae Sortes*, or the ancient practice of opening Virgil and accepting as a guide to action the first line seen. The book was Dryden's translation and the line at which he opened was this:

" *Go, let the gods and temples claim thy care.*"

VIII

And then Emerson fell in love. It was with no maiden, with lowered eyes and parted hair brought down to hide demure ears, but with a member of his own sex. His unnatural, monkish life at the age of seventeen had produced its own rebellion. Too much food for the intellect and not enough for the emotions. His apathy had persisted until his spirits had sunk to the bottom of a vacant and colorless well. His interior shell, however, was not yet opaque enough to shut out all the rays from the external world. He was susceptible to the presence of young girls, but he seldom saw any and of their society he had none. His imagination, yearning for the mystery, the romance, which adolescence demands from the world as its due, was bound sooner or later to focus itself upon some object, and at length it paused before a face seen in the freshman class. It belonged to a youth slightly younger than himself. Then came the necessity for a confidant. There being none except his journal, its pages received the following:

"There is a strange face in the freshman class whom I should like to know very much. He has a great deal of character in his features and should be a fast friend or bitter enemy. His name is —— [he recorded the name, but later erased it.] I shall endeavor to become acquainted with him and wish, if possible, that I might be able to recall at a future period the singular sensations which his presence produced at this."

In his senior year Emerson had as his roommate his brother Edward, whose presence mitigated his loneliness but could not allay his absorption in the more romantic tie. The face of the stranger still troubled his imagination, and he wrote:

"I begin to believe in the Indian doctrine of eye fascination. The cold blue eye of —— has so intimately connected him with my thoughts and visions that a dozen times a day, and as often by night, I find myself wholly wrapt up in conjectures of his character and inclinations. We have had already two or three long prolonged stares at each other. Be it wise or superstitious, I must know him."

With an ink wash Emerson then executed a portrait sketch,

perhaps from memory, of a youth with curly hair, a full jaw, and a thick neck. Beneath, he wrote these lines:

" Perhaps thy lot in life is higher
    Than the Fates assign to me,
While they fulfil thy large desire,
    And bid my hopes as visions flee.
But grant me still in joy or sorrow,
    In grief or hope, to claim thy heart,
And I will then defy the morrow
    Whilst I fulfil a loyal part."

The very next day he inscribed in his journal this confession and appeal: " I find myself often idle, vagrant, stupid, and hollow. This is somewhat appalling and, if I do not discipline myself with diligent care, I shall suffer severely from remorse and the sense of inferiority hereafter. All around me are industrious and will be great, I am indolent and shall be insignificant. Avert it, heaven! avert it, virtue! I need excitement."

There followed a period of struggle during which he doubted whether the youth was worthy of his unexpressed devotion: " My opinion of —— was strangely lowered by hearing that he was ' proverbially idle.' This was redeemed by learning that he was a ' superior man.' " The romance-at-a-distance continued almost to the end of the term, and then Emerson wrote:

" Well, I am sorry. . . . The anecdote which I accidentally heard of —— shews him more like his neighbors than I should wish him to be. I shall have to throw him up after all, as a cheat of fancy. Before I ever saw him, I wished my *friend* to be different from any individual I had seen. I invested him with a solemn cast of mind, full of poetic feeling, and an idolater of friendship, and possessing a vein of rich sober thought. For a year I have entertained towards him the same feelings and should be sorry to lose him altogether before we have ever exchanged above a dozen words."

There was one more disturbed entry before Emerson turned his thoughts to other interests:

" I am more puzzled than ever with ——'s conduct. He came out to meet me yesterday, and I, observing him, just before we met, turned another corner and most strangely avoided him. This morning I went out to meet him in a different direction, and stopped to speak with a lounger, in order to be directly in ——'s way; but —— turned into the first gate and went towards Stoughton. All this without any apparent design and as if both were intent on some tremendous affair."

This entry he afterwards blotted out with ink, as if to say " finis." There is no mistaking Emerson's language and actions as here described; they are those of a lover; but even at this early age they were in perfect accord with the sentiments recorded in the essay of his maturity, *Friendship*. " It is almost dangerous to me to ' crush the sweet poison of misused wine ' of the affections. A new person is to me always a great event, and hinders me from sleep. . . . Yet even in the golden hour of friendship, we are surprised with shades of suspicion and unbelief. We doubt that we bestow on our hero the virtues in which he shines. . . . We are armed all over with subtle antagonisms, which, as soon as we meet, begin to play, and translate all poetry into stale prose. . . . Why insist on rash personal relations with your friend? . . .

Let him be to me a spirit. A message, a thought, a sincerity, a glance from him, I want, but not news, nor pottage. . . . Though I prize my friends, I cannot afford to talk with them and study their visions, lest I lose my own."

So Emerson permitted this youth, as he later permitted many other admired persons, to disappear from his life without more than a few passing words. Did he fear to penetrate their interior shells lest in so doing, as he said, he lose his own? More than once he acquired a friend whom at first he praised extravagantly, only at a later period to withdraw into what he called his "insulation," leaving the friend puzzled and bewildered.

The young man for whom Emerson had this first secret admiration probably would have responded poorly to his admirer's exalted ideas. His name was Martin Gay, of Hingham, known to his classmates as "Cool Gay." His interests were almost exclusively scientific. He became a physician and passed most of his life in Boston, where he died in middle age. There is no evidence that, despite their nearness, he and Emerson ever met again. Though for years they lived only twenty miles apart, Emerson never sought Gay out. Emerson was an idealist, but he kept his ideals weighted with that skepticism which is sometimes termed common sense.

IX

In his junior year, Emerson won some notice and a Bowdoin prize with an essay, filled with juvenile rhetoric, on "The Character of Socrates," and earned a few dollars, which he sent to his mother, by "school-keeping" during

winter vacations at various bleak villages. Such employment
revolted him, and in one diary entry he described a situation,
somewhere in a mountain log-house, in terms which for
Emerson were almost profane:

" When I came out from the hot, steaming, stoved, stink-
ing, dirty, A-B spelling-school-room, I almost soared and
mounted the atmosphere at breathing the free, magnificent
air, the noble breath of life. It was a delightful exhilaration;
but it soon passed off."

He made a moderate showing in most of his college courses,
but in mathematics, especially analytical geometry, he continued to suffer anguish, from which he was glad to hurry to the
consolations of Chaucer and Montaigne, Plato and Plutarch.
In the next year he was second to Josiah Quincy in a " dis-
sertation " contest, Emerson's entry being, " The Present
State of Ethical Philosophy," and won a declamation prize
of thirty dollars with which he hoped to buy his mother a
coat; but it went to settle a baker's bill.

When he was eighteen years old, he was graduated from
Harvard, standing number thirty in a class of fifty-nine. He
failed of election to the Phi Beta Kappa Society, which admitted only those students who had distinguished themselves.
He was chosen Class Poet only after six other students had
declined to serve. In the commencement exercises he had the
part of John Knox in a colloquy on Knox, Penn, and Wes-
ley, but forgot part of his lines and had to be prompted. In
after years his classmates could remember him for nothing
that he did, but only for his hesitating but measured speech,
and courteous, suave manners.

He left college without regret — " I have not much
cause," he wrote, " I sometimes think, to wish my Alma

Mater well, personally." He had a sense of foreboding as to the future. Harvard had not removed a sense of inferiority. " I've less faculties and age than most poor collegians," he wrote. " But when I am out of college I will, *Deo volente,* study divinity and keep school at the same time — try to be a minister and have a house."

As was the case with his father, events and the will of his elders were pushing him reluctantly into the ministry. Ever since the opening of the century, gentle Unitarianism had been gaining ground over cold Calvinism, and it was the younger faith which was calling him to help administer another kick to the older. He tried to regard his mission cheerfully. " We must accept Fate," but, " We can only obey our own polarity."

Chapter Six

I

AT the age of nineteen, Emerson found himself being furtively inspected by a class of young ladies, and, even as he dealt out " the safe and cold details of languages, geography, arithmetic, and chemistry," he quaked with tremors arising from his imagined lack of personal authority and his alternating fear and admiration of their attractions. Having been brought up without the sanative presence of sisters or of other young women, he felt that he was launching himself upon a dark sea where he was pathetically unprepared as a navigator. The school belonged to his brother William, who had established it in his mother's home in Federal Street, Boston, and had called Ralph to be his assistant. One of Emerson's private pupils was Elizabeth Palmer Peabody. They used to sit opposite each other at the study table, neither daring to lift an eye from their books. Aside from his terror of his pupils, Emerson had no heart for school-teaching; it was merely a means of earning money to add to the family funds and to assist his younger brothers through college, while he prepared himself for the Harvard Divinity School. He got through the tedious days by following an ordained routine of recitations and " compositions," and in the evenings he shut out loneliness and ennui by writing in his journals long, solemn notes on morals, genius, and the laws of compensation.

However, the old enemy of his college days — " apathy " or " indolence," due to continued low vitality and lack of stimulating interests — frequently returned to bedevil him, and his ceaseless introspection produced nothing except despair. " Never mistake yourself to be great, or designed for greatness," he admonished himself, " because you have been visited by an indistinct and shadowy hope that something is reserved for you beyond the common lot. It is easier to aspire than to do the deeds." Bowed beneath the weight of nineteen summers, he saw endless cycles of dismal school-teaching ahead of him, while Martin Gay was " advancing his footing in good company and fashionable friends." Nine months had passed since his graduation and he was not yet great. What must Aunt Mary think of him? World-woe descended and enmeshed him. " I am a hopeless Schoolmaster . . . toiling through this miserable employment even without the poor satisfaction of discharging it well, for the good suspect me, and the geese dislike me."

Three months later he was in no better spirits. Waves of self-pity rolled over him, succeeded by troughs of self-contempt. He crept to his diary and wrote: " In twelve days I shall be nineteen years old; which I count a miserable thing. Has any other person lived so many years and lost so many days? . . . Too tired and too indolent to travel up the mountain path which leads to good learning, to wisdom and fame, I must be satisfied with beholding with an envious eye the laborious journey and final success of my fellows."

But what frightened him even more than his intellectual apathy was his emotional coldness. He feared it might be permanent. In all his nineteen years he had not had one genuine romance, or emotional flare, except the aborted affair with Gay, to illumine his thought and soften its ice. He arraigned himself:

" Look next from the history of my intellect to the history of my heart. A blank, my lord. I have not the kind affections of a pigeon. Ungenerous and selfish, cautious and cold, I yet wish to be romantic; have not sufficient feeling to speak a natural, hearty welcome to a friend or stranger, and yet send abroad wishes and fancies of a friendship with a man I never knew." His despair at finding himself unable to touch any of the warmer currents of life found vent in this cry: " There is not in the whole wide Universe of God (my relations to Himself I do not understand) one being to whom I am attached with warm and entire devotion — not a being to whom I have joined fate for weal or wo, not one whose interests I have nearly and dearly at heart; — and this I say at the most susceptible age of man."

II

He had no choice, however, but to keep grimly on with his teaching for two years. William then left him in sole charge of the school to go to Germany where he studied divinity at Göttingen. Doubts attacked William there, and not even a consultation with Goethe, who advised him to continue his present course, resolved them; and he cut the knot by returning to America, becoming a lawyer, and escaping to New York.

About this time Ralph notified his friends that he preferred in future to be called Waldo. This preference probably marked some internal change, although his low spirits continued. His Aunt Mary detected them in his letters, but could not understand them. Since he was earning a comfortable salary and could live on little, she deemed his circumstances "too easy and rhyme-like." As a Calvinist, she preferred to see him bleed and suffer. From her solitude in Maine she trained on him a saturnine eye and, seizing her mocking pen, wrote this to the pilgrim floundering in his Boston slough of despond:

"Is the Muse become faint and despond? Ah, well she may, and better, far better, she should leave you wholly till you have prepared for her a celestial abode. Poetry, that soul of all that pleases; the philosophy of the world of sense; the Iris, the bearer of the resemblances of uncreated beauty — and yet, with these gifts, you flag! Your Muse is mean because the breath of fashion has not puffed her. You are not inspired at heart because you are the nursling of surrounding circumstances. . . . Still, there is an approaching period I dread worse than this sweet stagnation — when your Muse shall be dragged into *éclat*. Then will your guardian angel tremble!"

She urged him to retire to a rural seclusion where solitude and contemplation of Nature might enable him to recover himself. Waldo, accompanied by William, shortly afterwards had two weeks in the country, but found that lounging among the trees and grasses induced only "a soft, animal luxury," which was the very enemy of thought. His aunt informed him he should have gone alone. "Solitude," she added, "which to people not talented to deviate from the beaten track is the safe ground of mediocrity (without offending), is to learning and genius the only sure labyrinth, though sometimes gloomy, to form the eagle-wing that will bear one farther than sun and stars."

The similarity of phrases here to her nephew's subsequent remarks on the same theme, quoted in Chapter Five, is most marked; revealing how strongly not only her thought but her very language lingered in Emerson's memory.

In his correspondence with his aunt at this time, appeared a reference to Oriental literature which indicates that it was also to his aunt that he owed, among so many other influences, the introduction to Eastern wisdom which subsequently developed into one of his major delights.

" I am curious to read your Hindoo mythologies," he wrote. " One is apt to lament over indolence and ignorance, when he reads some of those sanguine students of the Eastern antiquities, who seem to think that all the books of knowledge and all the wisdom of Europe twice-told lie hid in the treasures of the Bramins and the volumes of Zoroaster."

To obtain a few areas of color in his monotonous existence, he eagerly welcomed news of novelties in literature and philosophy, and started a correspondence with several of his college mates in which he implored them to advise him of all that was new and stimulating in their own experience or reading. He even tried to become interested in Boston politics, and to his classmate, John B. Hill, he made copious offerings of information in the hope, no doubt, of an equal return. He wrote of the rise in Boston of a middle-class party, led by " demagogues " and " murmurers," which, wedging itself between the old factions of Federalists and Democrats, hoped to loosen the grip the Boston aristocracy of merchants, bankers, and lawyers had long held on affairs.

" My books," wrote the nineteen-year-old young conservative, " warn me of the instability of human greatness, and I hold that government never subsisted in such perfection as here."

He made to Hill other revealing observations, among them this one, which demonstrates that even at this early age he was questioning (in that day, wrote Henry James the elder, " there was nothing in New England but questions ") the religious *status quo* and was pointing himself toward his real mission.

" When I have been at Cambridge and studied divinity, I will tell you whether I can make out for myself any better system than Luther or Calvin, or the liberal besoms of modern days. I am tired and disgusted with preaching which I have been accustomed to hear."

It was to Hill again, in 1823, when he was twenty years old, after his mother had moved to Lower Canterbury in what was then rural Roxbury, that he wrote he was trying to acquaint himself with Nature, confessing his instigator was his Aunt Mary, who, though living in distant Maine, kept upon her nephew her powerful, urging hand:

" I am seeking to put myself on a footing of old acquaintance with Nature, as a poet should. . . . My aunt (of whom I think you have heard before, and who is alone among women) has spent a great part of her life in the country, is an idolater of Nature. . . . She was anxious that her nephew might hold high and reverential notions regarding it, as the temple where God and the mind are to be studied and adored, and where the fiery soul can begin a premature communication with the other world."

III

In desperately low spirits Emerson continued his " school-keeping " for three years, teaching not only at Boston but at Chelmsford and Cambridge. His pupils remembered him as dignified and aloof, but always kindly. In an age when the birch did not spare the child, he never punished a boy by any ruder measures than requiring him to read portions of Plutarch's *Lives*, and, even in moments of acute annoyance, he never vented any exclamation more violent than " Oh, sad! " Since chief reliance was placed on pure memory, or, rather, pure memorizing, he showed his pupils how to remember through association, and taught them historical facts by the aid of rhyme.

Meantime, he read voluminously, and filled his journal with long notes on abstract subjects, such as history, genius, justice, society, etc. One of his entries on invention indicates that he foresaw the rise of the phonograph and radio; and he predicted an engine in which the scholar might put in a pin and hear poetry, two pins and hear a song.

But there were moments when the acquirement of mere book knowledge appeared to be a groping futility. He wished he could go back and be a contemporary of Noah. " Men's thoughts were their own then." he wrote. " Noah was not dinned to death with Aristotle and Bacon and Greece and Rome." He thus confessed his miserable state of mind in this chaotic period, and his uncertainty as to what in life he should be and do. " Unknown troubles perplex the lot of the scholar whose inexpressible unhappiness it is to be born at this day. A chaos of doubts besets him from his outset. Shall he read or shall he think? . . . Shall he nourish his faculties in solitude or in active life? "

The introspective young schoolmaster might have spared himself these wrestlings and vacuities. Events, his own constitution, and his Aunt Mary had already decided for him. " A man's power," he afterwards wrote in *Fate*, " is hooped in by a necessity, which, by many experiments, he touches on every side, until he learns its arc." The arc of his own power he was now about to learn.

Chapter Seven

I

"IN a month I shall be legally a man," he wrote on April 24, 1824. "I am beginning my professional studies and I deliberately dedicate my time, my talents, and my hopes to the church." Having arrived at this responsible age, he felt it to be time to subject himself to a thorough inspection. "I cannot dissemble that my abilities are below my ambition. . . . I have, or had, a strong imagination, and consequently a keen relish for the beauties of poetry. . . . My reasoning faculty is proportionately weak. . . . I inherit from my sire a formality of manners and speech, but I derive from him or his patriotic parent a passionate love for the strains of eloquence. I burn after the *aliquid immensum infinitumque* [something immense and infinite] which Cicero desired." He concluded that he was justified in choosing theology "for the highest species of reasoning upon divine subjects as rather the fruit of a sort of moral imagination than of the reasoning machines, such as Locke, and Clarke, and David Hume."

Of certain faculties, then, he was sure, but as to how he should exercise them he was not so certain. There were other questions which he desired to put to older and more experienced minds. He went hopefully to Dr. Channing, whose assumption of the Federal Street pulpit in the very year of Emerson's birth had been a triumph for Unitarianism in Boston; but Channing was absorbed in his own problems; and Emerson found it hopeless to expect the famous preacher, of whom Bronson Alcott said: " He never converses but holds monologues," to take any other viewpoint than his own. He consulted other clergymen, who, after expressing sympathy, retreated behind a cloud of words. In a new despair he addressed his brother in Germany: " Why talk you not of my studies — how and what I should do? "

Though dreading her possible sarcasm, he at last threw himself upon his Aunt Mary in Maine as being the " faithful lover of these mysteries of Providence," and hurled at her a series of terrible questions. Among other things he begged this solitary maiden lady to explain, in a universe ruled by an omnipotent and wholly beneficent God, the presence of evil.

" *What*," he demanded, " *is the origin of evil?* "

" *What becomes of the poor slave . . . who has never heard of virtue and never practised it, and dies cursing God and man?* "

" *How is it that a Benevolent Spirit persists in introducing onto the stage of existence millions of new beings in incessant series to pursue the same wrong road and consummate the same tremendous fate?* "

His manner suggested his hope of being raised from the pit. " You have not thought precisely as others think. . . . Some revelation of nature you may not be loath to impart, and a hint which solves one of my problems would satisfy me more with my human lot." In these formidable questions may be detected Emerson's desperate searching for something permanent, something deep-laid, to which he might anchor his confused thought while his physical faculties were contending with a world whose events and pursuits were becoming more and more devoid of meaning. He had arrived at a crisis from which he was too dispirited, too frightened, to rouse himself. His aunt answered in the only manner possible — by avoiding the particular and presenting him with the general. Not even her aggressive, decisive mind had a remedy to offer except her own Calvinistic faith. She spoke of " subjects veiled in something of (God's) own awful incomprehensibility, soothed only by the faith which reason leaves, but can never describe." She wished he were not returning to Cambridge. " Would to God thou wert more ambitious — respected thyself more and the world less." For his present state of mind she felt herself partly to blame. She ought to have praised the Emerson brothers less and criticized them more. " It was pretty, it seemed best, to tell children how good they were! " Now she could only say, " The time of illusion and childhood is past, and you will find mysteries in man which baffle genius." She offered no light on these mysteries — his the task of resolving them. " May you," she prayed, " be among others who will prove a Pharos to your country and times."

II

Thus was it impressed on the bewildered young man that he could expect no solution, or even help, from the older and the presumably wiser. He must fight out the battle for himself. He was Adam born into a new world, confronting a future into which the thought of the possibility of evil had entered. The curse of consciousness had been passed upon him. The Garden of Eden was behind him and already he was in the outer jungle. He made this forlorn confession:

" The last evening I spend in Canterbury. I go to my college chamber tomorrow, a little changed for better or worse since I left it in 1821. I have learned a few more names and dates; additional facility of expression; the guage of my own ignorance, its sounding-places and bottomless depths."

Returning to Harvard, he occupied a room in Divinity Hall, low, dismal, and damp. For a month he struggled to subdue his depression and then he collapsed. The physical symptoms of his breakdown were a stricture in his chest, rheumatic twinges in one hip, and failing eyesight. Too much narrow solitude, too much sedentary brooding, too many undigested books. His whole being rebelled. Nature, demanding that life be lived and not evaded, drove him out of his shadowy room to his Uncle Ladd's farm at Newton. Emerson's life, as compared with that of other conspicuous men, proceeded so smoothly, rising from the earth towards the sky with scarcely a visible joint or gradation, that it reveals few turning-points; but his enforced exchange at the age of twenty-two of a cell for a farm was one, for it led to a useful experience.

Chapter Eight

I

EMERSON disliked any meeting artificially brought about. He preferred leaving his encounters with men to chance; or, as he preferred to call it, fate; " If we are related," he once wrote, " we shall meet." On this farm he worked among the common laborers, hoping to regain his health. " One of these men was a Methodist, and, though ignorant and rude, had some deep thoughts. He said to me that men were always praying, and that all prayers were granted."

It was virtually Emerson's first association with the " powerful, uneducated persons " afterwards celebrated by his pupil-at-a-distance, Walt Whitman. Hitherto, his circle had exclusively comprised the refined, the learned, and the genteel. In his affliction he had applied to these persons for a hint, an idea, a ray of light, that would lead him out of his present confusion. From them he had received only empty phrases or dead formulas. But here was a man who uttered a striking thought with a certainty, a conviction, that lodged deep in Emerson's imagination. He had found a catalyst for his whirling, fractious thoughts.

" I meditated much on this saying," he continued, " and wrote my first sermon therefrom; of which the divisions were: (1) Men are always praying; (2) All their prayers are granted; (3) We must beware, then, what we ask. This sermon I preached at Waltham, in Mr. Samuel Ripley's pulpit, October 15, 1826." A farmer afterwards said to him: " Young man, you will never preach a better sermon than that."

This laborer's name was Tarbox. Emerson never forgot him. The field-hand permanently joined that group, much reduced in subsequent years, who " gave a transcendent expansion to his thought, and kindled another life in his bosom." Tarbox's remark became not only the germ of Emerson's first sermon, but the basis of his pregnant essay, written years later, on *Fate*, in which appears Tarbox's quiet observation after it had passed through the alembic of Emerson's mind:

" *The soul contains the event that shall befall it, for the event is only the actualization of its thoughts; and what we pray to ourselves for is always granted.*"

The insertion of the phrase " to ourselves " is characteristically Emersonian. Tarbox had another effect on his fellow-laborer. He convinced Emerson that in his search for wisdom he must no longer confine his attention to books or to genteel, urbane persons; he must look to life itself and draw his deductions from his own deeps.

II

It was several months before his mind, overfed with reading and writing, was again ready for new tasks. He then resumed school-teaching at Chelmsford, but was obliged to leave that village in midwinter and take charge of his brother Edward's school at Roxbury. Breaks in the family ranks, due to ill health, were now occurring rapidly. Edward had been obliged to postpone activities for a time and seek recuperation in the Mediterranean. Peter Bulkeley had already been isolated on a farm. Waldo completed the term for his brother and then taught during the summer at Cambridge, to which place his mother had returned. Among his pupils were John Holmes, brother of Oliver Wendell, and Richard Henry Dana, Jr. Emerson's health did not permit him to take the regular courses at college, but he attended lectures and gathered material for sermons. Confessing his " cold feelings and slow tongue," he wrote long letters to his Aunt Mary, imploring her for oracles that would " awaken a sympathetic activity in torpid faculties "; but that lady was powerless to impart any store of her demoniac energy to her drooping nephew, and in September, 1826, he made this melancholy observation: "Health, action, happiness — how they ebb from me! Poor Sisyphus saw his stone stop once, at least, when Orpheus chanted. I must roll mine up and up and up how high a hill."

Despite his poor preparation, the Middlesex Association of Ministers admitted him to the fold on October 19, and five days later he delivered Tarbox's sermon. But his weakness continued, and he feared death would prevent the attainment of his ambition — " the foolish ambition," he called it, " to be valued." His friends became alarmed and his uncle, Samuel Ripley, at length induced him to board a ship for Charleston, S. C., where his friend, Robert Gourdin, brother of his Harvard roommate, who had meantime died, was ready to welcome him and where a Unitarian colony was already forming. But he found the November air even in Charleston too crisp for a " luke-sick " man, and after a few days he sailed farther south to St. Augustine, Florida. It was the first time he had ever been so far from home, and though he noted the increased grace of manners and the delicious air, at first his New England soul, nourished grimly on the belief in Purpose and the preciousness of Time, contracted like the sepals of a Calvinistic anemone at the sight of Southern laziness and slackness, accompanied by not a little dinginess and dirt.

" What," he wrote from St. Augustine, " is done here? Nothing. It was reported in the morning that a man was at work in the public square, and all our family turned out to see him."

III

In the course of his several weeks at St. Augustine, between spells of homesickness for the " genial cold " of New England and strolls on the beach, during which he idly drove a green orange over the sand with a stick, he noted, with an eye trained to a keenness which he often ascribed to his more observant brother Charles, some of the oddities of the old Spanish town. There were the iron frames in which criminals had been hung up to starve to death; a priest attending a masquerade in the character of a drunken sailor; the cathedral, " full of great coarse toys "; and the simultaneous occurrence at the same place of the meeting of the Bible Society and a slave auction — a symptom of that pervading dualism in American character by means of which the right hand remained piously ignorant of what the left might be doing. He also met several persons who gave him novel material for his notebook, among them a North Carolinian who told him of Methodists in his State who jumped and barked about a tree, shouting that they had "treed Jesus."

IV

Although to his journal he confessed, "I do not love the look of foreign men," by the time he had reached the end of his visit in April his congealed arteries had thawed a little toward the somnolent old town whose "fragrant airs and simple hospitality" he celebrated in verse; and well he might, for St. Augustine had enabled him to survive a dangerous crisis. To his aunt he acknowledged that his ailments had been not only physical but "metaphysical." He had been sick in mind as well as body; but now his thin frame was clothed with eleven more pounds and his spirits had become so brisk that he was once more able to write letters to his brothers in his customary humorous vein. He had had time to reflect and re-collect himself; his pains and dreads had placed him, he believed, "in a connexion with God that furnished a solution of the mystery of his being." But the soft old Florida town had done even more for him: it had provided him with a friend of the kind at that moment most necessary to him. "If we are related, we shall meet." He hinted to his aunt that he had encountered a wonderful person. He hastily warned her he was not talking of women. "Alack-a-day! it surely is not so."

This friend was of a character most likely to excite a glow in the young provincial preacher — "a philosopher, a scholar, a man of the world . . . very candid and an ardent lover of truth "; but he was more — he was a nephew of Napoleon Bonaparte (who, with the exception of Shakespeare, was Emerson's most exalted hero) and a son of Napoleon's sister, Caroline, and of one of his generals. This was Achille Murat, whose father, Joachim, had been King of Naples. Achille, after the execution of Joachim, had fled to America, married a Virginia lady, who was a grandniece of Washington, the former Miss Willis of Fredericksburg, and become a planter near Tallahassee, Florida. At the moment, he was about to start for Bordentown, New Jersey, to visit his uncle, Joseph Bonaparte and his own brother Joachim, whose American wife was keeping a school for young ladies there.

The contained Puritan and the expansive Latin touched poles at once; " everything good is the result of antagon- isms." They instantly fell into avid discussions, the thin and pallid young clergyman gazing at his companion admiringly as Murat, who was an admitted atheist and skeptic, with great sweeps of his arms and a torrent of talk, heaped his avalanches of scorn upon those who believed that the chief end of man was to "tree Jesus." Emerson stood by and nodded occa- sionally, sighing gently with relief. These orotund invectives, these fierce and bristling epithets, were the very ones he would have liked to use, had not his constitution rendered him incapable of uttering them.

Most of their conversations took place on the ship which was bearing them northward. Previously Emerson seems to have spent several days with Murat on the latter's plantation near Tallahassee, where Mrs. Murat was so impressed with the sweetness of the young guest that she afterwards silenced her husband with his name whenever " a harsh expression found its way up his throat." It is a pity we have no record of these shipboard discussions; for though Murat was no match for Emerson in penetrative intellect, he was his superior in poise and knowledge of men, and he had an acute understanding of the slim Yankee's fellow countrymen, of whom he had written to Count Thibaudeau in " Letters of a Citizen of the United States to One of his European Friends." Murat rejoiced in his American citizenship, believed that its freedom would introduce something new to the world, and admired the people of the new republic; but certain of their traits amused and baffled him. He noted their extraordinary love of calculation and " figuring "; their worship of young girls; their readiness to undertake great enterprises at a moment's notice; their trick of atoning for weekday cheating by the rigid observance of a dismal Sabbath day, and by their condemnation of dancing, especially the lascivious waltz; their passion for fierce competition in all activities; their indifference to aesthetics but yearning for short cuts to culture; and their determination to obtain a uniform observance of a moral code which regarded the gayer arts with bleak suspicion. Murat described the first performance of an opera company from Paris, whose opening ballet caused the scandalized women of the audience to withdraw, leaving the men behind to laugh loudly from the shelter of their side-whiskers.

However, from what remains of their correspondence and of contemporary notes made by Emerson, we can guess at the substance of the arguments that passed between the two men. The New Englander replied to the Frenchman's attacks on the historic foundations of the Christian belief by contending that organized Christianity, despite admitted

weaknesses, had a certain social utility in keeping men moral
— in short, it had a police value; and that it was possible
for a belief which was suited to the present needs of society,
though, absolutely speaking, it might be false, to be relatively true. Murat felt compelled to admit that "in a barbarous time of obscurity and ignorance," Emerson's theory
might be more useful, but argued that his own contentions
must be accepted by seasoned minds. The ardent Frenchman
went on to Point Breeze, New Jersey, whence he wrote to
Emerson, saying that he purposed, on his return home, to
compose a monograph "on how we can have an *absolute*
notion of truth." But his subsequent return to Europe, where
he hoped to assist in settling the tumults there, prevented
any further communication; and although Murat was eventually restored to his Florida farm, the two men never met
again. On Emerson's part further meetings were unneces-
sary; he had obtained from the hearty Frenchman what he
required — an increased clarification of his thought, some
of the cloud in which had already been precipitated by Tarbox, the field-hand. Like Tarbox, the agile Frenchman appeared in Emerson's subsequent writings. His lineaments are
seen in *Manners* and in *Society and Solitude*. In the latter
the grateful essayist said:

"If we recall the rare hours when we encountered the best
persons, *we there found ourselves*, and then first society
seemed to exist. That was society, though in the transom of
a brig, or on the Florida keys." [The italics are ours.]

V

Emerson returned to the North by easy stages, pausing at Alexandria, Washington, Philadelphia, and New York, and rejoicing to find he could preach without pain, though not yet rid of the stricture in his lungs. In June he was again at the Old Manse in Concord, where his mother was the guest of Dr. Ripley. He was heartily glad to be there and thought the very trees recognized him and nodded a welcome. " They know me as their son," he wrote. He took another room at Divinity Hall, Cambridge, but his lack of vigor would permit no serious study. He preached several Sundays at the First Church, Boston, and later at Northampton, New Bedford, and Lexington. But his health improved so slowly as to make him doubt whether he would not precede his brother Edward to the cemetery. He was still fighting a losing battle with the unconscious half of his nature which, though rigidly kept down, was still unreconciled to his entering the ministry as then constituted and which was refusing to grant him harmony with himself until he should choose the work suited to his constitution. A quotation from Goethe, which he copied in his journal, mirrored his state of mind:

" What good were it for me to manufacture perfect iron, while my own breast is full of dross? What would it stead me to put properties of land in order, while I am at variance with myself? "

To his aunt he wrote of promptings in the direction of painting and poetry, and to William he confessed: " I meditate, now and then, total abdication of the profession, on the score of ill health. . . . Very sorry, for how to get my bread? Shall I commence author? Of prose or verse? "

Meantime, Edward Bliss Emerson was breaking down completely under the intensified stimulation which Murat had deemed so terrifying a feature of Yankee life, and which had been brought to an unnaturally sharp focus upon the Emerson boys. Edward, like his brothers, was not allowed to grow and expand as his powers gradually developed, but must get ahead, must achieve, must outdo, must be great, by next week. In the summer of 1828, Waldo was compelled to record the beginning of the end: " Yesterday we brought Edward down to Charlestown. His frenzy took all forms. . . . There he lay — Edward, the admired, learned, eloquent, striving boy — a maniac."

VI

Waldo himself might not have escaped a like fate except for that protective integument within, and that very trait for which he often condemned himself — a tendency to what he called " silliness," manifested by a desire to snicker or giggle.

" I court laughing persons," he wrote at this very period, " and after a merry or only a gossiping hour, when the talk has been mere soap-bubbles, I have lost all sense of the mouse in my chest, am at ease, and can take my pen or book." He recorded with obvious pleasure a visit to the room of George W. Burnap, a fellow divinity student, afterwards a minister. Burnap made fun of Dr. Watts and thought it " the greatest phenomenon " that " the church should go chanting his hymns for centuries, mistaking the effusions of belly-ache for the inspirations of David." He also confessed another "peculiarity of humor," which he deprecatingly called a "propensity for strolling."

"I deliberately shut up my books in a cloudy July noon, put on my old clothes and old hat, and slink away to the whortleberry bushes, and slip with the greatest satisfaction into a little cowpath where I am sure I can defy observation. . . . I solace myself for hours with picking blueberries and other trash of the woods, far from fame behind the birch trees. I seldom enjoy hours as I do these. I remember them in winter; I expect them in spring. I do not know a creature that I think has the same humor, or would think it respectable."

And so he had to find relaxation furtively, in a guilty and sinful spirit, as if the Holy Ghost were keeping watch on him. Even this vivid sketch, so full of a simple beauty, he felt he must conclude by saying: "But the only will I find in idleness is unhappiness."

So read and study on, his demon urged. Work, for the night is coming. Fill the hours to the brim with purposeful toil. Leave no white margin around, no blue space within your grim composition. Permit nothing that is not hard or gritty to remain. One of four termini await you: you will be famous, you will be rich, you will be an invalid, or you will go to an insane asylum. "Why do you work so hard?" he asked himself. "Have you forgotten that all the Emersons overdo themselves?"

Chapter Nine

I

AT the age of twenty-four, Emerson was still afraid of young women. Their presence palsied him, so that he could neither act nor speak without a deepening of his sense of inferiority. Their lightness made his gravity appear to be stupidity, their stifled laughter seemed to make audible a creaking in his joints. So self-conscious was he that it was easy for any woman to put him out of countenance. " Nature," he observed, " wishes that women should attract man, yet she often cunningly molds into her face a little sarcasm, which seems to say, ' Yes, I am willing to attract, but to attract a little better kind of man than any I yet behold.' "

On a visit to Concord, New Hampshire, in December, 1827, he met for the first time a dainty young girl who made him conscious neither of his hands nor his hesitating speech. On the contrary, the very look in her eyes dissolved the awkwardness from his limbs, while her receptive serenity filled his arteries with a new sense of power; his locked tongue was loosed, a sudden desire to talk welled up, and he was astonished at the unaccustomed ease in his mind, at the good things he was able to say. Almost for the first time in his life he wished to be listened to at length. He talked so much that he frightened himself and made abrupt pauses that he might notice in her any sign of fatigue. He even ventured to be silly, uttering nonsensical things at which she laughed freely. It was her capacity for laughter which fastened on him the final fetter, and he fell as madly in love as if for twenty-odd years he had not schooled himself to be cold and self-contained.

Her name was Ellen Louisa Tucker, daughter of Beza Tucker, a Boston merchant. After her father's death, her mother had married again and become Mrs. W. A. Kent of Concord, New Hampshire. Ellen was only sixteen years old, but her slight form was already roundly molded, and in mind Emerson found her singularly mature. Her eyes were large, full-orbed, and sympathetic. Her face was oval, her hair curly, her lips full; while her whole appearance was invested with a daintiness and fragility that made the gawky young clergyman afraid to touch her. His regard for her was hallowed by a reverence for an unearthly quality which in his eyes made her Beauty itself. He could never refer to her except as " Friend " and even in his gayest moments she remained " beautiful friend." He was now no longer the staid preacher but " a watcher of windows. . . . The day was not long enough, but the night, too, must be consumed in keen recollections; when the head boiled all night on the pillow with the generous deed it resolved on; when the moonlight was a pleasing fever, and the stars were letters, and the flowers ciphers, and the air was coined into song."

Just how they met is not recorded, but references in Emerson's writings to mysterious communications that flash from eye to eye, make it likely that she came to hear him preach in the New Hampshire church; that over the heads of hearers they exchanged looks; and that after the service he contrived to be introduced to her.

EMERSON AS A YOUNG CLERGYMAN

From a drawing by John W. Alexander

Though deeply smitten, Emerson was not the man, even at twenty-four, to yield to any impulse, however pure — after due analysis and examination — it might appear to be; and he went away for a year. But the head, even of an Emerson, could not boil on a pillow for a year of nights with impunity, and at length he found an excuse to return to New Hampshire. The ostensible reason was the necessity of travel and diversion for the sick Edward, recently released from his asylum. When Emerson saw Ellen again his cool veins throbbed, and he could no longer refrain from speaking out. Haltingly he began a preamble setting forth the poverty of his prospects. How could he, a poor preacher with scarcely all his ministerial feathers on, presume to . . . ? Gently but tersely she interposed.

" I do not wish to hear about your prospects," she said.

Emerson was not then acquainted with the practical, far-seeing nature of woman; Ellen had already measured her man, and while he was fumbling his words and being miserable, this poised and delicate maid had already accepted him. After that there was naught to do but be, as he shyly wrote to William, " as happy as it is safe in life to be." He added, " She is seventeen years old, and very beautiful, by universal consent." In his journal for December 21, 1828, he wrote: " I have now been four days engaged to Ellen Louisa Tucker. Will my Father in Heaven regard us with kindness, and as he hath, as we trust, made us for each other, will he be pleased to strengthen and purify and prosper and eternize our affection? "

II

Emerson had meantime been occupying the pulpit of the Reverend Henry Ware, Jr., at the Old North (Second Unitarian) Church in Boston while the pastor was recovering from an illness, and when Mr. Ware was appointed professor in the Cambridge Divinity School, Emerson was chosen in his stead. Now for the first time in his life the clouds over his head began to give place to a clear blue. He was head of an important church, and his overwhelming sense of darkness and solitude had already been dispersed by the entrance into his life of a worshipped being. His spirits rose gently and with them his health.

But there was too much Calvinism latent in Emerson to permit him to exult too freely in the present moment. From the hill of good fortune he could not resist a glance down at the valley shadows in which there might be lurking his father's God, quiescent now but capable of dreadful interventions. Many persons said they loved this Deity, but no one quite trusted him. And so he wrote to his Aunt Mary for assurance that the bogey-man would not hurt him. " Can this hold? " he asked. " Will God make me a brilliant exception to the common order of his dealings which equalizes destinies? "

Scarcely had this uneasy letter been dispatched when the news came that his bride-to-be was very ill. The malady was the same which was constantly threatening himself and his brothers — tuberculosis. But in the course of the summer she improved, and by September, 1829, she was deemed well enough to be married. Emerson and she at once began house-keeping in Boston, his mother living with them. He was twenty-six years old, she eighteen. Emerson afterwards recalled " that sort of fearful delight with which the bride-groom sits down in his own house with the bride saying: ' I shall now live with you, always.' "

Chapter Ten

I

"IT is the best part of the man, I sometimes think, that revolts most against his being a minister."

This passage from Emerson's diary for January 10, 1832, indicates his interior struggle while he was for three years outwardly carrying out the duties of his pastorate with entire devotion. His preaching was in general acceptable to his congregation, although some of the older pew-holders thought he dwelt too much on ethical speculations and not enough on doctrine. The younger people, however, liked his simple delivery, his illustrations drawn from familiar scenes and objects, and in especial his clear, vibrant voice, over which he had obtained excellent control. The rhetorical scrolls and arabesques to which the example of Edward Everett and Daniel Webster had once tempted him, he had discarded as unsuited to him, and his speech had thereby gained in sinew. Margaret Fuller was one of the young people who came to hear him, and at once, in her impulsive way, resolved to know him better. But at no time was his full heart in his work. He hated the "official goodness" to which he was bound. He felt himself chained to habitual words and routine texts, while he wished to arouse his auditors with "the great circling truths." It is significant that of the 171 sermons preached during this period, he afterwards permitted only two, delivered on official occasions, to be published.

" The whole world holds on to formal Christianity," he wrote, " and nobody teaches the essential truth, the heart of Christianity, for fear of shocking, etc. . . . This accommodation is a loss of so much integrity and of course of so much power."

Power, and the freedom to exert it — that is what he craved. He was beginning to feel the rise of his own forces, and yet forms enclosed and muffled him. Even in the pastoral duties of visiting the sick and preaching funerals he was ineffective. He had cultivated no bedside manner, and his attempted condolences trailed off into triteness and conventionality. It was this long period of repression from which he no doubt derived the vigor and defiance which he later packed into *Self Reliance*, that essay which at the time was an elixir to a famished Young America.

From his semi-failures in the outer world he retreated to his books and drew inspiration from his " Citizens of the Universe " — Coleridge, Carlyle, Landor, Wordsworth, and Goethe. He was delighted to find that science, which was to influence the whole literary thought of the nineteenth century, could supply him with fresh material, and he eagerly read Newton and Cuvier. He was charging himself with ideas to the bursting point; a rupture, a breaking through, could not much longer be delayed.

But before he could gird himself for action, his bride suffered a relapse and he was compelled to take her South. He returned to his duties, but performed them like a man only half alive. He could think of nothing but Ellen, her gayety, her childish laughter, alternating with moods of a charming gravity. He tried to absorb himself in books — " a man's library," he once wrote, " is a sort of harem " — but when the laggard spring came he could only push them aside and compose poetry, forcing his heavy hand to write lightly, as in " Ellen at the South ":

" O'er ten thousand, thousand acres,
    Goes light the nimble zephyr;
The Flowers — tiny sect of Shakers —
    Worship him ever.

Hark to the winning sound!
    They summon thee, dearest, —
Saying, ' We have dressed for thee the ground,
    Nor yet thou appearest.' "

But even these delicate summonses failed to arouse her from the passive mood into which she had fallen. She had ceased to fight her ailment and " did not think she had a wish to get well." One day the following spring, just as he was preparing to go South and join her, appeared this abrupt entry in his journal:

" Ellen Tucker Emerson died, 8th February, Tuesday morning, nine o'clock."

II

There were no more entries for five days, and then he wrote:

" This miserable apathy, I know, may wear off. I almost fear when it will. Old duties will present themselves with no more repulsive face. I shall go again among my friends with a tranquil countenance. Again I shall be amused. I shall stoop again to little hopes and little fears and forget the graveyard. But will the dead be restored to me? . . . No. There is one birth and one baptism and one first love. . . ."

The death of Ellen was one of the three calamities which gave Emerson the most formidable shocks of his life. At this time he was only twenty-seven years old, and he needed all the steadiness of his carefully equilibrated being to endure a loss for which he had been only partly prepared by her long illness. Every morning in all weathers he went to visit her grave in Roxbury, and for years his journal received his short, barely suppressed cries of mourning.

By April, however, he had recovered himself, and was able to write: " the troubled water reflects no image. When it is calm it shows within it the whole face of heaven." And the next day: " The days go by, griefs, and simpers, and sloth, and disappointments. The dead do not return, and sometimes we are negligent of their image." And four years later he could say, " I loved Ellen, and love her with an affection that would ask nothing but its indulgence to make me blessed. Yet when she was taken from me, the air was still sweet, the sun was not taken down from my firmament, and however sore was that particular loss, I still felt that it was particular, that the universe remained to us both, that the universe abode in its light and in its power to replenish the heart with hope."

III

Something unaccountable and strange is detectable in Emerson's attitude toward his first wife. In his numerous references to her and to their life together occurs none of the endearments, none of the pet names, which men spontaneously bestow on fragile and attractive women. He worshipped her, but from a distance; as if she were a goddess or angel who had graciously but temporarily lent her shining presence to his life. No closeness, no intimacy, is revealed in the tone of calm grief with which he wrote of her. She remained his " friend," his " beautiful friend," his " enchanting friend." He was incapable of speaking of her in more passionate terms, as he was incapable of passion itself. Stranger still are his references to the compunctions which assailed his later and more mellow memories of her. He mentions these compunctions in his journal, and in the very introduction to his essay, *Love,* occurs this mystifying passage:

" Let a man go back to those delicious relations which make the beauty of his life, which have given him sincerest instruction and nourishment, he will shrink and shrink. Alas! I know not why, but infinite compunctions embitter in mature life all the remembrances of budding sentiment, and cover every beloved name."

There is a suggestion that he wished he had known how to be more tender and demonstrative toward Ellen and his dead brothers, but " alas! " he confessed at another time, " even for those I really love I have not animal spirits." Neither human impulse nor warm spontaneity resided in the adult Emerson. It is probable that his affection for Ellen he intellectualized; in the same way that he intellectualized every other relation, toward person or thing, in which he entered. " With thought, with the ideal, is immortal hilarity, the rose of joy," . . . he again wrote in *Love.*

" But with names and persons, and the partial interests of today and yesterday, is grief."

IV

With the passage of years his grief entered a new and even cooler phase, and with his dislike of the dismal he was able in *Compensation* to arrive at this conclusion:

" The death of a dear friend, wife, brother, lover, which seemed nothing but privation, somewhat later assumes the aspect of a guide or genius; for it commonly operates revolutions in our way of life, terminates an epoch of infancy or of youth which was waiting to be closed, breaks up a wonted occupation, or a household, or style of living, and allows the formation of new ones more friendly to the growth of character."

This was his way of saying that although under the impact of Ellen's death his internal shell had rocked and wavered, it had not been shattered and was now again firm in its seat. There is no denying that there was indeed compensation for Emerson, as concerned his career, in the death of Ellen; for, since he was no longer a husband or prospective father of a family, his hands were at last free to cut the exacerbating tie that had for years bound him to a formalized pulpit.

Chapter Eleven

I

WHEN on the morning of the ninth of September, 1832, seven months after Ellen's death, Emerson arose and, in a serene voice that vibrated only a trifle with hidden feeling, began to address his congregation, some inkling of what was about to transpire had already seeped into the air, and rows of eyes, some glittering with a half-sympathetic curiosity and others smoldering with a half-suppressed hostility, fastened themselves upon his thin body, his mild, blue-eyed face.

Other presences, forewarned that another battle in the long war in which they had all participated was about to take place, must have been there also; and in the darkness of backgrounds and corners might have been detected the shades of venerable figures — popes and prelates, St. Augustine and Martin Luther, John Calvin and John Knox, Michel Angelo and Immanuel Kant, Copernicus and Isaac Newton. The Reformation and its uterine sister, the Renaissance, were 400 years old in Europe; but in the New World they had barely arrived, encased in the broadcloth of a gentlemanly Unitarianism.

Unitarianism — liberal, believing in one God, and wishing to be on good terms with all the world — had captured Harvard College, most of the important Boston pulpits, and churches in a few of the larger American towns; but over the rest of the country lay the shadow of Calvinism — harsh, theocratic, autocratic, dogmatic — teaching that men, even at birth, were depraved and despicable objects, and as such were to be watched, herded, suspected, and regulated until at death those few who had been chosen by a childishly wilful Jehovah should be admitted to a heaven whose streets were lined with organized institutions. The spirit of Calvinism had taken possession of the Presbyterian, Methodist, and Baptist churches, and even rebellious Unitarianism had not entirely divested itself of ancient remnants, particularly in ritualistic observances. Calvinistic preachers, of the kind described by Emerson as "God's police," had, each Sunday since colonial days, laid down doctrines whose cathartic violence was not unsuited to a rural population which every day observed evidences of total depravity not only in man but in animals, tools, and the earth itself, and had rendered services thus described by Emerson at a later day in Concord:

"The Church aërates my good neighbors and serves them as a somewhat stricter and finer ablution than a clean shirt or a bath or a shampooing. . . . These people have no fine arts, no literature, no great men to Boswellize, no fine speculation. Their talk is of oxen and pigs and hay and corn and apples."

In Boston, however, and in other American centers where an optimistic merchant and nascent manufacturing class had begun to heap up wealth and comforts, the bony chair of Calvinism, bare of ornament and full of protruding nails, was too uncomfortable to sit in; and it had been succeeded by the comforting upholstery of Unitarianism, which taught that man, under the right conditions, was a worthy and even a noble soul, and that Jesus Christ was not his God but his sympathetic brother.

To understand what Emerson did on this day, it is important to keep these distinctions clear; for confused history has somehow identified Calvinism with Puritanism, which was another thing and had a different lineage. Puritanism had its birth in a revolt against what it deemed to be superfluous and distracting religious ritualism. It did not, in its beginnings, hate harmless human joys, or try to regulate human behavior. A Calvinist might be also a Puritan; but a Puritan was not necessarily a Calvinist (Emerson, for example, was a Puritan, but not a Calvinist); and it is not Puritanism which has left to American civilization its legacy of dogma, intolerance, and dark suspicion of all the creations of man, but the doctrines of John Calvin, who was born in France and at intervals suffered from biliousness.

II

Emerson's discourse on this day differed profoundly in structure and style from his later essays and lectures. Whereas these last were whimsical, jagged, and often contradictory, his sermon was measured, logical, and carefully proportioned, proceeding clearly and directly from opening statement to firm conclusion.

His theme was the observance of the Lord's Supper. After pointing out that in religious history there had been neither unanimity nor uniformity in regard to its nature and celebration, he openly proclaimed his opinion that when Jesus ate the Passover supper with his disciples, he did not intend to establish an institution for perpetual observance, and he condemned the contemporary mode of celebrating it as "inexpedient." " Jesus," said Emerson, " was a Jew, sitting with his countrymen, celebrating their national feast."

Before his hearers had recovered from the shock of contemplating Jesus as a Jew among other Jews, the calm young pastor gave them another: he laid impious hands upon St. Paul. Nowadays the authority of Paul, the Roman citizen who belonged to the upper caste of the proudest Jews of his time, has waned somewhat, and it is recognized that Paul tried to establish what was virtually a new religion, differing markedly, and in some respects basically, from that taught by Jesus Christ as reported in the Synoptic Gospels; but at that time Paul's influence was supreme, and it was unspeakably shocking to hear a home-bred young clergyman ascribe this institutionalized rite of the Communion wholly to Paul and then to say: " There is a material circumstance which diminishes our confidence in the correctness of the Apostle's view"; namely, Paul's belief that Christ's second coming would shortly occur.

Emerson then summed up his own objections to the ordinance of the Lord's Supper as tending " to produce confusion in our view of the relation of the soul to God "; he affirmed that the symbolism of bread and wine was Oriental, and therefore " foreign and unsuited " to New Englanders.

" To eat bread is one thing," said Emerson. " To love the principles of Christ, and resolve to obey them is another. . . ." After referring to his impending resignation, he intimated, in this terse language, his indifference as to how his views should be received: " It is my desire, in the office of a Christian minister, to do nothing which I cannot do with my whole heart. Having said this, I have said all. . . . That is the end of my opposition, that I am not interested in it."

It was in these closing words that Emerson entirely cut himself off from his church and proclaimed that he was finished with it. The leaders of the congregation had already been consulted and had unanimously refused to relinquish the rite in question. The pew-proprietors were subsequently called together and voted thirty to twenty-four to accept his resignation; but they generously continued his salary for the present, probably owing to the disbelief that Emerson, bone of their bone, would reject an eventual reconciliation.

III

It may be imagined how great was the sensation caused in the close-knit church circles of Boston by Emerson's bold nailing of his thesis on the door of the Second Church. Discussion was agitated and warm, and when it was seen that Emerson would accept no compromise, there were not lacking those who deemed him crazy. The brilliance of the Emerson brothers was not denied, but it was clear that mingled with it was a vein of errancy.

Emerson's resignation brought him the relief he had expected. He smiled when he heard his admirers describe his action as bold, noble, and self-sacrificing. He knew he had simply made an effort " to suit his external condition to his inward constitution." He wrote his elder brother of the " peace and freedom which I plainly see before me, albeit afar "; but he was not sure what he would do now. He contemplated the establishment of a review similar to those English ones he had admired, but better — a magazine in which "the soul of a man should speak out, and not the soul general of the town or town-pump."

But even while he was listing his possible contributors, a depressing reaction set in. He had not the stamina fit to cope with the stresses of the past few months, and his old maladies reappeared. His mother, alarmed, wrote to Edward, who had gone to Porto Rico in the vain hope of mending his broken health, and had been joined there by Charles, who also had been driven from his law studies by incipient consumption, urging him to return and care for "the lonely brother." Both brothers returned, the dying Edward for his last visit. Charles wrote to his Aunt Mary in the November following Ralph Waldo's September resignation: "Waldo is sick. His spirits droop; he looks to the South, and thinks he should like to go away. I never saw him so disheartened." In December he wrote again: "Waldo is meditating a departure for Italy. . . . I do not doubt he may write and be a fine thinker, all alone by himself; but I think he needs to be dragged closer to people by some practical vacation, however it may irk his tastes."

The Reverend Dr. Ware and other friends had, meantime, convinced Emerson of the benefits of a transatlantic voyage; he was quite ready to be swayed and readily accepted the passage to Italy pressed upon him. Aboard a cargo vessel he sailed from Boston on Christmas Day, 1832. He was bound for Malta and Naples; but he well knew where he should eventually land — to sit at the feet of his four Buddhas, to ride out with the Four Horsemen of the European Apocalypse — Carlyle, Coleridge, Wordsworth, and

Landor. He had not yet reached the stage where he, the persistent traveller, could say: " Men run away to other countries because they are not good in their own "; " only the light characters travel "; " there is a restlessness in our people that argues want of character"; and, finally, " Can we never extract this tape-worm of Europe from the brain of our countrymen? "

Almost a hundred years have passed since Emerson made his first visit to Europe, and the tape-worm is still where it was. And he, the leader of the advance guard in the revolt against Europe, was as much a victim of it as any present-day summer tourist.

Chapter Twelve

I

ALMOST at once Emerson found diversion for his pallid thoughts in admiring the busy seamen and their practical skipper, their indifference to gales and their attention to the work in hand. He had an almost feminine admiration, a Nietzschean worship, for gross, hairy men who suggested the presence of that which he always regarded with shining eyes — Power. They were *plus* men, and " all *plus* is good." They had muscle and stomach; " the first wealth is health "; and they swore and cursed in a rich and satisfying manner.

" Men of this surcharge of arterial blood cannot live on nuts, herb-tea, and elegies; cannot read novels and play whist; cannot satisfy all their wants at the Thursday Lecture or the Boston Athenaeum."

He admired them as he always secretly admired " strong transgressors like Jefferson or Jackson," the " bruisers," the " gross and peccant " men who, though " not clothed in satin," get the thing done, and whose excess of virility " brings its own antidote." In contemplating the versatile sailor, " tailor, carpenter, cooper, stevedore, and clerk, and astronomer besides," he forgot himself; pulpits and libraries sank below the horizon; and at length he was thanking " the sea and rough weather for a truckman's health and stomach."

His spirits rose even to the point where he could jauntily salute the Europe just beyond the fog:

" Sleep on, old sire, there is muscle and nerve, and enterprise in us, your poor spawn, who have sucked the air and ripened in the sunshine of the cold west, to steer our ships to your very ports and thrust our inquisitive American eyes into your towns and towers and keeping-rooms. Here we come, and mean to be welcome. So be good now, clever old gentleman."

He used his leisure for a bit of self-examination — " wherever we go, whatever we do, self is the sole object we study." He found reason to castigate himself: " I seem on all trivial occasions to be oppressed with a universal ignorance. . . . Is it the hard condition upon which the love of highest truth is given — such extreme incapacity for action and common conversation as to provoke the contempt of the bystander, and even of kindred and debtors? "

II

He landed at Malta five weeks and three days from the day of sailing. His New England eyes were almost at once affronted by the mass of swarming human life, and at an English chapel he heard a sermon preached and Watts's hymns sung " with greedy ears." He was only mildly wrought upon by the sight of quaint buildings and handsome faces — " that which is finest in beauty," he confided to his journal, " is *moral*," underscoring the word firmly.

Syracuse, however, with Arethusa's fountain and Hyblaean honey, pleased the poet in him. At Naples he braced himself against the beauty of the bay lest he be " overawed by names," and insisted it was " only the same world of cake and ale, of men and truth and folly "; and even while he wandered through its sensuous streets he remembered Zion, lovingly recalling " the fogs of close, low pinewoods " and "blue violets out of black loam."

In the museums, the busts and statues of Grecian gods and great Latins surprised him " with a moral admonition " — " These are the countenances of the first-born, the face of man in the morning of the world." He remarked how they contrasted with " the frivolity and sensuality " of the mob. This was characteristic; Emerson hated mobs and masses just as he hated sweat and smell. He thought they drowned that in which he tenaciously believed — the perfect individual. He permitted himself an outburst: " Goethe says he shall never again be wholly unhappy, for he has seen Naples; if he had said *happy*, there would have been equal reason."

In Rome he tried to brace himself against the beauties of sculpture and painting, but was compelled to write: " It is vain to refuse to admire; you must in spite of yourself." He saw a papal procession, but Emerson was descended from those men who had substituted the meeting-house for the cathedral, and his Puritan eyes rejected the parade even as a spectacle: " There is no true majesty in all this millinery and imbecility."

In Rome he made an entry in his journal which disclosed the true Emerson. He encountered a New England face there which made well-nigh all of Italy acceptable. It belonged to a friend named Lewis Stackpole, and to Emerson he appeared " as fresh and beautiful as a young palm tree in the desert." Through Stackpole he met other resident

Yankees and was instantly at peace. Emerson was only momentarily interested in things, no matter how beautiful in form or color. His primary interest was in persons, and among these he was ever seeking the individual whom he could idealize and adore.

" Ah, great Rome! " he wrote. " It is a majestic city, and satisfies the craving imagination. And yet I would give all Rome for one man such as were fit to walk here, and could feel and impart the sentiment of the place."

The bent of his mind was not artistic, or historical, or antiquarian, or archaeological; it was biographical. " God's greatest gift is a Teacher," he wrote despairingly to his Aunt Mary, " and when will he send me one full of truth and of boundless benevolence and of heroic sentiments? "

In Florence he saw his first ballet, and diligently tried to remember Goethe's injunction that one's judgment before a work of art should be purely aesthetic. In vain. His reaction was moral — " I could not help feeling the while that it were better for mankind if there were no such dancers."

III

In Florence he tried very hard to be interested in what artist friends eagerly showed him, but his spirits were not really kindled until Horace Greenough, the American sculptor, took him to visit one of his four heroes — Walter Savage Landor, then living in solitary splendor, after numerous quarrels in his native England and publishing his *Imaginary Conversations*. It was the first time Emerson had seen in the flesh any foreign writer of eminence, and as Landor was

this, and was an upper-class Englishman, too, he was prepared to be properly awed and impressed. Landor received
him courteously and invited him to come back another day
for breakfast. At this second interview, Landor, sitting amid
his " cloud of pictures," indulged in the whimsy which a
great European might permit himself in the presence of an
earnest and inquiring young Yankee. Almost at once his host
discovered that Emerson venerated the name of Socrates,
whereupon Landor called Socrates " a vulgar old sophist."
Emerson, blue-eyed, open-mouthed, and serious, could not
perceive that he was being " spoofed," and that his host was
merely having a little morning target-practice on his guest's
most precious idols. Landor went on to denounce vulgarity
as being particularly offensive in a wise man, and veered
from this to proclaim Washington, Phocion, and Timoleon
as the three greatest of men, pointing out the deep signifi-
cance of " the similar termination of their names "! While
Emerson was still pondering this revelation, Landor hung
wreaths on Lord Chesterfield, for whom Emerson had an
aversion on the ground of his "slippery morality." " It is
inexcusable in any man who pretends to greatness," Emerson
wrote indignantly in his day's journal, " to confound moral
distinctions." The American then countered on Landor by
admitting his ignorance of Southey — Southey, his host's
friend and hero! After that Landor cut loose and smeared
Emerson's idols one by one. They parted coolly, Emerson to
go to his hotel and write restrainedly to his brother Charles:
" Landor does not quite show the same calibre in conversation as in his books," and Landor subsequently to return to
England, where at Bath he replied to Emerson's published
account of the interview in a book which was supposed to be

a refutation, but which was only more of Landor's petulant fault-finding.

Emerson was now a trifle uneasy as to what he might expect from the three remaining literary Riders-to-the-Sea, but of one he was reasonably sure. " I hope better things of Carlyle."

IV

From Florence he passed through Bologna, Ferrara, and Padua to Venice, which " looked for some time like nothing but New York . . . a most disagreeable residence . . . always a smell of bilgewater." He experienced a growing irritation against foreign sights, and even against his companions, gay Wall and Robertson. " I have no skill to live with men," he wrote after a breathless day. " No boy makes so many blunders or says such awkward, contrary, disagreeable speeches as I do."

He was dragged through the rest of Italy, feebly trying to be enthusiastic at Brescia and Milan, until he reached Geneva, and thence, " protesting all the way," he visited Ferney, the home of Voltaire, whose work he compared to that of a " buzzard and tarantula." He was in a state of revolt against all he had seen. " The charm of Italy," he wrote, " is the charm of its names. I have seen as fine days from my own window. Then what Boswellism it is to travel! Illustrate, eternize, your own woodhouse. It is much cheaper, and quite possible to any resolute thinker."

V

Arriving in Paris, his companions eagerly looked to him for the raptures expected of all good Americans there. It was June, but Emerson was nervous and sight-saturated. " The gardens of the Louvre looked pinched and the wind blew dust in my eyes, and before I got into the Champs Élysées I turned about and flatly refused to go farther." He had merely " come to a loud, modern New York of a place." The French were " a vain nation." His exacerbation increased until it alarmed him and in his diary he admonished himself: " Be cheerful. What an insane habit is this of groping into past months, and scraping together every little pitiful instance of awkwardness and misfortune, and keeping my nervous system ever on the rack."

He tried to interest himself in the life of the streets, went to a dinner given to Lafayette, and attended lectures at the Sorbonne, hearing Jouffroy, Thenard, and Gay-Lussac; but he was too homesick to be genuinely absorbed. " A lecture at the Sorbonne is far less useful to me than a lecture that I write myself," he declared. He added that to Paris he would prefer his inkstand.

It was only at the Garden of Plants that he felt a glow, and his meditations among the specimens there were reflected in his writings for many years. His revulsion against art and too close association with human beings — he could find no confirmation for his belief in the perfect, self-sufficient individual among the sodden masses of Europe — invested the works of Nature with a new charm. " I am moved by

strange sympathies; I say continually, ' I will be a naturalist.' " He noted, apparently for the first time, " how much
finer things are in composition than alone." It was his discovery of the category of relation — that no one thing has an absolute existence, but is what it is by virtue of its relation to
other things. " We are not strong by our power to penetrate
but by our relatedness." He felt an exhilaration. " Here we
are impressed with the inexhaustible riches of nature. The
universe is a more amazing puzzle than ever, as you glance
along this bewildering series of animated forms . . . the
upheaving principle of life everywhere incipient, in the very
rock aping organized forms. Not a form so grotesque, so
savage, nor so beautiful but is an expression of some property inherent in man the observer." His exaltation found expression later in the poem *Each and All*, the central lines of
which are:

> " Nor knowest thou what argument
> Thy life to thy neighbor's creed has lent.
> All are needed by each one;
> Nothing is fair or good alone."

During the last few days of his visit, he became a little
more friendly toward Paris and even found objects and
customs to praise; but no returning exile was ever gladder
than he to turn his face toward England. No man ever
gained less from a Continental tour than the young clergyman whose thoughts continually reverted, amid the pictures,
the cafés, and the lusty crowds, to cool Concord and his
inkstand. He had passed through uncounted cities like
a man in a trance, anaesthetized to all external objects.

He had scarcely been detained by any building, ruin, bust, or picture. He had not come to see them anyway; he had been searching for " moral truth," and he had not found any.

VI

London was " immense," but " very dull." The sights made only a slight impression upon him; but he was gratified to behold at the funeral of Wilberforce, the anti-slavery agitator, one of his beloved men of action — the Duke of Wellington. At the first opportunity he escaped to the suburb of Highgate, and after much inquiry, for no one knew the name of the object of his search, he found Coleridge, then within a year of his death, living with his friend and protector, Mr. Gillman. It was near noon, but Coleridge was still in bed and Emerson had to go away and return an hour later. Coleridge was " a short, thick old man, with bright blue eyes and fine, clear complexion." Between pinches of snuff, which sprinkled his suit and cravat, he greeted the young Unitarian minister with a violent attack on Unitarianism. Emerson felt compelled to remind him that he was born and bred a Unitarian.

" Yes," said Coleridge coolly, " I supposed so."

He had once been a Unitarian himself and knew its " quackery." It was " an unspeakable misfortune " that Dr. Channing, whom Coleridge said he had once looked up to — nay, looked *at* — with interest, should have " turned out a Unitarian after all." He was afraid that Channing loved the good in Christianity and not the true. " The Trinitarian doctrine is realism," declared Coleridge. " The idea of a God is not essential, but super-essential."

For an hour Coleridge went on with his monologue, critical and denunciatory. He ignored the young American and gave him small opportunity for remark or question. Finally Coleridge, observing that he did not know whether his visitor " cared about poetry," offered to recite some of his verses and then declaimed the poem which ends:

> " In vain they try
> To end my life, that can but end its woe.
> Is that a deathbed where a Christian lies?
> Yes! but not his — 'tis death itself there dies."

And there the unilateral interview ended and Emerson crept away. " As I might have foreseen," he wrote, " the visit was rather a spectacle than a conversation, of no use beyond the satisfaction of my curiosity." But he was still hopeful. Two of his four heroes had failed to ride grandly across the sky for his edification, but two remained; they surely would " give one the satisfaction of reality, the sense of having been met, and a larger horizon." On to Ambleside then, and to Scotland, home of the Edinburgh Reviewers.

VII

Ambleside, close to the Scottish border, was to Emerson particularly holy ground, for there, on Rydal Mount, lived the poet in whom he had found certain deficiencies — " there is something hard and sterile in his poetry" — but who nevertheless represented " the high-water mark which the intellect has reached in this age," and who had vastly influenced his thought in the direction of Nature and its healing teachings. Wordsworth was then sixty-three years old, and Emerson's first sight of him was disconcerting. He was a " plain, elderly, white-haired man, not prepossessing," and he was not wearing an aureole, but green goggles. To the former schoolteacher from America, Wordsworth said: " Schools do no good. Tuition is not education." He considered that " society was being enlightened by a superficial tuition out of all proportion to its being restrained by moral culture." He spoke at length of his visitor's country. Twenty-eight years before it came, he thought a civil war was needed there, to teach the necessity of knitting the social ties stronger.

" There may be in America," he said, " some vulgarity of manner; but that's not important. That comes of the pioneer state of things. But I fear they are too much given to the making of money; and secondly, to politics. . . . I fear they lack a class of men of leisure — in short, of gentlemen — to give a tone of honor to the community."

Wordsworth thought that necessary reforms should be obtained by moral, constructive action, and not physical violence. Indulgence in sin threatened society with the gravest mischiefs. " Faith is necessary to explain anything, and to reconcile the foreknowledge of God with human evil." In discussing books and writers, he gave relatively low rank to Emerson's admired Virgil, and deemed Lucretius a far higher poet. Emerson ventured to ask his opinion of Carlyle.

" I think him sometimes insane," said Wordsworth promptly.

Carlyle, he said, was clever and deep, but too defiant of

sympathy. In obscurity he was worse than Coleridge. At mention of Goethe, Wordsworth drew himself up and began to thunder. He denounced *Wilhelm Meister* as " full of all manner of fornication." He had thrown the book across the room rather than finish it. When he had silenced Emerson, he led the way out to the garden where he showed his visitor the gravel walk on which thousands of his lines had been composed. A new edition of his poems could be had at the booksellers', he mentioned. Being unable to read, owing to inflamed eyes, he carried hundreds of lines in his head. Among them were three sonnets written only three days previously on Fingal's Cave.

" If you are interested in my verses," he said, " perhaps you will like to hear these lines."

Wordsworth then mused for a moment, struck an attitude " like a schoolboy declaiming," and launched with animation into a recitation of the three sonnets. Emerson was appalled to find himself attacked by one of his old fits of " silliness." He wished to be grateful and respectful, but instead he repressed with difficulty an impulse to giggle. He needed all his self-command to hear Wordsworth through.

After further desultory conversation, the old poet escorted the young American part of the way to his station, talking vehemently, while Emerson tried not to show how glad he was to be escaping. " Alone we are whole, but when we meet we become fractions."

VIII

At Edinburgh, Emerson was disturbed to find that Carlyle not only did not live there, but was virtually unknown to the inhabitants. Only after much search was he able to obtain the Scot's address from the secretary of the university. Meantime, he preached in Edinburgh at the Unitarian chapel. Alexander Ireland, who became his guide and friend, records that nothing like Emerson's sermon had ever been heard there before — "the pregnant thoughts and serene self-possession of the young Boston minister" charmed his Scottish audience, while he himself deemed the preacher's voice "the sweetest, the most winning and penetrating of any I ever heard."

Emerson crossed the Highlands to Glasgow and thence to Dumfries, where he had to hire a gig to take him the sixteen miles over heath and rock to Craigenputtoch — in Gaelic, "Hill of the Hawk" — and at last sat down with Thomas Carlyle and Jane Welsh in their nook, "the loneliest in Britain," with "not a person to speak to except the minister of Dunscore," who was unfriendly.

Carlyle, then eight years the elder, had not yet made the descent upon London where he was to become Chelsea's sage, and was known only to a narrow circle as a translator from the German, with an errant admiration for German thought and philosophy, upon which he wrote copious articles in reviews and encyclopaedias in a twisted, repulsive style. At first glance the trepidant Emerson was satisfied that here was his man; he "never saw more amiableness" than was in his countenance. He liked Jane, too: "a most accomplished, gracious woman," who considered Emerson angelic, although she afterwards was mean enough to say that what Emerson had, he owed to her husband.

It may be imagined with what curiosity the cynical Carlyle,

looking from under his cliff-like, saturnine brows, surveyed his visitor, with a face as open as any field of bluets. Of course the conversation early got around to books and Carlyle quickly discovered the American's love for geniuses and his particular adoration of Socrates and Plato. This was the opening desired by the railing Scot. He never read Plato, he said, and dismissed Socrates as despicable. In his broad Scotch he went on to declare that for real genius he preferred pigs. He described at length how he had tried to confine his own pig in a pen, built with much toil and ingenuity, but the animal had put his wits to work and discovered how to let a board down and so escape. The burden of the Scot's discourse was that man was a very interesting, "plastic little fellow," but for genius not to be compared to a moor-bred pig.

No more than in Landor's case did Emerson at first realize that the Scot was having sport with him. He had not yet seen around his host, or grasped that on occasions half, and sometimes more than half, that Carlyle said and wrote was for effect only; and that some of his most fantastic utterances, however stratified with truth, were made in a spirit of sour jest or bitter sportiveness. He therefore listened with his ingenuous smile while Carlyle, pleased by his own jests, went on to ridicule the intellectual broils of the moment — "Mydoxy and Thydoxy, Pantheism and Pottheism." He made fun of the very magazines in which he appeared: Blackwood's was the " Sand Magazine " and Fraser's the " Mud Magazine." He admired Nero's death — "What an artist do I die." He liked America because its workingmen could have meat for their labor. He ridiculed his own profession and its mediums, in terms how familiar! — " No newspaper is trusted now; no books are bought, and the booksellers are on the road to bankruptcy."

Carlyle considered John Stuart Mill the best mind he knew: " more purity, more force," but Mirabeau (to Emerson a " scrub ") was his present hero. It was Rousseau's *Confessions* that had convinced him he was not a dunce. He excoriated England, then as now full of workless men, for its treatment of paupers. "Government should direct poor men what to do," he said. He admitted the attraction of London for him. " London is the heart of the world, wonderful only for the mass of human beings. I like the huge machine. Each keeps its own round. The baker's boy brings muffins to the window at a fixed hour every day; and that is all that the Londoner knows or wishes to know of the subject."

While Mrs. Carlyle prepared the evening meal, he took Emerson out for a walk over the hills, whence they could see the peak of Criffel and look down into Wordsworth's country. The two men sat down, and Emerson, to Carlyle's disgust, instead of gazing upon the mountainous beauty, introduced the topic of the immortality of the soul. Carlyle was indulgent but brief. " Christ," he said, " died on the tree; that built Dunscore yonder; that brought you and me together. Time has only a relative existence." He pitied the man who had no worship, no reverence for anybody, but condemned Calvinism and Unitarianism as narrow and limited.

However, Carlyle, for all his burlesque and whim, could not long hold out against the innocence and naïveté of Emerson, and by the next day he had accepted the foreigner as a friend. " I saw him go up the hill," he said afterwards. " I didn't go with him to see him descend. I preferred to watch him mount and vanish like an angel."

So was founded a friendship which persisted for forty-four years and which was kept arterial by a correspondence that endured till both men were grey and old. On Emerson's part the friendship was active, idealistic, and fond; on Carlyle's it was passive, indulgent, and only occasionally responsive. Emerson urgently desired a spiritual brother, and Carlyle, at times making a face, accepted the fraternal rôle. Their correspondence is one of the most celebrated in literature; it is also one of the most curious. Emerson wrote from an adolescent country, thinly peopled, but ambitious, rash, and confident; Carlyle from a hoary land, heavy with people, tradition, and treasured iniquity, making changes only with laborious effort. It was as if Emerson warbled with the voice of a New England wood-thrush, clear, cheery, and flute-like, from a solitary but flowered glade; while Carlyle, from London's matted mass, answered with eructations.

The two men, despite trenchant differences, of which each was aware, had sufficient ground on which to meet. Their early histories were similar — each had been intended for the ministry but had revolted against its halters. Each was by nature a prophet, Puritan, and seer; the one an ancient Jeremiah, the other a new John the Baptist. Both were at bottom Romantics, already shaping themselves as leaders of the reaction against classicism and dogmatic authority. And both, frail Scot and frailer Yankee, were incurable hero-worshippers, believing in the Strong Individual, with grim purpose and iron will, who would one day purge the world of moss-grown sins. Emerson lived to see him in the flesh. And he failed to recognize him.

IX

From Carlyle's home Emerson went to visit Wordsworth, with the results already described; and then with lightened heart turned his musing face homeward. His gallery of gods had been found to be all too human and he was eager to be back at his own inkstand. "A man not too old feels himself too old to be a vagabond," he observed. "The people at their work accuse me by their looks for leaving my business to hinder theirs. These men make you feel that fame is a conventional thing, and that man is a sadly 'limitary' spirit. You speak to them as children, or persons of inferior capacity, whom it is necessary to humor. . . ."

From Manchester to Liverpool he had his first ride on a railway, travelling twenty-one miles in an even hour. At his Liverpool hotel he exchanged remarks with a stranger who proved to be a fellow countryman, Jacob Perkins, the Massachusetts inventor, who in his time had "made everything except money," and who was in England trying to sell some of his numerous devices. Emerson was delighted with Perkins; he was a diverting contrast to moral poets and such; he was a man who "could do things," and at once became that type of inventing Yankee with his head full of wheels and ratchets which Emerson loved to refer to. Ever avid for illustrations, Emerson put a pail under the inventor and drained him of information regarding steam engines, then so new to the world. Perkins, elated, took him out and showed him the toyish little locomotives then regarded as colossal monsters; they had grandiose names such as "Goliath" and

" Pluto." Perkins said they should not travel over fifteen miles an hour — it racked the engines to go faster. He then astonished his pupil by saying he expected to see the ocean " navigated by *steam*." Emerson was so impressed that in his diary he underscored the word.

On September 4, 1833, he took a sailing vessel, 516 tons, for New York, seeing " the last lump of England recede without regret." In his cabin he was able to sit at ease before his writing paper for the first time in months, draw a long breath, review his experiences, examine himself, and summarize his conclusions. He did not at the time comprehend all that his foreign tour had done for him; but his present reflections he set down firmly.

First, he convicted his four literary grandees of deficiency of "insight into religious [*i.e.*, spiritual] truth." They had failed to " fill the ear — fill the mind," and he wrote, " I shall judge more justly, less timidly, of wise men forevermore." He recalled Carlyle's amiability, but could not share his disposition to grudge the peasant his Calvinism. " I see or believe in the wholesomeness of Calvinism for thousands and thousands. I would encourage, or rather I would not discourage, their scrupulous religious observances." This was in line with Emerson's previous conclusion that Calvinism had a useful police function in keeping men at least mechanically moral.

One result of his tour was indubitable: Europe had cured him of his provincial reverence for Europe. " We go to Europe to be Americanized." Further reflections expanded his renascent patriotism. " I am thankful that I am an American as I am thankful that I am a man. It is its [England's] best merit to my eye that it is the most resembling country

to America which the world contains." Here is discernible
that revolt against European domination in which Emerson's
chief literary contemporaries were to join. Washington Irving had been almost entirely European in manner and outlook, but James Fenimore Cooper had pointed out a native
path which succeeding writers were to follow and widen.

And then after a day or two more of solitary musing,
Emerson's credo, which was to govern his subsequent life
and teachings, came to him in almost solid form. It was like
a Mosaic tablet handed down out of the blue. Visible in it
are the threads and spores found in virtually all his writings.
At the age of thirty, sitting in his vessel's cabin, while the
wind was still, he wrote these firm sentences without altering a word:

" A man contains all that is needful to his government
within himself. He is made a law unto himself."

" All real good and evil that can befall him must be from
himself. He only can do himself any good or any harm."

" Nothing can be given to him or taken from him but
always there is a compensation."

" There is a correspondence between the human soul and
everything that exists in the world; more properly, everything that is known to man."

" Instead of studying things without the principles of
them, all may be penetrated unto within him."

" Every act puts the agent in a new condition."

" The purpose of life seems to be to acquaint a man with
himself."

" He is not to live to the future as described to him, but
to live to the real future by living to the real present."

X

He landed in New York October 9, 1833, and went to his Uncle Ladd's farm at Newton to rejoin his mother. On invitation he preached at various places, and even appeared in his old pulpit at the Boston Second Church. By December he was able to write, " I please myself with contemplating the felicity of my present situation. May it last."

Thus did Emerson signify his re-creation. His European trip had cleansed his mind of certain fogging notions and put his own intellectual legs under him. Dispersed were his old pains, his introspective aches, his haltering apathy, even his grief. His sense of inferiority had been lifted; he had matched his own mind against four foreign intellects and had discovered his own was not to be scorned. He was refreshed and newly equipped for the task he was about to undertake; but at the moment he could scarcely have been aware that during his thirty years a new sort of America had merged which would eventually be, by the very conditions of its birth and being, fertile to his gospel. New England agriculture was rapidly giving place to manufacturing; the first textile spindles were already turning at Waltham, Lawrence, and Lowell. Steam, electricity, and hot-blast furnaces were creating forward-looking towns in which there was no place for the slow peasant and his dour Calvinism. A middle-class was arising, liberal and optimistic, eager to do, to clear, to build, to trade. Westward and southward the population was pushing in great waves, delighting in the discovery of lands, rivers, metals, minerals. The pioneer, California bent, had already left the Middle West to the settler; and on the settler's heels had come the speculator, the merchant, and the manufacturer.

For hardy, ingenious, romantico-practical men of the motor type it was a golden age, and independence and individualism were the twin devices on their banner. The infant Union of States was becoming economically, socially, free of England; but the circle of independence would not be complete until they were spiritually, culturally, free. Who would sound the trumpet for the advance that would close the gap?

Chapter Thirteen

I

HIS return from Europe was followed by a pause of several weeks, during which he gave himself to solitary reflection and woodland rambles, and some study of the sciences, particularly geology, chemistry, and physics. He eagerly followed the experiments of Faraday in England and drew on them to illustrate lectures on natural history which he was preparing against the day when he should again have a platform. He blessed his solitude and bided his time.

" By going much alone," he wrote, " a man will get more of a noble courage in thought and word than from all the wisdom that is in books."

Then occurred a fortunate circumstance. The settlement of his wife's inheritance from her father's estate gave him an annual income of about $1200, which relieved him of the more pressing economic worries — a fact which immensely influenced his subsequent career and thinking.

He considered establishing a home in Berkshire, where he might house his mother, and take care of Edward, who was still ill in Porto Rico; also Charles, whose encroaching malady was already causing periods of despondency. He also revived his former notion of establishing a periodical which would " speak truth without fear or favor," but distractions intervened. On invitation he preached for several weeks at the Unitarian Church in New Bedford, whose minister had been called elsewhere. Emerson gave so much satisfaction that a tentative offer of the pastorate was made to him, but this was withdrawn when he let it be known that he would not carry out the Communion or offer prayer. He was now adamant against forms.

He profited, however, by his stay at New Bedford among the Quakers, whose tranquillity he admired and whose obedience to the inner light deeply impressed him, so much so that he was afterwards accused of being too much under the sway of Quaker teachings. He made a firm friend of Mary Rotch, a Quaker lady whose wisdom he was fond of quoting for years afterward. The Friends also supplied him with many anecdotes of the kind in which he delighted.

" Mary," said a New Bedford Friend who wished to be more than that to a certain lady, " it has been revealed to me that I should marry thee."

" Abner," she said, " when it has been revealed to me, I will tell thee."

II

He continued his desultory preaching for several years, chiefly at country churches, where his clear voice and unpretentious illustrations from Nature pleased his congregations, regardless of the latent heresy of his doctrines. At East Lexington a lady said: " We are a very simple people and can understand no one but Mr. Emerson."

However, although he might respond to occasional calls, he was definitely finished with the ministry, and saw a more receptive field and a less constricted platform among the lyceums then springing up in the country, in response to a spontaneous demand from a people who had few books to read and little leisure in which to absorb them. Seeking practice, he promptly accepted an invitation from the Boston Society of Natural History, and in November, 1833, he began his career as a lecturer with a paper entitled, " On the Uses of Natural History." He had at last found his niche, his place and sphere, and he fitted into it as die to matrix.

On the platform he was not less the preacher than in the pulpit, but without the confining clerical collar; and he had the satisfaction of knowing that for what he had to pour, there was a receptacle waiting to be filled. He was accurately expressing himself when he afterwards wrote: " What we need is not knowledge, but vent." The lecture platform as vent not only relieved Emerson of his apathy, his ill health, and his internal warrings, but caused profound modifications in his outlook. It gave him what he had previously lacked: direct, if selected, contacts under pleasing conditions with the body and corpuscles of human life, and so lessened his intellectual anemia, his spiritual stasis, giving his mental life elasticity, color, and firmness. From this time forward there were no more apathies, sinkings, and clouded introspections. His writing manner, too, underwent considerable alterations; his style became that of a man talking to listeners rather than writing for readers. His sentences Carlyle truly compared to a bag of duckshot, held together by canvas.

III

His first paper was followed in four weeks by a second entitled, " The Relation of Man to the Globe," and a few months later he delivered for the Natural History Society its annual address. In these lectures, founded largely on his observations at the Garden of Plants in Paris, he declared that the task of natural science was " to explain man to himself," to indicate his true place in the system of being, and to point out his connection with universal life. He almost trenched upon the borders of evolution theory then not yet framed [Darwin was at that very moment voyaging in the Beagle], deeming it a sublime fact that " man has been prophesied in nature for a thousand thousand ages before he appeared . . . the meaner creatures containing the elements of his structure and pointing at it from every side." But he hoped science, in its pursuit of facts, would not overlook poetry. " The naturalist should be subordinate to the man," and there was danger that the savant might become a mere " apothecary, a pedant." He saw a new hope for America in the study of its own natural history, for " all American manners, language, and writing are derivative . . . after the English manner."

In his journal at this period he indicated how he was further pursuing a parallel thought:

" The subject that most needs to be presented, developed, is the principle of self-reliance. . . . My own bosom will supply, as surely as God liveth, the direction of my course."

IV

Early in 1834 he addressed the Boston Mechanics' Institute on "Water" — a curious title, but characteristically Emersonian; for he saw everything as fluid — rocks, trees, institutions, even society itself: "society is a wave"; "the old statesman knows that society is fluid." For his material in this lecture he drew heavily on his talks with Jacob Perkins.

In the same winter he lectured twice on his travels in Italy and wrote a poem for the annual meeting of the Phi Beta Kappa Society in Cambridge. All these occasions he utilized as a means of discovering his thought and perfecting its expression. He constantly admonished himself to show more courage, to utter himself boldly. "Dear God that sleepest in man, I have served my apprenticeship of bows and blushes, of fears and references, of excessive admiration."

He repeatedly counselled himself to spend his life "within," to "penetrate facts for the law, and events for the cause." At the same time he warned himself against attaching followers, for the "least wisdom cannot be communicated, but must be acquired by every soul for itself." His excitement mounted as he felt himself yielding larger results the more he explored himself; and he recorded anticipations which have since been largely verified by modern electro-magnetic studies. For example: "The magnet is a marvel when we simply see it spontaneously wheel to the north, and cling to iron like one alive. The wonder diminishes when it is shown to be only one instance of a general law that affects all bodies and all phenomena, light, heat, electricity, animal life."

While he roamed the woods, he was constantly on the watch for " the Idea which would integrate the particulars " — the Idea " according to which the Universe is made." At length, on May 21, 1834, he wrote down this declaration:

" I will thank God of myself and for what I have. I will not manufacture remorse of the pattern of others, nor feign their joys. I am born tranquil, not a stern economist of Time, but never a keen sufferer. I will not affect to suffer. Be my life then a long gratitude. I will trust my instincts."

But even an Emerson, seeking Idea and recording Law, is not exempt from the mundane, and while he was enjoying the exultation of self-discovery and self-realization, a young man living next door was learning to drum. Nightly while Emerson kept his studious vigils, the youth practised beats, rolls, and tattoos until Thought was shredded and Idea drowned. Finally Emerson confessed: " I should like to reward his music with a wreath of *Smilax peduncularis* " [the common briar].

V

The words " Reason " and " Understanding " constantly appeared in his writings at this time, always capitalized. These terms he had probably got from Coleridge. By the Understanding he meant that everyday, practical faculty of arriving at rapid judgments which is ordinarily called common sense. " It works in time and space." The Reason was the deeper and far more reliable faculty; it perceived relations rather than facts, and instead of the part saw the whole. It was " the universal mind." It was virtually what a later psychology call the Unconscious, whereas the Understanding corresponded to the superficial Conscious. Indeed, Emerson occasionally used these very terms, as in this observation: "Blessed is the child; the Unconscious is ever the act of God himself." And again: " The age of puberty is a crisis in the life of the man worth studying. It is the passage from the Unconscious to the Conscious."

Emerson sought diligently to train himself to rely strictly upon this Unconscious, this " Reason." " Go to the bard or orator that has spoken and ask him if what he said were his own. No; he got it he knows not where, but it is none of his."

VI

An entry occurs in this portion of his journal which reflects his daily strivings to clarify his ultimate thought, to cut himself loose from all current influences and props:

" It is extremely disagreeable, nay, a little fiendish, to laugh amid dreams. In bed I would keep my countenance, if you please."

It has been already observed that Emerson resented being made to laugh aloud. Is this an indication that during his sleep his Unconscious thus revenged itself? Emerson was a notable dreamer by night as well as by day, and his writings, especially his essay on *Demonology*, testify that his sleep was frequently visited by strange and disturbing fantasies. At another time he seems to have thought that certain dreams were more connected with the Understanding (Conscious) than the Reason (Unconscious). " My dreams," he wrote in his forty-ninth year, "are somewhat arch and satirical, if I dare give them all the meaning they will bear. If they mean anything, they are surprising bits, yet by no means from a divine plane, but from a great sagacity on the Franklin level."

VII

In October of this year, 1834, came the news of Edward Bliss Emerson's death in Porto Rico, and Emerson wrote: " So falls one pile more of hope for this life."

By contemporaries Edward had been adjudged the most brilliant of the Emerson brothers. He had shone as a teacher, as a poet, and as a student in Daniel Webster's law office. Even the younger brother, Charles, was deemed superior in ability to Ralph Waldo, who lacked the social gifts that would draw notice; in society he was awkward and silent, and, if he took part in conversation at all, what he said was without novelty or sparkle.

To Edward's death was due a decision momentous for Emerson. In his desire to be near the ailing Charles, who had set up a law office in Concord and was about to marry Miss Elizabeth Hoar, he easily persuaded his mother to accept the invitation of Dr. Ripley to come and live in the Old Manse, and they moved at once to the Concord house built by Emerson's grandfather, the Revolutionary chaplain, and afterwards made famous by Hawthorne, who there wrote *Mosses from an Old Manse.*

From this time forward Emerson was never long absent from Concord. In it he found his spiritual as well as his physical home. The staid village founded by his dissenting ancestor, Peter Bulkeley, with its squarish houses and inhabitants who looked like their houses and elms, provided him with the outward circumstances that perfectly accorded with his inner life. The word decorum was the map of the community. Satan himself, on his rare visits, was ill at ease there; he was ignored socially; he fancied his advancing age was being noticed, and was relieved when he could escape to more fertile centers. Indicating his awareness that he was about to begin a new life, Emerson wrote this dedication:

" *Hail to the quiet fields of my fathers! Not wholly unattended by supernatural friendship and favor, let me come hither. Bless my purposes as they are simple and virtuous. . . . Henceforth I design not to utter any speech, poem, or book that is not entirely and peculiarly my own.*"

VIII

Despite this bold declaration, Emerson was not yet wholly sure of himself; and it was a sound instinct which led him to seek at this period the society of his younger brother, Charles. Although he had fewer years, Charles had had more direct experience with men and things; his was the more precise and certain mind; and Emerson was glad to lean on him and draw sustenance from his learning, his wit, his spontaneity. Ralph Waldo's thought was constantly turned inward; it was Charles who gave him eyes. " His senses were those of a Greek," said Emerson. " I owe to them a thousand observations. To live with him was like living with a great painter." During long walks and readings and animated discussions, Emerson found himself strengthened and sharpened. Charles's observations readily fell into aphorisms which the elder treasured and stored: " The spirit of Stoicism saith, ' Be high-minded and fear not.' Christianity says, 'Be not high-minded but fear ' "; " The south wind makes everybody handsome "; " As fast as Mrs. X rows, Mr. X backs water "; " Tomorrow I go to my Sunday School. That ever I should be a shepherd — I who cry inly as a weak lamb to be folded and fed "; " The nap is worn off the world." During a year of close association, Emerson's love for his younger brother became what in a man less cool would have been a major passion; it mounted to a worship which, however, never found expression until after Charles's death.

IX

Among the towns at which Emerson occasionally preached was Plymouth, where he found the " families and the faces almost as tranquil as their pines." He of course stood on the Rock, and noted " the fine objects in Plymouth from men and women down to vegetables." These fine objects drew him back again and again. Among them was a Miss Lydia Jackson, sister of Dr. Charles T. Jackson, the surgeon and one

of the discoverers of anaesthesia. She caused in him a pertur-
bation, also doubts which caused him to examine a picture of
himself critically. It depressed him; he found his features
" ugly," and recalled the story of Erasmus, who said: " Look
I like this picture? So am I the greatest knave that liveth."

Nevertheless he succeeded in becoming engaged to her,
he being then thirty-two years old, and he at once perceived
the world to be growing richer and better. " When I recol-
lect the charms of certain women, what poems are many
private lives, each of which can fill our eye . . . then I feel
the riches of my inheritance in being set down in this world."
He also experienced a new humility and wrote: " If any eye
rest on this page, let him know that he who blotted it could
not go into conversation with any person of good understanding without being presently gravelled."

He began to look for a house to rent, with the intention of
building one later on the hill rising between the Old Manse
and the tract called " Peter's field " or " Caesar's woods," so
named after the freed slaves who had once had cabins there;
but on August 15, 1835, he bought the wooden Coolidge
house, built about 1825 by a Concordian named John T.
Coolidge for $7800. Emerson paid $3500 for the property
including slightly over two acres of land.

Here was founded the Emerson home, which in later
years numerous pilgrims deemed beautiful; but which at the
time he spoke of as " a mean place, and cannot be fine until
trees and flowers give it a character of its own." He found
the house was set too low, but chose it because it was in the
outskirts of the village on the Cambridge Turnpike, well
beyond the shadows of other houses. " A cow," said Emerson,
" does not need so much land as my eyes require between me

and my neighbor " — a saying which proved his kinship with those early pioneers, who when a neighbor settled within fifty miles felt instantly crowded. The land was sandy and quickly drying, and on the north the high tableland screened it from the worst effects of Arctic storms. Eastward were visible the Lincoln hills. Southeast and south were the orchard and the garden open to the sun. Behind the house a path led to a meadow through which a brook flowed to the quiet Musketaquid, the " Grassy River " of the Indians, who still sometimes camped there. Beyond lay fields and woods through which there were walks to The Cliff and to the pond called Walden. The main house was originally L-shaped, but Emerson's additions made it virtually a square. Here was to come Emerson and his bride; here he was to give to the name of a homely village the luster of a permanent beauty; here he was indeed to make eternal his very woodhouse.

X

On September 14, 1835, he was married in the Winslow House at Plymouth. His wife, at his request, at once altered her name from Lydia to Lidian, so that a comfortable consonant would interpose between the vowels *a* and *e*. She readily gave way to him in everything, making no objection to Concord though secretly hoping they might live in Plymouth. In person she was gracious and dignified: her friends sometimes called her " the Abbess." She was one of the modest, unexacting women of her time, readily obscuring herself that her husband might grow great. Like Emerson himself, his two younger brothers, and his former wife, she was tubercular; but in her new home she soon conquered the ailment. In her quietly capable hands the household and its affairs flowed as smoothly as Musketaquid itself; and with her Emerson truly dwelt in Concord, sheltered, tended, adored.

Emerson drove his bride back to Concord in a chaise. The stable-owner had provided him with reins of a festal yellow. When Emerson saw them he was shocked; such things were not seemly, and he exchanged the yellow reins for the usual black.

XI

Although he had previously lived in Concord, and had friends and relatives there, Emerson did not at first take more than a very temperate part in the village life, except for silent attendance at town meetings, even after he had been appointed " hog-reeve," charged with the duty of pursuing, rounding up, and impounding wandering rooters. He did not encourage aimless visits, and the Concordians showed no disposition to intrude. Indeed, they paid little attention to him (" who in Concord," he wrote, " cares for the first philosophy in a book? "); in no way did they consider him a coming man or even a to-be-respected citizen; and as his wife was a stranger and he himself, though courteous, remained slightly aloof, they were content to let him alone. This was agreeable to Emerson. " The northwest wind, with all his snows," he wrote, " took me in charge and defended me from all company."

He was content to devote himself to his writing and to his bride. As they became better acquainted, he began to call her

" Mine Asia " and " Queenie." Her native wisdom, serene and gently uttered, sometimes astonished him. "I, as always," he wrote, " venerate the oracular nature of woman. The sentiment which a man thinks he came unto gradually through the events of years, to his surprise he finds woman dwelling there in the same, as her native home."

Chapter Fourteen

I

SHELTERED as Emerson was, he could not avoid occasionally hearing those distant shouts which even in Concord proclaimed that somewhere a world was in tumult. The Abolition cause was rising, vocal and aggressive, and anti-slavery agitators were sometimes guests at his home. A few months after he had established himself in his velvety domesticity, William Lloyd Garrison was dragged through the streets by a Boston mob. The papers were black with accounts of "movements" — against slavery, against Masonry, against tariffs, against Andrew Jackson — for whom Emerson at first had an aversion but whom he later admitted to the circle of those secretly admired men of deeds who were "half orator, half assassin." He was not aroused, however — "A man feels," he wrote, "that his time is too precious, the objects within reach of his spirit too beautiful, than that his attention should stoop to such disfigurements . . . yet welcome would be to him the principle out of which these proceed, for all the laws of his being are beautiful."

He preferred to write, to muse, and to begin his long correspondence with Carlyle; and one day he was moved to relieve the "extreme deadness" of the community by inviting the Scot to come thither and live. What would have been the effect on staid, uniform Concord of this tossing, maladjusted soul, this sulphuritic hurler of epithets at his fellows, the imagination backs at surmising; and the possible effect on the artless Emerson, who hated noise, complaint, and combat, would be even more difficult to estimate. Such a dynamitic situation, however, never came into being. Fate, ever kindly disposed toward Emerson, caused Carlyle to decline the invitation, thus keeping Concord history on its meted course.

Carlyle's *Sartor Resartus* had been recently appearing in *Fraser's Magazine*. Emerson had shown the numbers to his fiancée and to other friends, among them Dr. Le Baron Russell, who took them to James Munroe and Company, raised subscriptions for a book, and persuaded Emerson to write a preface. It was the first appearance of *Sartor* in book form, for British publishers would have none of it. This was the beginning of Emerson's long and faithful services to Carlyle in America. He became virtually the Scot's literary agent, and even performed for him a peculiarly loathsome task — keeping accounts in figures. He also advanced sums for Carlyle's account out of his own pocket.

As a lecturer Emerson continued to expand. In 1835 he read papers in Boston on Michael Angelo, Luther, Milton, Fox, and Burke; on "Correct Taste in English Literature"; on Concord history for the town's 200th birthday; and delivered ten lectures on "English Literature." In 1836 "The Philosophy of History" was given in twelve lectures, and in 1837 there were ten more on "Human Culture." These occasions were fairly well attended, and Emerson was listened to with respect, but without particular enthusiasm. His "Concord Hymn," sung to the tune of "Old Hundred" at the completion of the battle monument, did considerably more than his early lectures to win the notice of his neighbors. And gradually, very gradually, they began to accept him as their own.

II

In his thirty-first year Emerson was compelled to postpone his lectures and once more assume the roll of caretaker to the sick, for Charles had begun to droop. Emerson took him to William's home in New York, where his mother was visiting. It was the recollection of these mournful journeys, made for himself as well as others, that no doubt led Emerson, in his subsequent writings, to exalt " frolic health " and gave him an aversion against sick men's complaints. . . . " The only wealth is health."

Charles was to marry in the autumn, and Emerson had already begun to add rooms to his house in which he and his bride were to live. It was not believed that Charles's condition was grave; and Emerson resumed his lectures, only to be summoned quickly to his brother's bedside. He arrived too late, and could only write to his wife: " You must be content henceforth with only a piece of your husband; for the best of his strength lay in the soul with which he must no more on earth take counsel. How much I saw through his eyes! "

Yet, as he had previously written, he was " never a keen sufferer "; he believed even in " the compensations of calamity," and soon he was again tranquil and even cheerful in the company of the new friends, who were beginning to resort to his house. In the late summer he wrote William that A.

Bronson Alcott, "the world-builder," had spent a day with him and that his wife at present had a guest, "an accomplished lady," Miss Margaret Fuller.

III

In September of the same year, 1836, occurred two events important not only in Emerson's history but in American literary annals. One was the appearance, without the name of its author, of a little book entitled, *Nature*. Emerson had already seen print in the *North American Review*, but this was his first venture in book form. He had begun the writing of it in the Old Manse and completed it in the quietude with which his bride had at once invested his new home. He had labored over its points and gaps — "everything in Nature," he once wrote, perhaps with a sly double meaning, "has a crack in it"; but though not entirely succeeding in filling them, he had decided to publish the essay as it stood.

Even after Emerson was known to be the author, the little book earned only a few admirers, and twelve years were required to sell five hundred copies. Most of those persons who were not mystified by it, were hostile to it; and reviewers dealt with it as something repugnant. There was nothing in the imagination of the period which could respond to Emerson's lyric raptures. To the prosaic American mind Nature was neither interesting nor attractive; on the contrary, the common view, inherited from pioneer times still so fresh in memory, was that Nature was an enemy, harsh and forbidding, which was to be pushed back and kept at a distance. For example, the most conspicuous object of the landscape — the forest — was a mere lurking place for shadows, wild animals, and Indians; and its trees were to be attacked, cut down, and destroyed as if they were armed men.

The only comforting word from a high place came from Carlyle, who wrote from his new home in Cheyne Row, Chelsea, London, " Your little azure colored *Nature* gave me true satisfaction. . . . You say it is the first chapter of something greater. I call it rather the Foundation and Ground-plan on which you may build whatsoever of great and true has been given you to build. It is the true Apocalypse, this when the ' Open Secret ' becomes revealed to a man."

Emerson's introduction supplied the key to his general design: " The foregoing generations beheld God and Nature face to face; we through their eyes. Why should not we also enjoy an original relation to the universe? Why should not we have a poetry and philosophy of insight and not of tradition, and religion by revelation to us, and not the history of theirs. . . . Why should we grope among the dry bones of the past? . . . There are new lands, new men, new thoughts. Let us demand our own work and laws and worship."

Thus did Emerson notify an older culture that a New World was in being, had passed its adolescence, and now must have its own voice and own expression. These were the first trial notes of the trumpet which he was to sound again and again; but, as is so often the case with trumpet calls, they were heard better at a distance than near by. Europe heard them, and, though it did not clearly comprehend, cocked its ears; but Emerson's countrymen, though hearing, were busy with other concerns — the elders with lands, with markets, with building, and accumulation; the younger with sickly, introspective thoughts which Emerson called "the soul's mumps and measles and whooping-coughs." Only here and there was there a youth who listened and was moved. "I was simmering, simmering, simmering," said Walt Whitman. "Emerson brought me to boil."

IV

There were other young men who, though not directly affected by Emerson, yet enjoyed to some degree the advantage of walking through the swath which he had cut in the undergrowth. "Is it not singular and not at all unpleasing," remarked Emerson in his thirtieth year, "the fact that almost all great men have been so yoked together by the accidents of their lives, and few or none stand alone, but all in a genial constellation?"

There was indeed a constellation then existing, although only a few of its luminaries had as yet twinkled in the firmament. Among them were Irving, Cooper, Bryant, Hawthorne, Whittier, Holmes, Thoreau, Melville, and Poe. All, with the exception of the first three, were Emerson's juniors. All, like him, were products of the opening years of the nineteenth century, and were alike subject to its fermentations and its needs. And all were in various degrees inspired by the face of that Nature which Emerson gazed upon delightedly, as if it had been newly created for him and his generation. It was indeed a New World into which they had been born, clear-eyed and verdantly fair. To Poe alone was it old. Too old.

V

In his little book Emerson considered Nature in two aspects: as an object, or system of objects, apprehended by and delighted in by the senses; and as a subjective creation to be comprehended only by the metaphysical or spiritual eye. He left no doubt as to which vision was his own:

" I become a transparent eyeball; I am nothing; I see all; the currents of the Universal Being circulate through me; I am part and particle of God. . . . Nature always wears the colors of the spirit. . . . The beauty of Nature re-forms itself in the mind; and not for barren contemplation, but for new creation. . . . But Beauty in Nature is not ultimate. It is the herald of inward and internal Beauty. . . . Things are emblematic. Every natural fact is a symbol of some spiritual fact. . . . We learn that the dread universal essence, which is not wisdom, or love, or beauty, or power, but all in one, and each entirely, is that for which all things exist, and that by which they are; that spirit creates; that behind Nature, throughout Nature, spirit is present. . . . Once inhale the upper air and we learn that man has access to the entire mind of the Creator; is himself the Creator in the finite."

This lyric doctrine, through meditation distilled and compounded from Emerson's copious reading — from Plato and the Neo-Platonists, from Wordsworth and Swedenborg, from Kant and Coleridge and Berkeley and the Hindoo scriptures, entirely counter to Calvinism and even at variance with Unitarianism — presented far too impalpable a dish for the handy New England palate to relish; and Professor Bowen, of the Harvard chair of Natural Theology and Moral Philosophy, was only the agent of a suspicious and bewildered public when in the *Christian Examiner* he discharged both barrels of his indignation at *Nature* and condemned it in an article ominously entitled, " Transcendentalism."

VI

This word, though relatively new, had gradually come into circulation as a useful tag which could be safely affixed to a body of novel and abhorrent views. In its day, Transcendentalism corresponded roughly, in the minds of the scornful, to what almost a century later was called Bolshevism, as signifying something raffish and nonsensical, hopelessly theoretical and disagreeably threatening. It was a " movement," and any notion containing a suggestion of motion, flux, or change, could not fail to be regarded with suspicion by the solid and the anchored. Its beginnings were nebulous and groping, being no more than flocculent shreds of unease which eddied around and around seeking center and expression.

Remotely it derived its stimulus from the new German idealistic philosophy; from Kant with his *a priori,* intuitive concepts, and Hegel with his " process of becoming," and from the general ferment of ideas which had assailed intellectual Europe in the first third of the nineteenth century; in France developing into the middle-class revolution of 1830, and in England producing the Wordsworths and Carlyles who had reacted against rising mercantilism with its devotion to " things "; but immediately it had its source in a dissatisfaction with the New England which was reactionary in religion and utilitarian in philosophy.

In this New England there was no outlet, and scarcely an occupation, for the idealistic youth fresh from school and college, except in commerce and the professions which served the commercial classes. Indeed, the graduate, who in college had most diligently studied the classics, found himself by that very diligence out of step with a world preoccupied with machines and percentages. And so, while the merchants and manufacturers, the contractors and shippers, were joyfully circling a race-course in which sudden profit was the hare, the young intelligentsia stood apart, unable to find vent in trade and powerless to create a satisfying milieu of their own. Their inertia was accompanied by introspection and a gnawing concern about their souls — " diseased with theological problems," as Emerson described them. Those who forsook religion withdrew into the intellect, " and the result was monstrous," said Emerson. " A canine appetite for knowledge was created . . . but it did not bring peace or beneficence." A dreadful marasmus took possession of the younger strata of society, inducing a melancholy state of mind adequately described by Charles Emerson, who was one of the conspicuous victims of it, when he said to Ralph Waldo, " The nap is worn off the world."

These pools of dissatisfaction attracted to their edges the most varied kinds of dissenting, eccentric, or maladjusted persons — men who hated the noise and clamor of the prevalent Jacksonianism, who scorned current theology, who saw evil in the country's nascent industrialism, who suspected the Freemasons, who hated slavery and whiskey, who condemned flesh-eating or predicted ruin for a universe that used white, bolted flour. And so there arose advocates of Dr. Sylvester Graham's new bread, of phrenology, of mesmerism, of tariffs, of free trade, of hydropathy, of the protection of ground-worms, slugs, and mosquitoes, and of countless other cults and schemes, some sane, others entirely lunar.

It was in an instinctive but not clearly defined desire to find a voice and outlet for this movement of dissatisfaction that led Emerson one day in September, 1836, to talk with three friends, all young Unitarian preachers, "on the state of current opinion." One of them was the Reverend Dr. Frederic Henry Hedge, a member of the younger intelligentsia which had been reading Carlyle and Coleridge. He had studied in Germany and had brought back word on the new influences current there. A week later they called together a dozen or more friends at the home of George Ripley in Boston and vaguely discussed the founding of a journal. The next meeting was at Emerson's Concord home and a nucleus was formed which never framed a program but which met for occasional discussion for several years. It was at first called the "Hedge Club," or the "Symposium." Among those who attended then or later were Dr. Channing, Bronson Alcott, John S. Dwight, Ephraim Peabody, Elizabeth Peabody, Convers Francis, Orestes Brownson, Theodore Parker, Caleb Stetson, James Freeman Clarke, Sarah Ripley, and, occasionally, H. D. Thoreau and Margaret Fuller.

Scoffers nicknamed this set the Transcendental Club. The attitude of the old school toward them and their like was well stated by the redoubtable John Quincy Adams, when he wrote:

"The sentiment of religion is at this time, perhaps, more

potent and prevailing in New England than in any other portion of the Christian world. For many years since the establishment of the theological school at Andover, the Calvinists and Unitarians have been battling with each other upon the Atonement, the Divinity of Jesus Christ, and the Trinity. . . . A young man named Ralph Waldo Emerson, a son of my once-loved friend William Emerson, and a classmate of my lamented George, after failing in the everyday avocations of a Unitarian preacher and schoolmaster, starts a new doctrine of Transcendentalism, declares all the old revelations superannuated and worn-out, and announces the approach of new revelations and prophecies. Garrison and the non-resistant Abolitionists, Brownson and the Marat Democrats, phrenology and animal magnetism — all come in, furnishing each some plausible rascality as an ingredient for the bubbling caldron of religion and politics. Pearse Cranch, *ex ephebis*, preached here last week, and gave out quite a stream of Transcendentalism, most unexpectedly."

It was common to impute to the founders of Transcendentalism all manner of subversive projects. These they never had; they began with no purpose except that of conversation and an exchange of views. They merely called themselves " the club of the like-minded." " I suppose," said James Freeman Clarke, " because no two of us thought alike."

Emerson had no great expectations of them. " Their education and reading were not marked," he wrote, " but had the American superficialness, and their studies were solitary." This is scarcely a fair statement; the intellectual Transcendentalists would have gone farther if they had had more cohesion, but even so they attained no mean heights. Their devotion to ideals instead of markets was a healthful counter-influence to the grubby thing-worship of their time. And they attained an exhilarating vent for their powers. They had their glow, their day. If they erred, it was in following Emerson's dictum too strictly, and hitching their wagon too exclusively to stars.

VII

A third important event occurred in this fruitful year: a child was born to Emerson. As in the case of the winning of Ellen Tucker, he was awed into wonder and humility. Emerson could never accustom himself to the thought that he was subject to mundane events in the same manner as other men. Particularly was he overcome by the simple joys and events common to more practical-minded households. He could not grasp the fact that on October 30 he and Lidian were two persons and on October 31 they were three. There was some magic here, in the circle of which he felt he did not belong.

"How remote from my knowledge, how alien, yet how kind, does it make the Cause of causes appear to me! The stimulated curiosity of the father sees the graces and instincts which exist indeed in every babe, but unnoticed in others, the right to see all, know all, to examine nearly, distinguishes the relation, and endears this sweet child. Otherwise I see nothing in it of mine. . . . I seem to be merely a brute occasion of its being."

On further reflection, however, he descended to earth, and even permitted himself an ecstatic nursery word, which in an unaccustomed rush of emotion he underscored: "The contrast of size makes the little nestler appear so *cunning.*"

He sought to calm himself by turning away to abstractions, and in the same journal wrote as if the recent meeting of the Transcendentalists was still on his mind:

"This age will be characterized as the era of Trade, for everything is made subservient to that agency. . . . Superstition gives way; Patriotism; Martial ardor; Romance in the people; but Avarice does not. Meantime it is also a social era; the age of associations, the powers of Combination are discovered."

Busy, plebeian America rushes on, its men fighting for advantage like so many fish around a floating bait. Newly released energies, linked to virgin resources, create riches. Rifts open between classes and even between geographical sections. The mushroom rise of manufacturing creates a demand for labor. Irishmen and Germans flock in to take the places of natives who have risen in the social scale; installing in the Massachusetts mind a fear of low-paid foreign labor which is to culminate, despite a world's outcry, in the execution of Sacco and Vanzetti less than a century later. Finance grows swollen in the cities, but is temporarily subdued by Andrew Jackson, backed by a rising middle class. The South waxes sullen as it watches the effect of tariffs on the North. The West raises voices defiant of old idols in legislative chambers. Labor unions form and grow restive. Anti-slavery speeches are answered by the threats of Nullifiers. The clamor in the external world grows ever more raucous.

But Emerson remains in his study mornings and fills his afternoons with walks. "When I bought my farm," he writes, "I did not know what a bargain I had in the bluebirds, bobolinks, and thrushes, which were not charged in the bill. As little did I guess what sublime mornings and sunsets I was buying, what reaches of landscape, and what fields and lanes for a tramp."

Weekdays he takes rides into Boston to read and lecture, and on Sundays preaches at East Lexington. He expands and softens. It is the happiest period of his life; and visitors, among them Harriet Martineau from England, mark his serenity, and even gayety. The arrival of little Waldo has filled his cup. With an infinite delight he watches his first-born grow and begin to walk. All his previous life has been mere "preface." Henry Thoreau becomes the deep-eyed boy's chief playmate, and Margaret Fuller, on her frequent visits, hugs him with rapture, and wishes she had a child so charming.

Chapter Fifteen

I

EMERSON was often joined on his woodland rambles by Bronson Alcott, then teaching a novel kind of school in Boston. On a pleasant afternoon they would start out briskly and get as far as the first fence, where Alcott, who meantime had been reminded of an absorbing topic, would pause to make one more point before they climbed over. It could not always be disposed of in a mere five minutes, and Alcott would lean his back against the fence or sit down while Emerson furtively gazed around at the clouds or at the meeting of the land and sky which formed a line he always loved to contemplate. Higher and higher would rise the flood of Alcott's talk, filling Emerson's ears and pounding on his head like surf. The passage of an hour, two hours, would find the two men still standing on the hither side of the fence, Alcott still talking and Emerson gazing wistfully over at the fields which he was not to cross that day. Slowly they would return to the house for supper, Alcott to look up an authority among his host's books and Emerson to creep off to his bedroom where he would throw himself down, grateful for the enclosing darkness and for the poultice of silence.

Emerson, who hated much speaking, and who lived that he might observe and muse, was not always at one with

Alcott, who lived that he might talk; and once in a moment of impatience he said of Alcott, " he lives tomorrow, as he lived today, for further discourse." However, at first he admired the tall teacher extravagantly and praised him with encomiums such as he did not give to any other friend. He even felt inferior to Alcott. "He has more of the godlike than any man I have ever seen, and his presence rebukes and threatens and raises. . . . The most extraordinary man, and the highest genius of his time. . . . The scope and steadiness of his eye at once rebuke all before it, and we little men creep about ashamed." Somewhat later, after he had been well-nigh drowned by Alcott's rivers of talk, and had once or twice been forced to his bed by exhaustion after several days in the same house with him, Emerson confessed: " He is, to be sure, monotonous; you may say, one gets tired of his uniformity — he will not be amused, he never cares for the pleasant side of things, but always truths and their origin he seeketh after." At length he was provoked to say that "Alcott is a pail without any bottom," and finally he delivered this severe summing up of two men who were then his neighbors: " Alcott and Hawthorne together would make a man."

His early admiration for Alcott the Platonist was probably due to the fact that in Alcott he saw himself — himself free of those canny checks and balances which in Alcott's presence seemed mere chains and halters. Alcott was the complete Platonist, a Romantic plus. If Emerson might be compared to an airplane, occasionally soaring from the earth in long but gentle sweeps that never rose too far above the fences, Alcott was a helicopter, rising straight into the sky and heedless as to whether he should ever return to earth. Alcott's thoughts, which Margaret Fuller once said were so few that she could count them, had no relation to actuality and, indeed, scorned it. He could not understand why people should concern themselves with food and shelter when they could discuss Absolutes. He was perfectly capable of taking his family's last few dollars to market and returning triumphantly with an armful of books; or, when his wife needed warm clothing and his children shoes, of going out on a long lecture tour and forgetting to ask an admission price or take up a collection. He would turn from a determined quest after truth half-frozen and requiring to be nursed and put to bed by his half-starved womenfolk.

With all his lunar notions, however, he was an able teacher; he understood that education is to educe and not suppress; and his school in the Masonic Temple at Boston, where methods were followed which, though dangerously novel at the time, have since been incorporated in modern pedagogy, might become one of the Hub's chief prides, except for two deplorable circumstances. One was his discussion before his class of the process of human birth. It was gently and religiously done, but in upper-class Boston it was not admitted that babies came in any fashion except via stork, and the artless Alcott was assailed in the most vituperative terms. The school, however, might have survived this storm, had not Alcott admitted to it a Negro child. A few years later Bostonians were shedding their blood for Negro rights, but at the moment Alcott might better have let in a leper. Parents swooped down and took their children away bodily, and a mob formed which insulted him and might have illtreated the bewildered teacher had not his small daughter, afterwards celebrated as Louisa M.

Alcott, author of *Little Women*, interposed and protected him.

Alcott's school had for its aim the encouragement of children to think for themselves; and their naïve conclusions on the questions submitted to them — questions, chiefly, in the manner of the time, theological — have been preserved in *The Record of a School*, by Elizabeth Peabody, who was Alcott's assistant. Alcott himself had made a record of them in a little book, *Conversations on the Gospels*. It was at once attacked by the Boston *Courier*, organ of Conservatism, which quoted a Harvard professor as saying, " one-third of Mr. Alcott's book is absurd, one-third blasphemous, and one-third obscene." The charge of obscenity concerned a brief reference to the virgin birth of Jesus Christ. Emerson went to Alcott's defence in a letter which said that " any reasonable man will perceive that fragments out of a new theory of Christian instruction are not the best place for examination between the Price Current and the Shipping List." After the incident of the Negro child, attendance at Alcott's school dwindled until only four pupils remained. Three of them were the principal's own children. The school then expired. On Emerson's invitation Alcott removed to Concord and here, under a friendly wing, he was at peace for a time, until the next unearthly scheme took possession of him. He did day labor for the farmers, digging and hammering, and trying very hard to be practical. Emerson did what he could to keep him near to earth, reminding one of a frail, earnest man trying to hold down a very large dirigible with a very small rope.

Alcott once produced a book called *Psyche, or the Breath of Childhood*, and sent the manuscript to Emerson, who praised its power " to awaken apprehension of the Absolute," but sighed over its "want of compression," adding, " you are tempted to linger around the Idea in the hope that what cannot be stated in a few words may yet be suggested by many." He laboriously endeavored to correct Alcott's characteristic words and phrases in a list which is a perfect mirror of the two men. Where Alcott wrote, " seraphic life of the spirit," Emerson commented, " We can hardly be too frugal with words of this kind." Where Alcott wrote, " I would shadow forth truth not only to the head," Emerson advised, " Say vaticate or embody, and eye and ear. Embodiment is not English, and is pedantic in this place." Where Alcott mentioned "spirituality," Emerson's terse remark was, " I think we should leave spirituality to the Unitarian Association."

Somewhat later Alcott followed Emerson's example in invading the lecture field; and, in expounding a Platonic philosophy mixed with Kantian concepts, he used to tell his rural audiences that Man was divided into the Knower, the Actor, and the Thinker. Attracted by the sound of this first category, a pious lady one day arose and asked the speaker if this was the same Noah that was saved in the Ark.

II

One of Alcott's assistants at his Boston school was Margaret Fuller, who had left her lonely farm home at Groton in the hope of finding a mode of life more suitable to her energetic, vital nature. She had already heard Emerson preach at Boston, had admired him, and, from the moment that Alcott introduced her to Concord, she laid siege to the sage in an open, direct fashion that aroused all his reserves of caution and reticence. When Emerson wrote to his brother William that she had been visiting his wife, this was only half the truth; she was visiting Emerson no less. Then began a curious friendship, active and aggressive on her part; on his, passive and reluctant.

At first he was greatly taken with her; she stimulated him and made him feel his powers. " She is quite an extraordinary person," he told William, " for her apprehensiveness, her acquisitions, and her power of conversation. It is always a great refreshment to see a very intelligent person. It is like being set in a large place You stretch your limbs and dilate to your utmost size." But as she, on her repeated visits, advanced and began to attack his " fences," he drew back, although not entirely. Her interest in him flattered him, but he feared her headlong disposition. " She ever seems to crave," he wrote, " somewhat I have not, or have not for her." He passed through alternations of response and contraction, described as " strange, cold-warm, attractive-repelling conversations with Margaret, whom I always admire, most revere when I nearest see, and sometimes love; yet whom I freeze and who freezes me to silence when we promise to come nearest." She did not know, then, that although still a young man, he had already drawn around himself a line which he would permit no person to cross. " I prefer a tendency to stateliness to an excess of fellowship," he once wrote. " In all things I would have the island of a man inviolate." By now he was well aware of one of his chief limitations — lack of physical vitality. As he expressed it a few years later: " I have so little vital force that I could not stand the dissipation of a flowing and friendly life. . . . I husband all my strength . . . [and] no doubt shall be a well-preserved old gentleman."

Ellery Channing, the poet, said of Emerson: " Women do not like him; he cannot establish a personal relation with anyone, yet he can get on agreeably with everyone." This was not accurate; women did like him, as his many friendships with them proved; but he had no more room in his personal circle. His wife surrounded him with an affectionate and attentive domesticity, and he had already taken Elizabeth Hoar, his dead brother's fiancée, to be his sister, confidante, and intimate friend. He was indeed an island, not to be invaded except across icy moats. He so explained to Miss Fuller in a letter, perhaps the most remarkable he ever wrote for candid and wet-blankety self-revelation:

" None knows better than I, more's the pity, the gloomy inhospitality of the man; the want of power to meet and unite with even those whom he loves ' in his flinty way.' What amends can he make to his guests? he asked himself long since. Only to anticipate, and thus if possible mitigate, their disgust and suspicion at the discovery, by apprising them beforehand that this outside of wax covered an inside of stone. Ice has its uses, when deception is not thought of and we are not looking for bread. . . . Humbly grateful for every expression of tenderness which makes the day sweet and inspires unlimited hopes, I did not deceive myself with thinking that the old bars would suddenly fall. . . . Therefore, my friend, treat me always as a mute, not ungrateful though now incommunicable."

At another time when she taxed him with " inhospitality of soul," he replied that he wished he could " melt once for all these icy barriers, but great is the law."

Although the terms of Emerson's letters would seem to indicate otherwise, there is no evidence that Margaret Fuller, despite her persistent efforts, craved an intimacy with him other than an idealized one. Hand-reared by a father who had given her an almost masculine bent of mind, in the direction of abstract learning, his death had deprived her of an anchor, such as it was; and it is possible that in Emerson she saw another father, a kindly pope and father-confessor, in whose calm she could find a counter for her tossing emotions, a focus for her scattered talents. Cold as Emerson was in detaching himself from the tentacles she threw around him, his instinct in so doing was probably sound. His thin reserves would have been burned through by that eager flame, his last resources of energy ravaged by that passionate spirit. He perceived the essential difference of their temperaments, the impossibility of reconciling his ideology with hers. He wished to live subjectively, through reflection; she wished to live vitally, through action. She wished to be at the center of things, he on their rim. To him the ultimate good was wisdom, to her it was the joy of the complete use of functions. There was another wide disparity in their views of the existence of evil. Emerson would never recognize evil except as a negation of good; she accepted evil as the permanent partner of good. Emerson was in quest of principle; she said, "I seek the divine rather in Love than Law."

She was not offended when he withdrew behind his barriers; they continued an intercourse as correspondents and fellow editors; and at length she was content that he had left her to find her own center of stability. She even came to have a slight scorn for his one-celled life. She criticized "these tedious, tedious attempts to learn the universe by thought alone," and finally she wrote this conclusion: " I trow the fates which gave this place Concord, took away the animating influences of Discord."

The truth is, Emerson was scared of Margaret Fuller; most men were; she had more virility than they; and so she went away to Europe seeking what America could not give her, returning only to be drowned with her babe and husband, Count Ossoli, in sight of New York, the victim, as always, of storm. Emerson did not come to join the search for her remains. He sent Thoreau.

III

Although Emerson and Thoreau were fellow townsmen, they did not meet until after Thoreau, who was the younger by fourteen years, had left Harvard College. While he was a student, Emerson, at the instance of friends, had written to President Quincy, asking that the promising youth might be assisted by a grant from the college funds. After Thoreau returned to Concord and set up as a schoolteacher, he conceived an admiration for Miss Lucy Brown, a relation of Mrs. Lidian Emerson; and one day, in his woman-shy way, he tossed in an open window a sheaf of verses for her. An introduction to Emerson followed, and Thoreau was soon admitted to the small and sacred circle of those persons who were invited to ramble with the author of *Nature* and to come to his home to participate in Sunday evening meetings.

Emerson introduced the young teacher, then barely twenty-one years old, to his journal with an anecdote which reveals that, even at that early age, Thoreau was displaying the nonconformity which made his character so prickly: " I delight much in my young friend, who seems to have as free and erect a mind as any I have ever met. He told as we walked this afternoon a good story about a boy who went to school with him, Wentworth, who resisted the schoolmistress's command that the children should bow to Dr. Heywood [Concord's town clerk] and other gentlemen as they went by, and when Dr. Heywood stood waiting and cleared his throat with a Hem, Wentworth said, ' You needn't hem, Doctor. I shan't bow.' "

In Thoreau Emerson found that of which his brother Charles's death had deprived him — eyes; he also found in him a friend who fitted in between Alcott, who was made on Emerson's own pattern, and Margaret Fuller, who was his antithesis. He admired Thoreau for his ability to do things with his hands, for his strong legs, for "his simplicity and clear perception . . . everything that boy says makes merry with society." He was pleased with their agreement — " I am familiar with his thoughts; they are mine, quite originally dressed "; and although Emerson wished no "school " or following, he could scarcely fail to be secretly pleased when the gossips whispered that Henry was beginning to carry his head like Emerson and was even speaking in Emerson's tone.

It was not until much later, after Thoreau had served faithful years as the elder's helper and caretaker of his home and children, his planter and builder, that a rift appeared between the two men, a rift caused as much by a difference in superficial traits as difference in character. Thoreau was " with difficulty sweet"; " I love Henry," said Elizabeth Hoar, " but I do not like him." He was a fighter, and Emerson disliked combats, even if purely intellectual; Thoreau was motor and Emerson was sensory; Thoreau was an iron bar and Emerson a steel spring; Emerson was willing to bend and Thoreau was rigid.

" If I knew only Thoreau," wrote Emerson in what, for him, was almost a moment of exasperation, " I should think coöperation of good men impossible. . . . Centrality he has, and penetration, strong understanding, and the higher gifts — the insight of the real, or from the real, and the moral rectitude that belongs to it; but all this and all his resources of wit and invention are lost to me, in every experiment, year after year, that I make, to hold intercourse with his mind. Always some weary, captious paradox to fight you with, and time and temper wasted."

Henry, meantime, was nursing a choler against Emerson's outward bows and smiles. He saw them as a screen which Emerson kept between himself and the world, and behind which the real man hid himself insincerely:

" When I meet one of my neighbors these days, who is ridiculously stately — being offended — I say in my mind, ' Farewell! I will wait till you get your manners off. Why make politeness of so much consequence when you are ready to assassinate with a word? I do not like any better to be assassinated with a rapier than to be knocked down with a bludgeon. You are so grand that I cannot get within ten feet of you.' Why will men so try to impose upon each other? Why not be simple, and pass for what they [sic] are worth only? "

Each criticism had a base of justice. Henry was so intent on armoring himself as a complete person that he left rare openings through which a hand could be extended to his fellows; the individualist in him triumphed while the social man in him died. And Emerson's gracious manners too often concealed the fact that while he liked Man, the abstraction, he had an aversion from men, the mass. And yet, each, in his criticism of the other, drew his own ironical portrait. Thoreau, who could destroy a silly questioner with a sentence, objecting to assassination by a word! Emerson, the island-man, perceiving a defect in his neighbor's non-coöperation! It was rightly he who should coin the aphorism, " Consistency is the hobgoblin of little minds," or as he privately expressed it in his journal, " Damn consistency! " On the other hand, his habit of withdrawing himself was perfectly in accord with his belief that " men, as well as books, may be read too much."

IV

While Emerson was forming and adjusting these relationships which were to have a bearing on his life in little Concord, the outside world was rolling and tossing in one of those convulsions brought upon it by an undigested capitalism. In the spring of 1837 occurred a financial panic which affected virtually all the United States and no small part of Europe. Boston and New York banks suspended specie payments; the New Orleans Exchange was burned; merchants were ruined; mobs formed; and workingmen found themselves without a livelihood. Emerson was impressed by these " loud cracks in the social edifice," and his comments on the crisis revealed how far his countrymen had gone in the thing-worship which was beginning to sicken the Transcendentalists:

" It is true there are no men. Men hang upon things. They

are over-crowed by their own creation. A man is not able to subdue the world. He is a Greek grammar. He is a money machine. He is an appendage to a great fortune, or to a legislative majority, or to the Massachusetts Revised Statutes, or to some barking and bellowing institution. . . . Young men have no hope. Adults stand like day-laborers idle in the streets. . . . This is the causal bankruptcy, this the cruel oppression, that the ideal should serve the actual, that the head should serve the feet. . . . Let me begin anew; let me teach the finite to know its master."

A few weeks later he was invited to deliver the annual oration before the Phi Beta Kappa Society at Cambridge in August. His ideas had meantime become further sharpened and centered, and he welcomed the opportunity to vent his charged feelings.

" The hope to arouse young men at Cambridge to a worthier view of their literary duties," he noted in his journal, " prompts me to offer the theory of the Scholar's function. He has an office to perform in Society. What is it? "

PART TWO
Manhood and Mastery

Chapter Sixteen

I

WHEN on the last day of August, 1837, Emerson, who was dressed in the " reverend clothes " which accentuated his long, sloping shoulders, and his pallor, but slightly ruddied by recent work in his Concord orchard, stood before his audience of Harvard youths, their eagerness betrayed that they expected something momentous from this alumnus whose sayings were beginning to be talked about. The aisles and passages could hold no more, and even the windows framed peering faces.

Emerson began, as was his habit, slowly, in his resonant baritone in which every word was distinct. His very first sentences revealed that his auditors were not to be disappointed; for without preliminary flourishes he demanded the cultural independence of America. He called on them to put aside the Past and concern themselves with the Present, to have done with Europe and respond to their own country's needs.

" Perhaps the time is already come . . . when the slug-gard intellect of this continent will look from under its iron lids and fill the postponed expectations of the world with something better than the exertions of mechanical skill.

" Our day of dependence, our long apprenticeship to the learning of other lands, draws to a close.

" The millions that around us are rushing into life cannot always be fed on the sere remains of foreign harvests.

" Events, actions, arise, that must be sung, that will sing themselves."

He indicted the temporary state of society, the decay of faculties consequent upon subdivision and specialization, and the tendency of an encroaching mechanical age to convert men themselves into machines.

" The state of society is one in which the members have suffered amputation from the trunk, and strut about like so many walking monsters — a good finger, a neck, a stomach, an elbow, but never a man.

" Man is thus metamorphosed into a thing, into many things. The priest becomes a form; the attorney a statute book; the mechanic a machine."

It must have shocked his audience to hear Emerson assign a relatively low place to that revered being known as " the thinker " over whom he exalted " the man thinking." It was clear that by " thinker " Emerson meant that person whose views are second-hand, as derived from books, tradition, and current prejudices; whereas " man thinking " is he who permits his thoughts to be shaped and acted upon by the whole of Nature.

" The Scholar is the delegated intellect. In the right state he is *man thinking*. In the degenerate state, when the victim of society, he tends to become a mere thinker, or still worse, the parrot of other men's thinking. In this view of him, as man thinking, the theory of his office is continued. Him Nature solicits with all her placid, all her monitory pictures; him the past instructs; him the future invites." It is the scholar's business, he continued, to find the fact among the appearances. " It becomes him to feel all confidence in himself, and to defer never to the popular cry: Let him not quit his belief that a popgun is a popgun, though the ancient and the honorable of the earth affirm it to be the crack of doom."

A second shock ensued when, before an audience of book-nourished young men, he attacked their very shrine. " Meek young men grow up in libraries, believing it their duty to accept the views which Cicero, which Locke, which Bacon have given; forgetful that Cicero, Locke, and Bacon were only young men in libraries when they wrote these books." He reminded them that their own generation had its tasks to perform. " Each age must write its own books, or, rather, each generation for the next succeeding. The books of an older generation will not fit this." He put forward experience, instead of tradition, as the right material for thought. " Action is with the scholar subordinate, but it is essential. Without it he is not yet man. Without it thought can never ripen into truth." Again he sounded the call for cultural independence: " We have listened too long to the courtly muses of Europe. The spirit of the American freeman is already suspected to be timid, imitative, tame. The scholar is decent, indolent, complaisant. The mind of this country, taught to aim at low objects, eats upon itself. There is no work for any but the decorous and the complaisant."

He referred to the intelligent young men of the period, hesitant, discouraged, and inert, to whom he addressed this passage, the closing sentence of which we put in italics, because it remained a central point in the Emersonian gospel:

" What is the remedy? They did not yet see, and thousands of young men as hopeful now crowding to the barriers for the career do not yet see, that *if the single man plant himself indomitably on his instincts, and there abide, the huge world will come round to him.*"

There was the flower and fruit on the long stalk of Emerson's discourse. In this sentence was laid down the keel of the philosophy of individualism which shaped American thought for many subsequent decades and which, despite changed conditions, still influences it. The dictum did not originate with Emerson. It was the product of its day and soil; its spirit was in the air, and Emerson did but give it voice and expression. The great man, he often said, is he who is parallel to his time.

II

The address was received with mixed emotions; with " enthusiasm of approval," said James Russell Lowell, also with " grim silence of foregone dissent." To the younger men it was vivifying, as opening new vistas for ambition and energy; in its printed form 500 copies were sold in a month; their elders were either silent or growled as they saw authority mocked. But there was no doubt of the impression it left, and Emerson suddenly found himself wearing an aura from which he modestly shrank. It was noticed that he had increased in power; his delivery had that " fist " in it, that vigor and pungency, which it had previously lacked. He began to be famous, and his subsequent lectures on " Human Culture " in Boston drew much larger audiences, numbering at the close 500 persons. He kept an account of his revenues, noting with gratification the " pecuniary advantage of the Course ":

" Season tickets sold 319 for $620
" Single tickets sold 373 for 186
                                    _____
                                    $806
" Deduct error somewhere   13
                                    _____
                                    $793
" Deduct expenses   225
                                    _____
                                    $568 net profit "

" Thanks," he added, " to the Teacher, of me and of all, the Upholder, the Healthgiver; thanks and lowliest wondering acknowledgment."

III

In *Nature* Emerson had demanded a new way of seeing; in *The American Scholar* a new way of thinking; it was natural to expect that as a clergyman who was still wearing the vestments of his calling but who was gradually sundering all ties with pulpits, that he would soon proclaim the necessity of a new way of believing. This he did almost a year later, July 15, 1838, when he delivered his Divinity School Address before the senior class at Cambridge.

He began lullingly, with a poetical chant of praise to Nature and a passing slap at Calvinism: " Man is born to the good, the perfect "; and then with a bound he was defiling the very nest of orthodox Unitarianism — " If a man is at heart just, then, in so far, is he God."

Calvinism deemed man wholly depraved, redeemable only by God's grace, which was somewhat capriciously extended, but evocable through the intervention of the other two persons of the Trinity, Jesus Christ and the Holy Ghost. Unitarianism, rejecting the depravity of man, taught that he might approach the one God directly, without the help of either Jesus or the Holy Ghost; but it was not prepared to hear that man, in any respect or measure, could be God. A keen ear might therefore have heard subdued murmurs of protest — " this is atheism "; " this is pantheism." But Emerson proceeded as calmly as if he were unaware of the pain he was giving to devout and unquestionably worthy ears: " The good by affinity seek the vile. Thus, of their own volition, souls proceed into heaven, into hell."

Thus did Emerson glorify the Will, and assert that in man resides the determination of his own destinies. Man discovers truth, he declared, not by external aids, but by intuition. His guide is the moral sentiment, the faculty which intuitively distinguishes between the good and the bad, which perceives, " under what seem foolish details, principles that astonish. These laws refuse to be adequately stated. They will not be written out on paper or spoken by the tongue. They elude our persevering thought; yet we read them hourly in each other's faces, in each other's actions, in our own remorse."

This sentiment, which he called " the essence of all religion," he refused to admit was confined to New England, or to Europe, or even to the teachings of Jesus; on the contrary, he expressly declared that it " dwelled deepest in the minds of men in the devout and contemplative East. . . . Europe has always owed to Oriental genius its divine impulses. . . . The unique impression of Jesus upon mankind . . . is proof of the subtle virtue of this infusion."

Here was another statement which could not fail to give

offence to his Protestant auditors. They had always acted and taught as if Jesus had come on a mission exclusively to Anglo-Saxon Gentiles, and especially to New England Puritans; but Emerson's dicta would merely assign Jesus to a place in a long line of Oriental teachers, such as Buddha, Confucius, Menu, and Zoroaster, and would grant to Jesus attributes no greater than those of the ordinary man. Indeed, he described Jesus as " the one man " who " was true to what is in you and in me."

Emerson then attacked the whole of contemporary religious teaching. " I have heard a devout person, who prized the Sabbath, say in bitterness of heart, ' On Sundays it seems wicked to go to church.' " [This had, in fact, been only recently remarked by his wife, Lidian.] " Churches are not built on the principles of Jesus, but on his tropes. Christianity became a Mythus, as the poetic teaching of Greece and Egypt, before. He spoke of Miracles; for he felt that man's life was a miracle, and all that man doth, and he knew that this miracle shines as the character ascends. But the word Miracle, as pronounced by Christian churches, gives a false impression; it is Monster. It is not one with the blowing clover and the falling rain."

At this point there must have been new murmurs of " Pantheism! " but Emerson never took the trouble to deny the pantheism that anyone might detect in his teachings. He would never deny any random charges or be drawn into polemics. His method was to affirm and to continue affirming.

" It is my duty to say to you," he continued, " that the need was never greater of a new revelation than now. You will infer the sad conviction which I share, I believe, with numbers, of the universal decay and almost universal death of faith in society. The Soul is not preached. The Church seems to totter to its fall, almost all life extinct. . . . Wherever the pulpit is usurped by a formalist, there is the worshipper defrauded and disconsolate. We shrink as soon as the prayers begin which do not uplift, but smite and offend us. We are fain to wrap our cloaks around us, and secure as best we can a solitude that hears not."

Emerson made it plain that he had no intention of setting up a new religion, with new forms. " I confess that all attempts to project and establish a cultus with new rites and forms seem to me vain. Faith makes us, and not we it, and Faith makes its own forms. All attempts to construct a system are as cold as the new worship introduced by the French to the Goddess of Reason. Rather let the breath of the new life be breathed by you through the forms already existing, for, once you are alive, you shall find that they shall become plastic and new."

Emerson, however, did not leave the platform without stating his own creed, and giving those definitions of good and evil which explain his conduct in all subsequent affairs, public and private. This is his creed:

" *That the world is not the product of manifold power, but of one Will, one Mind; and that one Mind is everywhere active, in each ray of the star, in each wavelet of the pool; and whatever opposes that Will is everywhere balked and baffled, because things are as they are and not otherwise. Good is positive. Evil is merely privative, not absolute; it is like cold, which is the privation of heat.*"

At the time there were, as there have been since, persons who affected not to understand Emerson, although this declaration should have been clear enough to anyone. It upset the dogmas of Calvinism, and for them substituted principle. It denied the Unitarian concept of the immanence of God, substituting for it the doctrine that man is a part of God, as an inlet opening into a universal ocean of Mind. It countered the Western idea that a man lives and saves himself by Action, and laid equal emphasis on the Eastern idea that salvation comes through Being.

The world has concerned itself with other questions since, but at the time they were of vital consequence. The good Yankee of the period busied himself on weekdays with things and the acquisition of things by work, saving, order, and self-denial, but during his leisure hours and on Sundays he took his religion hard and seriously. He had divided his life into two compartments; in one he was the economic man, in the other the emotional — or, as he called it, the spiritual — man. This caused him to suffer from a grievous disunity, and in the endeavor to bridge the chasm between his outer and his inner life, he endured frightful lacerations. It was this struggle, often morbid, which formed the drama in Hawthorne's novels. And it was this disunity which Emerson strove to heal. Having integrated himself, he wished to impart the blessings of a unified life to others, and called on his countrymen to realize their connection with and subjection to " one Will, one Mind." He summed up his thesis in the opening lines of his essay on *History*: " There is one mind common to all individual men. Every man is an inlet to the same and to all of the same. . . . Who hath access to this universal mind, is a party to all that is or can be done, for this is the only and sovereign agent."

IV

It was to be supposed that doctrines so novel, so heretical, so revolutionary, pronounced before an audience of embryo preachers, would shake the ecclesiastical structure; they did. Theodore Parker, then new to the ministry, ably described their effect when he said, "My soul is roused," and again, " It caused a great outcry; one shouting, 'The Philistines be upon us! ' another, ' We be all dead men! ' while the majority called out, ' Atheism! ' The Dean said, ' That part of it which was not folly was downright atheism.' " In other quarters it was gravely questioned if Emerson could be called a Christian, and if, when he died, he would go to heaven. Father Taylor, who conducted a Methodist mission to seamen in Boston, disposed of the question by saying, " I am sure of one thing: if Emerson goes to hell, he will change the climate there, and emigration will set that way; but he knows no more of the religion of the New Testament than Balaam's ass did of the principles of the Hebrew grammar." Emerson himself declined to be drawn into a public discussion, and made no answer to published attacks. He wrote to the Reverend Henry Ware, his former colleague, in terms which indicate how fully he realized his deficiencies as a logician and fighter:

" I have always been — from my very incapacity of methodical writing — a ' chartered libertine,' free to worship and free to rail — lucky when I could make myself understood, but . . . I do not know what arguments are in reference to any expression of a thought. I delight in telling what

I think; but if you ask me how I dare say so, or why it is so, I am the most helpless of mortal men. . . . I shall go on just as before, seeing whatever I can, and telling what I see."

Showing his firmness in impenitence, he repeated virtually the same dicta a week later when he addressed the literary societies of Dartmouth College on " Literary Ethics "; but in that hoarily conservative institution, whose very president taught that slavery had the support of the Bible, no hubbub followed. His discourse simply bounced cleanly from the Dartmouth mind, leaving no dent behind. Here, Emerson again assailed the nation's immersion in the pursuit of wealth arising from invention applied to suddenly discovered resources.

" You will hear every day the maxims of a low prudence. You will hear that the first duty is to get land and money, place and name. ' What is this truth you seek? What is this beauty? ' men will ask with derision. If, nevertheless, God have called any of you to explore truth and beauty, be bold, be firm, be true. When you shall say, ' As others do, so will I: I renounce, I am sorry for it, my early visions: I must eat the good of the land, and let learning and romantic expectations go, until a more convenient season ' — then dies the man in you; then once more perish the buds of art, and poetry, and science, as they have perished already in a thousand thousand men."

The frequency with which Emerson recurred to this theme in his various papers and addresses indicated the extent to which prevalent thing-worship burdened his mind. He feared the effect of mere acquisition on the American temperament, and the loss to life of quality, consequent upon the replacement of simplicity by complexity. He diligently tried to induce his countrymen to think in terms of the process rather than the particularity, to regard the end as well as the means; but to the tough-grained Yankee mind abstractions such as Truth and Wisdom must have appeared to be far-off and misty goals.

Emerson vested his hope in the scholar, who "must reinforce man against himself. . . . Bend to the persuasion which is flowing to you from every object in Nature, to be its tongue to the heart of man, and to show the besotted world how passing fair is wisdom. Why should you renounce your right to traverse the starlit deserts of truth, for the premature comforts of an acre, house, and barn? . . . Make yourself necessary to the world, and mankind will give you bread."

The power of Emerson as an inspirer lay in his refusal to present programs or to suggest methods; he conceived it as his mission to delineate principles, to indicate tendencies, having faith in the tendency of evils to provide their own antidote; but he was sometimes criticized because he was reluctant to act himself and could not show others how to begin.

V

His curious dislike of translating his own thought into action was revealed in the same year, 1838, when a church meeting was held in Concord to discuss the proposed ejection, at the instance of powerful interests, of the Cherokee Indians from their eastern lands. Fraud and skulduggery were, with good reason, suspected; and here and there protests were made. Emerson wrote: "This tragic Cherokee business . . . will look to me degrading and injurious, do what I can. It is like dead cats around one's neck. It is like school committees and Sunday-School classes and teachers' meetings and the Warren Street Chapel and all the other holy hurrahs. I stir in it for the sad reason that no other mortal will move, and if I do not — why it is left undone."

It is much to Emerson's credit that he did move; for the whole transaction, one of a train through which the white man aimed at the Indian's early extermination, filled the land with a noisome odor. Though he told himself that " stirring in the philanthropic mud gives me no peace," he wrote a long and excoriating letter to President Van Buren which contained these sentiments:

" Such a dereliction of all faith and virtue, such a denial of justice, and such deafness to screams of mercy were never heard of in times of peace and in the dealing of a nation with its own allies and wards, since the earth was made. Sir, does this government think that the people of the United States are become savage and mad? From their mind are the sentiments of love and good nature wiped clean out? The soul of man, the justice, the mercy that is the heart's heart in all men does abhor this business."

The Cherokees were forcibly removed, however, to Oklahoma; their lands were seized by speculators; and the distaste that men felt was soon forgotten in the greater ferment of the anti-slavery agitation. As early as November, 1837, Emerson had made an anti-slavery address in the Concord Second Church, but for several years he declined to take part in active agitation, due to characteristic reasons. He had no sympathy with the South, but he could not bear the manners of the Abolitionists, their bigotry, noisy habits, and tendency to make a career out of much speaking. Emerson remained to the last a little afraid of the world and what it might do to him. He felt himself to be unfitted by nature to be a propagandist. He once said to Alcott, " by defying every settled usage in society, I should be sure to sour my own temper."

Chapter Seventeen

I

BY the time he had reached his thirty-fifth year, Emerson had worked out a way of life suited to his organic nature and he disliked being distracted from it. The secret of a good life, he had determined, resided in alternation. "Undulation, alternation, is the condition of progress, of life. . . . Solitude is naught and society is naught. Alternate them and the good of each is seen." He began to care less for books, and more for his wife, boy, neighbors, and garden. "If you do not quit the high chair, lie quite down, and roll on the ground a good deal, you become nervous and heavy-hearted. . . . The dog that was fed on sugar died." Domesticity and the serene joys with which Lidian had invested it had drawn him far out of his old shell. "The study of books is sickly, and the garden and a family, wife, mother, son, and brother, are a balsam. There is health in table talk and nursery play. We must wear old shoes and have aunts and cousins."

At length there came a day, the family being absent, when he was compelled to admit that self-sufficiency was no longer admirable, and that he was plain, downright, humanly lonely. "The self-subsistent shakes like a reed before a sneering paragraph in the newspaper. . . . He finds the solitude of two or three entire days, when mother, wife, and child are gone, tedious and dispiriting. Let him not wrong the truth and his own experience by too stiffly standing on the cold and proud doctrine of self-sufficiency." Four days later he was ready to abandon the doctrine of complete individualism to whomsoever would take it: " Solitude is fearsome and heavy-hearted. . . . Leave me alone a few days, and I creep about as if in expectation of calamity."

This abject confession was significant of a change in Emerson. The lance of theory had been shattered in the first large encounter with life — or, as he would have called it, Nature — and now, as if for the first time, he had learned that he, abstract Man, was in reality no more than husband, father, and son. It was his discovery that a man exists not alone in himself, but also in his relations; that man is individual, but also social.

It was perhaps in accordance with this realization that he gradually began to relax his aloofness and to discover Concord. The town had made the first overture in appointing him a hog-reeve. He now responded by helping to set up the Concord Athenaeum and Reading Room. He attended the town meetings, and noted with edification that the citizen who was so dull and wordless in personal contact could be a perfect lion in debate. He joined the Fire Association and dutifully attacked nascent forest blazes with his green bough. He joined the Social Circle, which comprised the village's twenty-five leading citizens, and regularly attended its Tuesday evening meetings. He attended the celebrations of the Light Infantry and the Artillery, which on occasions imported rival bands that, unable to subdue each other by toots and blares, sometimes embroiled their supporters in a glorious fist fight.

EMERSON IN HIS FIFTY-FIFTH YEAR

He began to take long walks through the village, wearing
·his shawl or long black cloak, responding to the greetings of
citizens and speaking graciously to every child on the streets.
He found new delights in the knobs and eccentricities of private character, and regretted the fame that caused grocery-
store gatherings to break up respectfully as soon as he entered.
"There is the hero who will not subscribe to the flagstaff or
the engine, though all say it is mean. There is the man who
gives his dollar, but refuses to give his name, though all other
contributors are set down. There is Mr. H., who never loses
his spirits, though always in the minority. Here is Mr. S.,
who warmly assents to whatever proposition you please to
make, and Mr. M., who roundly tells you he will have
nothing to do with the thing."

He perceived the division into castes and classes, and their
respective traits. "The high people in the village are timid;
the low people are bold and nonchalant, negligent, too, of
each other's opposition, for they see the amount of it and
know its uttermost limits, which the remote proprietor does
not." He even found something pleasing in the earthiness of
the inhabitants. In Concord, "people go a-fishing and
know the taste of their meat. They cut their own whippletree
in the woodlot; they know something practically of the sun
and east wind, of the underpinning and the roofing of the
house, and the pan and mixture of the soils."

More and more he looked to peasants and proletarians for
the homely wisdom derived from work and experience, not
to be found in books. He made eager notes of their sayings
and thirsted for more. He stood in helpless admiration before
George Minot, the woodsman and handy man who lived on
the slope of the opposite hill. George was equal to any task

and always knew a way to do the thing. When one day George said: " It's no use balloting, for it won't stay; what you do with a gun will stay so." Emerson went away pondering and wrote the remark down.

He took equal pleasure in Edmund Hosmer, the farmer who was his authority on all agricultural and orchard problems. Emerson's own knowledge of plant life was drawn wholly from books, and as often as he was moved to make some experiment, it was Hosmer's duty to hold the experiment down and keep it within root distance of the earth.

Somewhat later came Sam Staples, who when not the jailer was an auctioneer and farmer. It was Sam who said of Alcott, when the townspeople could not account for his preferring jail (during the war on Mexico) to the payment of a poll tax: " I vum, I believe it was nothing but principle! " Sam approved Emerson as a neighbor: " He kept his fences up."

There were the two inveterate anglers, Abel Davis and Old Goodwin. Of the latter Emerson observed that he could always catch pickerel, whereas, " if you have any moral traits, you will never get a bite." He even admired the two barroom keepers, Bigelow and Wesson, particularly the latter's philosophic saying that " I thought I was asleep, but knowed I wasn't."

And there was Deacon Parker, the canny store-keeper, whose hanging sign had become so shapeless, black, and weather-beaten that no one could tell whether it was of wood or metal. The Deacon himself could not remember. An argument arose one day, and to settle it the sign was taken down and analyzed. It was found to be a salted fish.

Among the occasional helpers on Emerson's farm, which by additional purchases had expanded to nine acres, were

Alcott and Thoreau. The latter studded the sage's bare acres with trees, and the former, not to be outdone, conceived the idea of a summer-house in which the sage could be sheltered while he took the air. He tried to build it unaided, but Mrs. Emerson, who was privy to Alcott's enthusiasms, called in Thoreau to assist; he remarked afterwards that he felt as if he had been " nowhere doing nothing." The summer-house was finally completed according to Alcott's own designs, and very original it was; but it had so many cleverly placed windows that the philosopher found it drafty, and its numerous openings admitted mosquitos which stung him out of his train of thought. It eventually became known as " The Ruin."

To Emerson's mind, however, the greatest of all the Concordians was his step-grandfather, the Reverend Dr. Ezra Ripley, occupant of the Old Manse and member of " the rear guard of the great army and camp of the Puritans," whose sayings he loved to record, particularly his habit of reproving, by inference, the capriciousness of the Almighty. When Emerson's brother Charles died, the worthy Doctor, in preaching the funeral, said: " This event seems to me loud and piercing, like thunder and lightning. While many aged and burdensome are spared, this beloved youth is cut down in the morning." On another occasion he said from the pulpit: " Mr. N. F. is dead, and I expect to hear of the death of Mr. B. It is cruel to separate old people from their wives in this cold weather." In dry times it was the custom for all ministers to pray for rain, and during an exceptionally severe drought Dr. Ripley said to a younger colleague with professional dignity: " This is no time for you young Cambridge men; the affair, sir, is getting serious. I will pray myself."

The grimness of the Puritan fathers did not deprive their lives of a certain beauty, and this Emerson recognized in a letter to his Aunt Mary when Dr. Ripley died:

" These Puritans, however in their last days they have declined into ritualists, solemnized the heyday of their strength by the planting and liberating of America. Great, grim, earnest men, I belong by natural affinity to other thoughts and schools than yours, but my affections hover respectfully about your retiring footsteps, your unpainted churches, strict platforms, and sad offices; the iron-grey deacon, and the wearisome prayer, rich with the diction of ages."

Knowing their rigidities, he enjoyed the incident when one of the older inhabitants of the village said to him: " There are only three persons, as far as I know, whose opinions are obnoxious to the members of our community; they are Theodore Parker, Wendell Phillips, and — if I may say so — yourself, sir."

And he valued the honesty of the Concord washlady, who said after she had heard him lecture in the local Lyceum: " I like to go and see him stand up there and look as if he thought everyone was as good as he was."

Emerson's sense of humor, which ripened and mellowed noticeably after he had become a family man, even enabled him to survive the visits of the eccentrics, fanatics, ne'er-do-wells, and other " devastators of the day," who flocked to his door in increasing numbers. " Fools and clowns and sots," he wrote, " make the fringe of everyone's tapestry of life, and give a certain reality to the picture " — " the sanity of society is the balance of a thousand insanities." At first he was inclined to resent the sacrifice of his time, but received his nondescript invaders with more equanimity after Mrs. Emer-

son had counselled him to " try to make humanity lovely to
them."

" When a zealot comes to me and represents the impor-
tance of this Temperance Reform, my hands drop," he wrote.
" I have no excuse — I honor him with shame at my own
inaction. Then a friend of the slave shows me the horrors of
Southern slavery — I cry, Guilty! . . . I cannot do all
these things, but these my shames are illustrious token that I
have strict relations to them all." Although Emerson listened
patiently to them, he had a dread of one-idea men. " Truth,"
he wrote, " is our element and life, yet if a man fasten his attention upon a single aspect of truth, and apply himself to
that alone for a long time, the truth itself becomes distorted,
and, as it were, false. . . . The *lie of One Idea*." The
italics here are his. He persistently refused to be drawn out of
what he regarded as his own orbit. " You must love me as I
am," he wrote. " Do not by your sorrow or your affection
solicit me to be somewhat else than I by nature am." He was
content, in Voltaire's phrase, to cultivate his own garden,
and rarely could be induced to make a visit or spend the night
under any roof but his own. " If I wake up in another man's
house," he wrote, " or in a hotel, or place of constraint where
I am come to do a forced work — come, not with ideal of
freedom, but with external compulsion of some sort — then
I feel an irritability, as much in the skin as in the soul, that
pesters and hinders me. . . . The commonest person of condition and fashion affects me more than is right, and I am
mute, passive, and let their world wag, let them make the
world, I being but a block of the same. I ought to go upright and vital and say the truth in all ways."

The other class of persons from whom he suffered most

were " the goodies " and those who would " pull up lilies and plant skunk cabbages in their places." As often as he thought of them he became almost vicious. " One had as lief curse and swear," he wrote, " as be guilty of this odious religion that watches the beef and watches the cider in the pitcher at table, that shuts the mouth hard at any remark it cannot twist nor wrench into a sermon, and preaches as long as itself and its hearer is awake. Goodies make us very bad. We should, if the race should increase, be scarce restrained from calling for bowl and dagger. We will almost sin to spite them." To certain individuals of this species he was hospitable with difficulty. " Here comes Eliza," he once said, " who caught cold coming into the world and has always increased it since."

His chief comforts when annoyed were his afternoon walks through the woods, the sight of the stars at night — " the calm, remote, and secular character of astronomical facts composes us to a sublime peace " — and the movements of little Waldo. He marked the day when the boy first walked alone, December 8, 1837, and between comments on cosmic laws sowed his diary with delighted sketches of domestic scenes. " Lidian came into the study this afternoon and found the towerlet that Wallie had built, half an hour before, of two spools, a card, an awl-case and a flower-box top, each perpendicularly balanced on the other, and could scarcely believe that her boy had built the pyramid, and then fell into such a fit of affection that she lay down by the structure and kissed it down and declared she could possibly stay no longer with papa, but must go off to the nursery to see with eyes the lovely creature.". . . " Baby warbles quite irresistibly, as if telling a secret, too, to all the house,

' Mamma ky, Mamma ky! ' thus blabbing Mamma's flebile tendencies."

But within his home as well as without he noted the symptoms of the restlessness and tension characteristic of the age. " The rights of woman, the anti-slavery, temperance, peace, health, and money movements; female speakers, mobs and martyrs, the paradoxes, the antagonism of old and new, the anomalous church, the daring mysticism and the plain prose, the uneasy relation of domestics, the struggling toward better household arrangements — all indicate life at the heart, not yet justly organized at the surface."

The world's unease sometimes overbore his own optimism, and he thought he was growing old. " After thirty the stream feels its banks," he wrote, and again: " After thirty a man wakes up sad every morning, except perhaps five or six."

Chapter Eighteen

I

THE panic of 1837 had left the country in a severe depression, and traces of the despondency and disillusion it produced are to be detected in Emerson's addresses of that and the following year — in the Phi Beta Kappa oration, the lectures on " Human Culture " in Boston, The Divinity College address, and the Dartmouth College Oration. However, the optimism of a young and energetic people could not but regard it as but a passing jolt, and the same prompt recovery that followed the panic of 1819 was cheerfully expected. But by 1839 it was evident that convalescence was going to be slow, and uneasy doubts arose as to the benefits of the new regime under which factory-made products were superseding hand-made articles and under which the careful labors of small farmers were giving place to the operations of great companies. Money continued to be scarce, work was hard to find, and the honest and thrifty were in no better state than the crafty and wasteful. A fermentation ensued during which men asked themselves, What shall we do to be saved? It was perceived that an age of quantity production was threatening to overwhelm the old, leisurely life of quality, and a thousand projects were framed by which men might avert or escape an impending chaos.

In the very year of the panic occurred the death of the

Frenchman, Fourier; and his idea of the mathematical organization of production and distribution by " phalanxes " was again revived for discussion, together with the productive-colony idea of Robert Owen, founder of the New Harmony colony in Indiana, who had introduced the words " Socialization " and " Socialism " into America. Simultaneously a new impetus was given to the Transcendental movement, with its endeavor to find a new ideal for this New England which was producing two-thirds of the country's manufactures, and whose people were now suffering most severely of all from the crash of a newly introduced economic order.

In such a crisis it was to be expected that Emerson would say something relative to this fermentation, to the critics of and rebels against the new, sordid, and uglifying materialism. This he did in the ten lectures on " Human Life " which began at the Masonic Temple, Boston, on December 5, 1838. He immediately threw himself on the side of the young and rebellious. He assailed society for its attempts to ignore and suppress them, for its obstinate clinging to the *status quo.*

" This *deliquium,* this ossification of the soul," he proclaimed, " is the Fall of Man. The redemption is lodged in the heart of youth. To every young man and woman the world puts the same question, Wilt thou become one of us? And to this question the soul in each of them says heartily, No. The world has no interest so deep as to cherish that resistance. No matter though the young heart do not yet understand itself, do not know well what it wants, and so contents itself with saying No, No, to unamiable tediousness, or breaks out into sallies of extravagance. *There is hope in extravagance; there is none in routine.*"

We italicize the last sentence for two reasons: first, to

indicate the shock that must have been felt by the audience in hearing the decorous Concordian come out on the side of extravagance; and, second, to indicate how far Emerson had come since he had broken with the organized church. He further raised the banner of youth in this language:

" The hostile attitude of young persons toward society makes them very undesirable companions to their friends, querulous, opinionative, impracticable; and it makes them unhappy in their own solitude. If it continue too long it makes shiftless and morose men. Yet, on the whole, this crisis which comes in so forbidding and painful shape in the life of each earnest man has nothing in it that need alarm or confound us. In some form the question comes to each: Will you fulfil the demands of the soul, or will you yield yourself to the conventions of the world? None can escape the challenge. But why need you sit there, pale and pouting, or why with such a mock-tragic air affect discontent and superiority? The bugbear of society is such only until you have accepted your own law. Then all omens are good, all stars auspicious, all men your allies, all parts of life take order and beauty."

Emerson thus proclaimed the necessity, which he defined at another time, of one's " organic position "; only this would make possible complete self-trust, complete self-reliance. To attain salvation on earth, Emerson, characteristically, put little faith in organization; he saw it as an individual problem:

" I am afraid that in the formal arrangements of the socialists [the Owen idea] the spontaneous sentiment of any thoughtful man will find that poetry and sublimity still cleave to the solitary house. The members will be the same men we know. To put them in a phalanx [the Fourier idea] will not much mend matters, for as long as all people want the things that we now have, and not better things, it is very certain that they will, under whatever change of forms, keep the old system." In short, Emerson clung to the belief that the solution lay with the scholar, *i.e.*, the ethical intellectual.

Emerson meant to put all his weight into these lectures, but at their conclusion he was disappointed. Apparently no one had been aroused, and he felt he had not fully expressed himself. In addition, the attendance had fallen off. "I, who rail at the decorum and harness of society," he wrote, " why should I not speak very truth, unlimited, overpowering? But now unhappily the lectures are ended. Ten decorous speeches and not one ecstasy, not one rapture, not one thunderbolt. Eloquence, therefore, there was none."

It is more likely that the dull response he encountered was due to his audiences' expectation that he would give them some definite conclusion, some aim or goal. His eloquence had been sufficient, but had led nowhere. His speeches often began dazzlingly, but ended in diffusion, or in a soaring to some ethical height to which his hearers could not follow him. He thought harder work was the remedy and re-solved to do better next time, and to spend, if possible, sixty hours on the preparation of each lecture instead of his cus-tomary twenty-one. But he brooded over his disappointment, lost appetite, and fell into an apathy closely related to ill-ness. And then his old ailment, a pain in the lungs, came back and assailed him. He went to the mountains for a rest, but returned little improved. He found himself unable to write, and gave no more lectures for the rest of the year. " I hate sickness," he wrote to Margaret Fuller, " in common with all men this side of forty, and am sour and savage when I anticipate the triumphs of the Philistines." More than ever he admired the " frolic health " of history's Titans and confessed to his journal: " We must envy the great spirits their great physique. Goethe and Napoleon and Humboldt and Scott — what tough bodies answered to their unweariable souls! "

Chapter Nineteen

I

WHILE Emerson was sunk in this lethargy, some of his companions of the Transcendental Club revived the old project of a journal which should express the new ideas afloat in the world.

It was to stand for " the exposition of absolute truth," wrote Emerson to his brother William. He added, " I will never be editor, though I am counted on as a contributor. My Henry Thoreau will be a great poet for such a company, and, one of these days, for all companies." To Margaret Fuller he wrote, " For the sake of the brilliant possibility I would promise honest labor of some sort for a year, but I should wish to leave myself in the latitude of supreme indifference, nay abhorrence of such modes of working forever after. But if your labors shall introduce a new age, they will also mould our opinions, and we shall think that you think."

In this manner did Emerson disavow in advance any responsibility for the journal, and indicate that if he sat in the wagon it would be in an inconspicuous seat behind Miss Fuller. It was first proposed to make the project a reality at a meeting held at the Reverend C. A. Bartol's house in 1839. Present besides the host were George Ripley, Theodore Parker, Hedge, Alcott, W. H. Channing, and Margaret Fuller.

Most of these persons were thirty-odd years old or younger, Alcott alone being as old as forty. Emerson was thirty-seven, and Thoreau was only twenty-three.

Several meetings were held before a name could be chosen or an editor selected. Alcott suggested *The Dial*, and this was the name accepted. After much pulling and hauling, Margaret Fuller, who had made a reputation as leader of a conversational class for young ladies in Boston, was chosen as editress. The selection of a young unmarried woman, however brilliant, for such a post was, at that time, a radical and daring step. Only a short time later the Abolition movement was virtually split in two by the furious opposition of certain Abolutionists to the appearance of women on the platform as speakers against slavery. They were perhaps comforted when one day Emerson told them, " Consistency is the hobgoblin of little minds."

None of *The Dial* group was clear as to what the magazine should contain and what its aim should be. Emerson himself hovered between two opinions: on the one hand, he wished it to be " universal and poetic"; on the other, that it might be " a degree nearer the hodiernal facts than my writings are," and that it " should lead the opinion of this generation on every great interest." He did not favor contributions from celebrated contributors, but hoped that its wit and verse might come from eight or nine persons. The editress, however, in a preliminary statement made it plain that her views differed from his in important particulars. " A perfectly free organ is to be offered," she wrote, " for the expression of individual thought and character." It was to " aim, not at leading public opinion, but at stimulating each man to judge for himself, and to think more deeply and more nobly by letting him see how some minds are to be kept open, not to accomplish any untoward object, but merely to afford an avenue for what of liberal and calm thought might be originated among us by the wants of individual minds."

After much travail and inward groaning, the first issue of *The Dial* emerged in July, 1840, as a quarterly at three dollars a year. Its published purpose was the discussion of principles rather than measures. No claim was made for its contributors except a common love " of intellectual freedom and the hope of social progress; who are united by sympathy of spirit, not by agreement in speculation; whose faith is in Divine Providence rather than in human prescription; whose hearts are more in the future than in the past, and who trust the living soul rather than the dead letter."

II

It was at once apparent that however firm had been Emerson's intention to keep his connection with *The Dial* a slightly distant one, the Emerson shadow was to lie heavily over the journal; for out of twenty-seven contributions three, including the long introductory article, were from his pen; and two others had been supplied by him from the writings of his dead brothers, Edward and Charles. The editress herself had furnished no less than four. Among the other writers represented were Thoreau, Alcott, Ripley, Parker, W. H. Channing, C. P. Cranch, John S. Dwight, Mrs. Ellen Hooper, and Sarah Clarke.

In his introductory article Emerson announced that *The Dial* was the voice of those persons who had learned " to reprobate that rigor of our conventions of religion and education which is turning us to stone " and who perceived that in New England society a revolution was in progress. They represented " a protest against usage, and a search for principles," and meant to dwell " not in dead time," but in a " state of life and growth." This journal could not " prescribe its own course," having "all things to say and no less than all the world for its final audience." It hoped to be " one cheerful, rational voice amidst the din of mourners and polemics."

No one was quite pleased with the first number; it contained several good things, but they failed to hang together. There was no unified impression, no solid impact. Margaret Fuller herself made a face over it; expected contributors had been slow or silent, and none liked his neighbor's offering.

Emerson's criticisms did not spare her feelings. Except for Alcott's " Orphie Sayings," he had found in the magazine " little that might not appear in any other journal." He hoped *The Dial* was not going to be too literary, but would " read the law on property, government, education, as well as on art, letters and religion. . . . It does not seem worth our while to work with any other than sovereign aims. So I wish we might court some of the good fanatics, and publish chapters on every head in the whole art of living. I am just now turning my pen to scribble and copy on the subjects of Labor, Farm, Reform, Domestic Life, etc., and I asked myself, why should not *The Dial* present this homely and grave subject to the men and women of the land? . . . I know the dangers of such latitude of plan in any but the best conducted journal. It becomes friendly to special modes of reform;

partisan, bigoted, perhaps whimsical; not universal and poetic. But our round-table is not, I fancy, in imminent peril of poetry and bigotry, and we shall not bruise each the others' whims by the collision."

In his journal he wrote: "It might well add such poetry and sentiment as will now constitute its best merit. Yet it ought to go straight into life, with the devoted wisdom of the best men and women in the land."

But neither poetry nor wisdom helped to sell *The Dial*; the only popular response was to Parker's articles on timely or controversial topics. One contribution by him, relating to a certain minister's differences with his parish on the subject of temperance in drinking, caused the entire issue to be sold out; while those numbers containing contributions by Emerson, some of which later became famous poems and essays, went to load the storage shelves. What the public wanted was the very opposite of what Emerson proposed they should receive; the public wanted measures, but *The Dial* editress continued firmly to offer them principles.

III

Margaret Fuller went on editing and writing no small part of *The Dial*; prodding dilatory contributors and at the last moment filling vacant pages with her own hasty writings; working without pay amid the numerous distractions brought upon her by her own uneven temperament.

Emerson, meantime, looked at each issue in growing disapproval. He said nothing to his fellow Transcendentalists, but relieved his feelings in his private writings. In the face of this " saturnalia of faith," his innate reserve and canniness began to re-assert themselves.

" After twenty or after fifty years," he once said, " you shall find the individual true to his early tendencies — men do not turn sharp corners "; and so he wrote:

" 'Tis necessary that you honor the people's facts. If you have no place for them, the people absolutely have no place for you. The earth and sea and air, the constitution of things, and all that we call Fate, is on the people's side; and that is a reasoner not liable to a fallacy. . . . The whole human race spend their lives in hard work, for simple and necessary motives, and feel the approbation of their conscience. . . . There must be, not a few fine words, but very many hard strokes, every day, to get what even an ascetic wants. . . . Let a man hate eddies, hate the sides of the river, and keep the middle of the stream. . . . Wisdom does not seek a literal rectitude, but a useful, that is, a conditional one — such a one as the faculties of man and the constitution of things will warrant."

And this was the man who only a short time previously had declared " there is hope in extravagance; in routine none! "

It is not strange that Emerson so often disavowed any claim to consistency; for scattered throughout his collected writings are on one page statements, admonitions, apothegms, which are the very opposite of his utterances on another page. It would be easy to set up parallel columns which on one side would display positive statements by Emerson and on the other their complete negations. He saw everything as bi-polar; this is true, also that other, according to the Hegelian law of antinomy. He instantly reacted against any over-enthusiastic word or action, and attempted to offset extremes by something from the other side. If one was prone to be fire, he was water. If one was stationary, he was all motion. To a marked degree Thoreau had the same trait; but in another person Emerson found it annoying, according to the law which makes other persons offensive in the degree that they have our own faults.

IV

Carlyle found *The Dial* too " aurora borealis-like," and thought it lacked " a stalwart Yankee man, with a coat on his back." The first criticism was just; it was full of streamers, bright and skylighting, but they lacked connection. If, however, he meant to imply that the magazine was in flavor too feminine, he erred; for Margaret Fuller was not even as "feminine " in mind as Emerson. What she was unable to bring about was organization, and so she allowed the journal to fret and worry her, and after two years she, pleading ill health, resigned it to Emerson, having been paid little or nothing of the annual $200 promised to the editor.

Despite its obvious faults, *The Dial* in her hands was no feeble or witless journal, and she was delighted when subsequently she visited England to find copies treasured there by persons of discrimination. She introduced or made better known to the reading public such writers as Thoreau, Lowell, and Charles A. Dana, and her own contributions on German literature, on criticism, on music and art, did a positive service for the contemporary intellect. Most noteworthy of all her contributions was her realistic and cant-free article in her last issue, " The Great Lawsuit, Man versus Men — Woman versus Women." No such discussion of the relations between the sexes had ever been published before in America; and when it appeared in a book re-named, at Emerson's suggestion, *Woman in the Nineteenth Century*, it signalled the approach of Feminism in the United States.

If Emerson was the Yankee man, with a coat on his back, desired for *The Dial* by Carlyle, he proved to be no more successful as editor than the Yankee woman with a skirt around her legs. The magazine continued to stumble along, changing its publisher often but attracting no more material support than before. However, under its new editor it became less diffuse and literary, and more timely and specific. It paid attention to contemporary movements and projects for improvement, and encouraged advocates of a better organized society.

In his new post Emerson was able to carry out certain plans particularly dear to his fancy. One was to give more space to Thoreau's writings. In two years Miss Fuller had given space to five of his poems; Emerson printed sixteen in his first editorial year, also admitting Thoreau's first prose articles.

Another project put immediately into execution was the publication of a series of selections from the bibles of the world. It represented Emerson's attempt to acquaint his countrymen with those Oriental scriptures, anteceding the Judaic and Christian eras, with which he had become more and more in love, and to show New Englanders that there were other and older faiths than those purely Nordic ones in which they had been brought up — "the grand expressions," said the introduction, " of the moral sentiment in different ages and races, the rules for the guidance of life, the bursts of piety and of abandonment to the Invisible and Eternal."

In Emerson's first number was an article on "Prayers" with the same aim: "Let us not have the prayers of one sect, nor of the Christian church, but of men in all ages and religions who have prayed well."

At this distance Emerson's purpose in these articles appears clear enough: it was to break down the prevalent devotion to inherited tradition, dogma, and fixity; and to substitute a consciousness of the fluidity which had brought the Here and Now. This would clear a path for the Young America in which he had an ardent, nay, a glowing faith. He remained insistently cheerful.

"Nature," he wrote, "has not lost one ringlet of her beauty, one impulse of resistance and valor. From the necessity of loving, none are exempt; and he that loves must utter his desires. . . . Man is not so far lost but that he suffers ever the great discontent, which is the elegy of his loss and the prediction of his recovery. . . . What shall hinder the genius of the time from speaking its thought? It will write in a higher spirit, and a wider knowledge, and with a grander practical aim, than ever yet guided the pen of poet. It will write the annals of a changed world, and record the descent of principles into practice, of love into government, of love into trade. It will describe the new heroic life of man, the now unbelieved possibility of simple living, and of clean and noble relations with men."

The teachings by which Emerson meant to stand were by now attaining increasing clarity and shapeliness. He was well aware that the old forms, whose quondam usefulness he was prompt to admit, could not permit the expansion of a lusty and optimistic nation, which must discover forms in which it could work, think, and live; under penalty otherwise of suffering from the spiritual miasma, the defeatism, that had already gripped a portion of its youth. (Why did his two brilliant brothers die so young? Why were almost the last words of Charles Emerson words of disillusion?)

Whether or not Emerson's remedy was the correct one, his diagnosis of the disease of the time was accurate — the tendency to be content with "good eating" under the shadow of the old institutions. To offset this, he constantly admonished his young countrymen to live less in terms of Time. Nature itself, he declared, though not deep, had immense "lateral spaces." He wanted men to follow nature's example in the use of these lateral spaces — in thought, in action, in living. Emerson was the Apostle of Great Spaces. The curse of the age he declared was diffusion where there should be concentration. "We have freedom from much nonsense and superstition, but we pay a great price for it. The old faith is gone, the new loiters. The world looks bare and cold. We have lost reverence, yet are timid and flattering. See the despondency of those who are putting on the manly robe; when they are to direct themselves, all hope, wisdom, and power sink flat down." So ensued a tendency to gloomy reflection, introversion, and morbid views.

Emerson conceived it as his mission to dispel this stasis, and give body and form to a new faith. "I am to celebrate the spiritual powers, in their infinite contrast to the mechanical powers and the mechanical philosophy of this time. I am to console the brave sufferers under evils whose end they cannot see, by appeals to the great Optimism self-affirmed in all bosoms."

In the very last number of *The Dial* he published as an essay what had already been given as a lecture in Boston under the title of " The Young American," and here once more he sounded the rallying bugle:

" I call upon you, young men, to obey your heart, and be the nobility of this land. . . . In America, out-of-doors all seems a market; indoors, an air-tight stove of conventionalism. Everybody who comes into our houses savors of these precious habits, the men of the market, the women of the custom. I find no expression in our state papers or legislative debate, in our lyceums or churches, especially in our newspapers, of a high national feeling, no lofty counsels that rightfully stir the blood. . . . They recommend only conventional virtues, whatever will earn and preserve property, always the capitalist. The ' opposition ' papers, so-called, are on the same side. They attack the great capitalist, but with the aim to make a capitalist of the poor man. . . . Here stars, here woods, here hills, here animals, here men, abound, and the vast tendencies occur of a new order. If only the men are well employed in conspiring with the designs of the Spirit who led us hither, and is leading us still, we shall quickly enough advance out of all hearing of others' censures, out of all regrets of our own, into a new and more excellent social state than history has recorded."

He was convinced that the American Republic was to be the banner-bearer in a new human advance. " It seems so easy for America to inspire and express the most expansive and humane spirit; new born, free, healthful, strong, the land of the laborer, of the democrat, of the philanthropist, of the believer, of the saint. These should speak for the human race."

For two years Emerson strove to make *The Dial* something other than " the herbarium that it is of dried flowers "; but Young America remained dispirited and Old America merely looked on and sniffed. Emerson had no aggression as an editor, and he dropped no tears when *The Dial* expired of its malnutrition, for other exigent events were demanding his attention.

Chapter Twenty

I

THE Roaring 'Forties had come, and Emerson, feeling the pulsations from the energetic, pushing life of the rifle-carrying men in the Rockies, California, Texas, West, and Southwest, sometimes waxed impatient with the stagnation of the settled East. " Our virtue [Emerson habitually used this word in its original sense, as derived from the Latin *vir*, a man] runs in a narrow rill; we have never a freshet. One would like to see Boston and Massachusetts agitated like a wave with some generosity; mad for learning, or music, for philanthropy, for association, for freedom, for art. We have sensibility and insight enough, if only we had constitution enough."

There was a sufficient madness about, although it was not of the kind which Emerson hoped for. In the very year in which *The Dial* was founded, a series of meetings was held in Chardon Street, Boston, to discuss current dissatisfaction with old religious forms and to devise, if possible, new forms more suited to the times. It was called by a group calling themselves " Friends of Universal Progress." Emerson, who attended but took no active part, thus described the assembly:

" A great variety of dialect and of costume was noticed; a great deal of confusion, eccentricity, and freak appeared, as well as of zeal and enthusiasm. If the assembly was disorderly, it was picturesque. Madmen, madwomen, men with beards, Dunkers, Muggletonians, Come-outers, Groaners, Agrarians, Seventh-day Baptists, Quakers, Abolitionists, Calvinists, Unitarians, and philosophers — all came successively to the top and seized their moment, if not their hour, wherein to chide or pray or preach or protest. . . . If there was not parliamentary order, there was life, and the assurance of that constitutional love for religion and religious liberty which, in all periods, characterizes the inhabitants of this part of America."

These conventions, of which three were held, were but symptoms of a bubbling and seething that affected almost the whole of New England and extended to the Middle West. It had its center in Massachusetts, for the reason that this State was the first to feel the effects of an industrialism which was rapidly altering the old modes of life and causing drastic changes in habit and custom. It was everywhere felt that a turning-point had been reached and that a crisis was impending which was menacing all the known values of life. The uneasiness had been converted into alarm by the quakings that followed the panic of 1837. In their anxiety men were moved to draw together to compare information and take counsel as to the future. If there was madness in their air, it was because men were secretly fearful; and the decade covered by the 'forties was filled with their schemes to establish order in those avenues of life and work where chaos seemed to impend.

It was at this moment and in the same year, 1840, that George Ripley, Unitarian minister and business manager of *The Dial,* came to Emerson with a project for buying the

Brook Farm at West Roxbury, nine miles from Boston;
where a group of the like-minded might establish a more
agreeable mode of living, with special attention to education
and religion. There is no evidence that Ripley was influenced
by Robert Owen's experiment in socialized labor, begun in
1824 at New Harmony, Indiana; for that had failed. Nor is
it likely that he had been affected directly by the teachings
of Fourier; for the tenets of Fourierism were at that time
known only to a few Americans, who were not in contact with
the Unitarians surrounding Ripley. It is likely that Ripley's
impulse was at heart religious rather than economic, and was
due to a kind of monastic desire for withdrawal from a sordid
world rather than a desire for a new society.

Emerson listened to Ripley, but parried for time, mean-
while writing to Carlyle: " We are all a little wild here
with numberless projects of social reform. Not a reading man
but has a draft of a new community in his waistcoat pocket. I
am gently mad myself, and am resolved to live cleanly.
George Ripley is talking up a colony of agriculturists and
scholars, with whom he threatens to take the field and the
book."

Simultaneously he confided to Margaret Fuller: " At the
name of a society all my repulsions play, all my quills rise
and sharpen." His skeptical sense of humor and his belief in
individualism stood in the way; and when Ripley and his
group called again he wrote: " I wished to be convinced, to
be thawed, to be made nobly mad by the kindlings before
my eye, of a new dawn of human piety. But this scheme was
arithmetic and comfort; a hint borrowed from the Tremont
House and the United States Hotel; a rage in our poverty
and politics to live rich and gentlemanlike; an anchor to

leeward against a change of weather. And not once could I be inflamed, but sat aloof and thoughtless; my voice faltered and fell. It was not the cave of persecution, which is the palace of spiritual power, but only a room in the Astor House hired for the Transcendentalists. I do not wish to remove from my present prison to a prison a little larger. I wish to break all prisons."

He at length wrote Ripley, " very slowly and, I may almost say, with penitence," of his decision against leaving Concord for Brook Farm; and so, when the community spread itself over the West Roxbury fields in the following year, it was without the presence of Emerson. " I approve every wild action of the experimenters," he wrote. " I say what they say, and my only apology for not doing their work is preoccupation of mind. I have a work of my own, which I know I can do with some success. It would leave that undone if I should undertake with them, and I do not see in myself any vigor equal to such an enterprise. So I stay where I am, even with the degradation of owning bank stock and seeing poor men suffer whilst the universal genius apprises me of this disgrace, and beckons me to the martyr's and redeemer's office."

His position as a property-owner — he wrote to Carlyle about this time that he was worth about $22,000 — his love of personal insulation, and his ardent belief that society was to be saved only through the leadership of individual genius, all were factors in the great refusal; but, larger than any, was his consciousness that he was only an inspirer and distributor of ideas, and that he was incapable of putting any of them into practice. He was the seeing eye, as he so often insisted, but not the working hand.

However, he was a frequent visitor at Brook Farm, where he beamed approval on the children at their lessons, on scholars plowing the fields, and on Hawthorne milking the cows; and after The Great Experiment had come virtually to an end with the burning of the Phalanstery in 1846, he felt it time to write this:

"The founders of Brook Farm should have this praise, that they made what all people try to make, an agreeable place to live in. All comers, even the most fastidious, found it the pleasantest of residences. It is certain that freedom from household routine, variety of character and talent, variety of work, variety of means of thought and instruction, art, music, poetry, reading, masquerade, did not permit sluggishness or despondency; broke up routine. There is agreement in the testimony that it was, to most of the associates, education; to many, the most important period of their life, the birth of valued friendships, their first acquaintance with the riches of conversation, their training in behavior." At this point he indulged in a bit of Emersonian satire: " The art of letter-writing, it is said, was immensely cultivated. Letters were always flying, not only from house to house, but from room to room. It was a perpetual picnic, a French Revolution in small, an Age of Reason in a pattypan."

Margaret Fuller and Bronson Alcott likewise remained separate from Brook Farm; but they, too, were occasional visitors, the former coming for solitude and the latter the reverse. Being individualists seeking an individual connection with the Absolute, they were not attracted by any of the numerous associations, communities, and phalanxes which arose in Massachusetts and elsewhere about the time that

Albert Brisbane wrote, *The Social Destiny of Man,* and later persuaded the Brook Farmers to study Fourier.

Some of these colonies were religious in purpose, others educational, and still others economic; but all, including Brook Farm, were social symptoms — rashes and growths indicating a sick and strained America; and all were inspired by a dread of America's nascent capitalism. Men did not know how to face and deal with this capitalism, and could only by instinct huddle together. But Emerson had a constitutional aversion for huddles.

II

However, his sensibility to all changes of temperature would not permit him to remain quite unaffected by these stirrings in the social body, and as often as he thought of Brook Farm and its devoted laborers he experienced a slight twinge of conscience. He could not coöperate on any large and public scale; but could he not do so in a discreet and private way, beginning in a very small fashion and gradually expanding as the experiment prospered? Was he without sin in enjoying a scholar's ease, while servants toiled that he might be comfortable? He at least might a little ameliorate their lot and at the same time prove to himself that he was not blind to the obligations of the social contract. His proposal was that henceforth the maid and the cook be given places at the family dining-table on a level of complete equality and democracy. There was precedent for this in the old-fashioned, early-American practice of having the hired help at the common meal, which practice he was sure would pave the way to a new and more democratic arrangement. The scheme was broached to Lidian, and she, who never dreamed of opposing her great husband's fancies, at once consented; and it was she who was delegated to go out to the kitchen and explain the matter to the two open-mouthed girls, while Emerson waited trepidantly in the study upstairs. Louisa, the maid, who was a gentle lass, made no demur, but Lydia, the cook, begged to be excused; she could not be rightly dressed to come to the big table, and a cook, what with her hands and the pots, etc., was not fit to be seen in company anyhow; no, she just couldn't. This attitude on Lydia's part was disappointing but, at any rate, a beginning could be made with Louisa, and it was so ordered. The next morning, after Mr. and Mrs. Emerson had taken their seats at breakfast, little Waldo was dispatched to the kitchen to summon Louisa to the table. He returned alone, reporting that Louisa, begging pardon, had already breakfasted and was now needed for company while Lydia ate.

Thus was democracy shot, virtually at sunrise and in its infancy, in the Emerson household, done to death by those whom it was meant to benefit. The project was not renewed, but was permitted to lie where it fell. Its failure gave Emerson food for meditation, also for renewed skepticism as to large-scale schemes of reform.

" I have not yet conquered my own house," he wrote. " It irks and repents me. Shall I raise the siege of this hencoop, and march baffled away to a pretended siege of Babylon? " His answer to himself was in the negative, and it was so ordered.

III

A second point on which Emerson's conscience was uneasy related to the amount of superfluous space in his house. It had been enlarged with the expectation that Charles Emerson and his bride would come to live there; and as it stood, Emerson felt that, in accordance with the new social conscience, it ought to shelter more persons. A solution was found by inviting the Alcotts, whose resources continued meager despite Alcott's belief that Spirit would provide all, to come there and live for a year. Mrs. Emerson's consent to this arrangement was not quite so hearty, but it was granted; as for Alcott, he was enthusiastic, foreseeing immense benefit to all concerned. Accordingly preparations were made to receive the struggling family of the philosopher, with their crop of little girls, into a common life of " labor and plain living," as Emerson expressed it; and all might have transpired beautifully except that Mrs. Alcott, who had agreed to take Emerson's proposal " under consideration," left it there. She never did come, and thus another glowing project came to ground.

Emerson now had new cause for meditation, and out of it came the conclusion that in cases where men proposed reforms involving a readjustment in family life, they would do well, before executing them, to consult the women; otherwise, severe and perhaps basic alterations might be necessary. Women, especially if mothers, seemed to look askance at man-made communities. " It was to them like the brassy and lacquered life in hotels. The common school was well enough,

EMERSON AS HE APPEARED IN HIS SIXTIES

but to the common nursery they had grave objections. Eggs might be hatched in ovens, but the hen on her own account much preferred the old way."

IV

Being, as he fancied, "a little of an agrarian at heart," Emerson's thought next turned to the land and the beneficence of manual labor. A new love of the land had infected the whole of society. Hardy young New Englanders were daily deserting factory-threatened towns for the West that they might have it in more abundance; great companies were speculating in it; and all the myriad labor-communities and phalanxes of the period were possessed of one idea — "Back to the Land! " — as if the earth might somehow bury and heal the fevers that had assailed the social body.

Emerson had hitherto rather prided himself on the hours spent in his garden and orchard, his fields and corn-rows; but now such casual, part-time labor looked puerile, wearing "a certain emblematic air, like the ploughing of the Emperor of China." He resolved to throw his weight more fully into the collar, and in smock and old clothes pare down some of the inequalities of life which pained him to contemplate. "Nothing great," he told himself, "was ever achieved without enthusiasm. The way of life is wonderful. It is by abandonment." And so with enthusiasm, with abandonment, he attacked the sullen glebe, wielding spade and hoe with a vigor which made little Waldo, who was witness to all his father's labors, uneasy as to the safety of the parental legs.

But it was of no use. To swing his implements "heated

and untuned " him; the smell of the plants " drugged him and robbed him of energy "; he became " the dupe of dandelions," of purslain and dock and chick-weed, which, as soon as one was pulled, disclosed four thousand more; vines and trees became invested with a subtle and malignant poison; melon hills and quickset hedges were duns and traps. His once-loved garden took on the face " of those pernicious machineries we read of, every month, in the newspapers, which catch a man's coatskirt or his hand, and draw in his arm, his leg, and his whole body to destruction." Between pauses for breath and the removal of perspiration, doubts began to assail him as to the soundness of his previous teachings, and if at that moment his essay on *Nature* had been begun, it would probably have been of entirely different import. Land was no longer Mother Earth, but a Jabberwock with claws. " No land is bad, but land is worse. If a man own land, the land owns him." He grew peevish and depressed at the recollection of his once fresh morning thought, at the drowning of the Ineffable Whole in this mess of weedy particulars. He concluded that "the genius of reading and of gardening are antagonistic, like resinous and vitreous electricity," and even permitted himself to say: " This pottering in a few square yards of garden is dispiriting and drivelling."

Mrs. Emerson, who had hovered in the background, became alarmed as she noted his drowsiness and languor, his tendency to sleep over his notes and papers; and in a secret hour she sent for Thoreau, her favorite among all of Concord's young men. As she poured out her fears to him, Thoreau smiled a Sphinx-like smile and nodded as she put certain questions. Comforted by this consultation, she awaited a season when her lord should be unharassed by the thought of tomorrow's odious agriculture, and then put forth certain suggestions. There were shelves to be put up, she said, and repairs to be made in the kitchen, and locks were needed for certain doors. He, Emerson, was too busy to attend to such things — of that she was well aware; but would it not be possible to ask Henry Thoreau to come around once in a while and look after these trifles? Henry was always so helpful and ingenious with his little kit of tools. Besides, little Waldo was always asking for him. Did Emerson not remember the day when Waldo asked Henry to be his papa?

Thus was the seed planted. It grew, and in a few days Emerson was writing to his brother that Thoreau had been invited to come and live with him for a year.

Thoreau was willing, for he was sick of school-teaching; he made the repairs around the house in his tight, thorough way — blushing slightly as often as he had to go through the kitchen, where Louisa and Lydia tittered at his bashfulness; pruned the trees and planted new ones; took the garden in his hands and made it behave in a fashion that caused Emerson to beam as he looked on; rode Waldo on his back; and quickly established himself as a vitally necessary member of the family.

" He is to have his board, etc.," wrote Emerson to William with restored cheerfulness, " for what labor he chooses to do, and he is thus far a great benefactor and physician to me, for he is an indefatigable and a very skilful laborer, and I work with him as I should not without him, and expect to be suddenly well and strong."

Thus did another threatened social failure transform itself into a shining success, with all the parties to it happy and relieved — Emerson to be free to get on with his first essays instead of being daily drained of life by a devouring earth; Thoreau to have a congenial occupation in association with the man he most looked up to; and Mrs. Emerson to have someone at hand who could drive a nail indubitably straight.

The association lasted, in its first period, for two years, necessarily causing certain modifications in both men. Emerson was a powerful absorber, and learned more from Thoreau of wonders in Nature than he had ever dreamed of before. Thoreau sharpened the elder man's eyes and fascinated him with details where previously he had been prone to see only mystic Wholes. Whether the younger man derived as much from Emerson is a question. There were observers who thought that in Thoreau Emerson spoiled a good naturalist. They believed he marred Henry's objectively scientific bent by inducing him to see Nature not as physical but metaphysical. Emerson was, except on the platform, a slow outgiver; but Thoreau throve by contact with Emerson's library and his lively family, which soon comprised two little girls, Ellen and Edith, as well as Waldo.

Emerson's defeat at the clutches of the dandelions and chick-weed was not bootless, for it furnished, as all things did, the more meat for his writings. " You must elect your work," he thenceforth taught. "You shall take what your brain can, and drop the rest." At times, under his pen, Nature had appeared to be something like an aeriform goddess and again something large, placid, and maternal, like a nice Jersey cow. He now wrote:

" Nature, as we know her, is no saint. She comes eating and drinking and sinning. Her darlings do not come out of the Sunday School, nor weigh their food, nor punctually keep the commandments."

Chapter Twenty-One

I

"I UNSETTLE all things. No facts are to me sacred; none are profane; I simply experiment, an endless seeker, with no Past at my back."

These challenging words might well have been the preface to the *Essays, First Series,* which Emerson published when he was thirty-eight years old as the fruit of the thought and meditation of his mature manhood. Nothing like this bayonetted writing had ever been seen in Europe-aping America before; but no sensation followed in Emerson's country; its readers merely knitted their brows over this shower of spikey sentences, regretted that the author saw fit to be so obscure, and remarked that he gave them a headache. A few reviews praised them with cautious reservations, but in Europe certain lighthouse-keepers greeted them as heralds. From Carlyle, who afterwards confessed that at first he had not recognized Emerson's genius, came this exalting message: "You are a new era, my man, in your new huge country. God give you strength, and speaking and silent faculty, to do such work as seems possible now for you." And the German, Herman Grimm, who at first was puzzled by the unfamiliar words, the sharp-edged paragraphs, confessed: "I found myself depending on the book, and was provoked with myself for it. How could I be so captured and enthralled, so fascinated and bewildered? . . . I felt the pure air — the old weather-beaten motives recovered their tone. . . . He presents familiar facts, but he presents them in new lights and combinations. From every object the lines of light run straight out, connecting it with the central point of life."

In these essays Emerson reached the summit of his writing. For the first time that " fist " which he had developed in his speaking appeared in his writing; his style was vigorous, pungent, athletic. Yet he wrote calmly, as one having authority, as an oracle delivering sentiments not to be disputed. His wisdom was like that of the Orient, as if each thought had been born complete and required no support from any other. Said Carlyle: " That this little book has no system, and points or stretches beyond all systems, is one of its merits. We will call it the soliloquy of a true soul; alone under the stars in their days." It was indeed a soliloquy, but a soliloquy conscious of an audience. It was meant to be heard and overheard. In it Emerson disclosed himself in his true character as a preacher-teacher, an American Confucius, a New England Zoroaster, a Massachusetts Buddha.

In the first three essays, *History, Self Reliance,* and *Compensation,* are the three chief tenets of Emersonianism: that man is a particular, an inlet, in a sea of universal mind; that he is to trust himself when he occupies his organic position; and that for whatever befalls him, good or ill, there is an offset, a balance, and a compensation. When in the vein, Emerson threw off thoughts like a shower of sparks, and he was responsible for a multitude of opinions; but all are in some degree variations of these three themes.

Though slow in attaining acceptance, this book of first

essays in time penetrated to all parts of the civilized world
and had an incalculable influence — all because when Emerson returned from his first visit to Europe, it was with the
resolve to " eternize his own wood-house " and cultivate his
own intellectual garden. Whatever may be said of its teachings, as a feat performed by a village freeholder, a frail
Unitarian preacher who began life in poverty with a feeble
constitution and an overwhelming inferiority complex, it deserves all the admiration it has had.

In his own country the essay which first attained popularity and has since had the most attention is *Self Reliance*.
It has been reprinted in a thousand forms, and in pamphlet
form has been distributed by elders to millions of young
people. It has formed a part of innumerable enforced reading
courses for the young. Its maxims and apothegms have been
incorporated in daily speech and placed before generations as
mottoes which the immature penman must copy. Nothing
has been omitted which could stamp its sayings on the young
American mind. What echoes do not these sentences awaken?

" To be great is to be misunderstood."

" A foolish consistency is the hobgoblin of little minds."

" Speak your latent conviction and it shall be the universal
sense."

" In every work of genius we recognize our own rejected
thoughts."

" Let a man know his worth and keep things under his
feet."

" Trust thyself: every heart vibrates to that iron string."

" All history resolves itself into the biography of a few
stout and earnest men."

❖ 207 ❖

This essay is peculiarly a gospel for young men. It is electric and vivifying. Its " hard words " please the practical-minded, while for the poetic and dreamy it is rousing to mind and blood. It has the flash of swords in it and trumpets of defiance. It summons to action, and creates the wish to do heroic things.

But *Self Reliance* has in the country of its birth suffered a fantastic fate. Its particles, lifted from their context and dissociated from the body of Emerson's teachings, have been used to create effects the very opposite of those which Emerson intended. Emerson meant to give to his countrymen a banner which should head a holy crusade; they seized it and galloped off in a direction which its builder could not foresee. They read the inscription, but because they were ignorant of Emerson's inspiration they read it superficially, and they used it for purposes of which the Concordian could never have dreamed.

Self Reliance contains sentences which are two-edged, particularly the following:

" *No law can be sacred to me but that of my nature.*"
" *Good and bad are but names, very readily transferable to that or this.*"
" *The only right is what is after my constitution, the only wrong what is against it.*"

These sentences, if isolated, are dangerous weapons to place in the hands of those shrewd and ambitious persons who wish to sink their scruples, and who rejoice to find their individual acquisitions thus seemingly justified and their private desires thus provided with a gospel of rationalization.

It is obvious from the rest of Emerson's writings that when he used the general *me* he meant the metaphysical *me,* the soul which, he taught, had access to the universal mind. The Emersonian " Self " is used in the same manner as the Hindoo " Self," as indicating a divine and godlike essence. His meaning should have been clear as expounded in this saying: " Who has more soul than I masters me, though he should not raise his finger," and again: " Truly it demands something *godlike* in him who has cast off the common motives of humanity and has ventured to trust himself for a taskmaster. High be his heart, faithful his will, clear his sight, that he may in good earnest be doctrine, society, law, to himself, that a simple purpose may be to him as strong as iron necessity to others."

Emerson also was obviously outlining a philosophy constructed upon his own experience. He had attained his success, his unification, his serene and satisfying life, only after he had cut himself loose from worn-out dogma and tradition, ceased to worship accepted gods and men, and based himself upon his own instincts as to what was suited to his constitution. He not only had no regrets for his course, but rejoiced in it; and it was, in consequence, natural for him to believe that what had been so eminently good for him must be good for others.

It happened, however, that, at the time Emerson's first essays appeared, his country was on the brink of a clearly marked transition phase. Though still adhering to the bony religion of Calvinism, it no longer believed in certain damnation and was freeing itself from the Calvinistic discipline. Coincident with the break from strict Calvinism came the development of Industrialism — whose large and relatively easy earnings caused a gradual desertion of farm-and-cottage life — and the opening of the West, with its promise of abundant land for all. The prospect was broad and exciting, and clever and enterprising men made ready to attack the country's tremendous unexploited resources. They needed no more apt rationalization for what they wished to do than that which Emerson seemed to provide for them in *Self Reliance*. And so out came the speculator and the profiteer, mingling with the pioneer, the settler, the explorer, and the founder of enterprises, chanting: " The only right is what is after my constitution," " Good and bad are but names."

Shrewd men laid their hands on savings, on credit, on rivers, on lands, on railroads, on minerals and metals, as fast as the Daniel Boones, the Davy Crocketts, the Kit Carsons, the Sam Houstons, the Frémonts, and Bonnevilles carried the settlement line westward and advanced to new frontiers, and along with much heroic, picturesque endeavor went gigantic stealings, frauds, and malefactions; Texas was taken from Mexico in a war which was denounced by Emerson, Thoreau, and Abraham Lincoln; California was invaded by gold-seekers; the Indians were pushed off their lands and herded into reservations; murderous struggles broke out in Missouri and Kansas; and new territories were added so fast that the country could not digest them and, in a fury of argument as to whether they should be slave-holding or free-soil, finally exploded convulsively in civil war.

The more unscrupulous leaders of these comorantic movements, were, of course, not directly influenced by *Self Reliance* or any other of Emerson's essays; they were not the sort of men who cared to read about universals or any other abstract concepts. Nor did Emerson found the philosophy according to which they acted. A theory of intense and reckless individualism was already permeating the atmosphere, and Emerson only gave optimistic form and substance to what was already in the minds of men confronting unexplored wildernesses, particularly when he said:

"Personal force never goes out of fashion. . . . Power first, or no leading class. In politics and in trade bruisers and pirates are of better promise than talkers and clerks." And again: "The consideration the rich possess in all societies is not without meaning or right. It is the approval given by the human understanding to the act of creating value by knowledge and labor. It is the sense of every human being that man should have this dominion of Nature, should arm himself with tools and force the elements to drudge for him and give him power. Everyone must seek to secure his independence."

Emerson meant to preach the doctrine of a spiritual self, entitled to base itself on its instincts because connected with a universal mind which was always beneficent; but by the time his essays had won notice and attention, currents leading on to material fortune had been set in motion, and his precepts were hailed as confirmatory of the new philosophy of personal acquisition, intent upon property and none too scrupulous about method. And his teachings betrayed just enough of his admiration for power, sheer cleaving power, and the display of it, to give basis to the belief that he meant it literally when he said: "No law can be sacred to me but that of my nature." Many an obese American fortune has been heaped up by methods which would seem to indicate that this dictum has been applied literally, and the perverted acceptance given to it has been responsible for some of the greasier phenomena in American life.

The exalted idealism preached in Emerson's essays has had so powerful an influence, that even the factory, the counting-house, and the business office have felt it necessary to take it into account and to pay to it a homage which has resulted in a curious form of hypocrisy. Business, we are told, exists not for profits, but for "service." Even the great corporations, which once were called soulless, and which once conducted themselves as if they did not care if they were, now publish advertisements which teach that their chief purpose is not to win dividends for their stockholders, but to promote the public welfare with an almost maternal care; and there is no sweatshop operator or real estate dealer so small as not to proclaim that his business is founded upon large "ideals." Quotations from Emerson, indeed, are often found upon the pastel-tinted placards which adorn the offices of the grimmest go-getters; and no one quite likes to admit that he is in trade for the purpose of revenue only, for "service" has become the thing. All these window-dressings are to some extent due to the eloquence by means of which Emerson made idealism popular.

II

Emerson's essays had an unexpected effect in another direction. One of his European readers was Friedrich Nietzsche, who came upon the essays when he was an exile at Pforta and re-read them several years later, at which time he became so enthusiastic that he recommended them to his

friends. In the writings of the German creator of the Super-
man there are numerous passages curiously parallel to those
of Emerson. For example, this extract from the preface to
The Twilight of the Idols might well have been written by
the Concordian himself:

" Nothing ever succeeds which exuberant spirits have not
helped to produce. Surplus power, alone, is the proof of
power."

The same is true of these passages from *Thus Spake
Zarathustra:*

" And if all ladders henceforth fail thee, then must thou
learn to mount upon thine own head: how couldst thou
mount upwards otherwise? Upon thine own head and beyond
thine own heart! . . . Up, upwards, until thou hast even
thy stars *under* thee! "

" Dare only to believe in yourselves — in yourselves and
in your inward parts! He who doth not believe in himself
always lieth."

" Instruments and playthings are sense and spirit: behind
them there is still the self."

And this might have been written by Emerson after his
first disillusioning visit to Carlyle, Wordsworth, et al, in
Europe:

" Never yet hath there been a Superman. Naked have I
seen both of them, the greatest man and the smallest man:
All-too-similar are they still to each other. Verily, even the
greatest found I — all-too-human! "

Emerson helped to stimulate the German into volcanic
utterance, but there is no evidence that Nietzsche borrowed
Emerson's sayings; for the German's fierce aphorisms had
their source in the same kind of soil from which the

American had revolted: stagnation, stodginess, and comfort-worship. Nietzscht's hatred of these things as found among the Germans of his day — his revolt being characteristically more violent than Emerson's — led him to create the Super-man, hard, self-reliant, ruthless, and conquering. The Ger-mans misunderstood Nietzsche just as the Americans mis-understood Emerson. Ignoring their prophet's modifying precepts, the Germans chose to be dazzled only by the figure of the Superman, and with this stuffed figure, clad in shining armor, brandished before the rest of Europe, they succeeded in frightening themselves and their enemies into a World War. Their opponents, in 1914, ascribed this dreadful Teu-tonic figure to the writings of Nietzsche. A rather comic con-sternation might have followed had it been pointed out that the German writer owed his inspiration, in part, to the gentle-man from Concord.

III

Imitation and uniformity were vices for which Emerson constantly criticized his countrymen at this, his most produc-tive period, and he emphasized his disgust in his address, "The Method of Nature," before the Society of the Adelphi at Waterville College, Maine, in the same year (1841), de-claring that too much attention was paid to " machinery, com-merce, and the useful arts. We are a puny and a fickle folk. Avarice, hesitation, and following are our diseases." At such a time, while the multitude of men gave " currency to de-sponding doctrines," the scholar's task was to " reinforce man against himself." But not even the scholar, with his perspective, could point to anything final; he could but observe Nature's perpetual tendency to change and metamorphosis, working towards an end in which there was no private will, "no rebel leaf or limb." Herein lay another statement of Emerson's inveterate optimism: concern yourself not too much about present evil — this too shall pass. The constant recurrence of Emerson to this theme reveals how deep was the uneasiness of the time, how doubtfully men stood before the fork in the road, having no courage to "shoot the gulf, to reconcile the irreconcilable." Daniel Webster was a symbol of the age: he passed Emerson in the street one day, looking black and moody, and would not meet Emerson's glance.

IV

Emerson himself was in low spirits most of this year of 1841, partly because his labors in field, study, and lecture hall had exhausted him, and partly, perhaps, because he, too, was subconsciously affected by the miasma in the air. He diverted himself by a visit to Nantasket where, much to his astonishment, the fish bit at his hook as readily as that of any ordinary individual. He took frequent rides in the stage coach that passed his house on its way to Winthrop Place, Boston, and took particular pleasure in watching the easy, picturesque attitudes of the working-people in the North End, feeling the painter in him stir and crave expression. He went one night to see Fanny Ellsler dance and admired her grace, but did not consider the sight of her filmy skirts and pink slippers good for college boys. He read copiously in Asiatic literature, rejoicing in its quietism; but most of all he consoled himself by long walks in the Concord fields and woods, sometimes with Jones Very, the mystic from Salem, who felt it an honor to wash his own face in the mornings because it was part of the temple of the spirit — but when possible he walked alone. He found he was more than ever unfitted for " a flowing and friendly life "; it dissipated his energies and depleted his low fund of vitality.

The visitors, who came to his house in numbers that increased in proportion to the spread of his fame, sometimes afflicted him like a pestilence; they talked too much and they stayed too long. Intellectuals, who visited him in the hope of being roused or edified, found him empty and silent — he was like an electric bulb from which the current had been turned off — and when they went away disappointed he closed the door behind them with a thankful sigh. It was sometimes with an effort that he made himself affable to the mendicants, peddlers, and ne'er-do-wells who hung about his doorstep; he tried dutifully to help them but without heartiness. He was happy when he could escape from all human beings to the shelter of the blueberry pastures, where he could eat his fill and refresh himself with spring water, when he could watch the changing lights on the still surface of Walden Pond, and when at night he could see the galaxies hanging in the sky.

V

Almost the one companionship of which he never tired was that of little Waldo. His son was now nearly five years old, with beautiful, grave face and deep blue eyes shaded by long dark lashes. Waldo, when not watching Thoreau carve a toy, learning his letters from his grandmother, or being adored by Margaret Fuller, loved to trot at his father's heels. In the study he would be quiet for hours, going about on soundless feet, but out-of-doors he exploded into questions. What was the microscope and the magnet for, and could he work the file and try the pincers? Wasn't it time to collect the eggs and let out the dog? His father was fond of bringing in his own firewood, and Waldo was never so important as when fetching his quota for his grandmother's room. He invented romantic, high-sounding names for things and was apt with explanations. When his sister came into the house crying, it was because she had stepped on his sand-house and got pushed. His father's policy in dealing with grievances was to divert his children's minds with a question or an order to go out and shut the front gate. For example, when Waldo had a nervous crying spell, Emerson would say: " Where's kitty? Go find kitty." The boy quickly learned the usefulness of this device, and when reproached for high crimes would say artlessly: " Where's kitty? " His father drew on him not only for ceaseless entertainment but for wisdom, with which he filled his notebooks and illumed his essays.

The northwest winds of January, 1842, looped fiercely over the ridge opposite Emerson's house and shook the screen of pines and firs on the right-hand side. They howled down the chimney like a challenge and a summons, and then Waldo fell ill of a fever. His cheerfulness made his parents think the ailment was nothing worse than scarletina, as it was euphemistically called; but when the boy grew much quieter, it was diagnosed as scarlet fever. The village heard the dread news but remained hopeful; and one morning little Louisa Alcott came to ask how was Waldo. Emerson met her at the door with a terrible look on the aquiline face, always so benignant.

"Child, he is dead!"

VI

Nothing ever happened to Emerson so rending as the death of his son. Nothing in his experience, his philosophy, his careful schooling of his emotions, availed him now. He was only a man bereft of his first-born, and no more than any other did he know how to reconcile himself to the fact that where yesterday there was a sunbeam, there was today only darkness and silence. His grief engulfed and palsied him; his inner defences, now virtually an integral part of him, were all but shattered. His only assuagement was to write the poem, "Threnody."

The passage of two years brought him nothing with which to reinforce himself, and when on the second anniversary his wife uttered the boy's name, the sound was like a bell-stroke in his father's heart. Succeeding years failed to heal, and on Emerson's deathbed almost his last words were, "Oh, that boy."

But "life," as he wrote, "goes headlong," and two months after Waldo's death he was calm enough to go to New York and read six lectures on "The Times." His purpose in part was to raise money for Alcott, who was possessed of another grandiose project: to go to England and spread there the gospel of education which his own country had so contemptuously rejected. At Ham, in Surrey, a school had already been named Alcott House, and its inspirer was eager to visit it. The New York trip not only brought Emerson $200 above expenses but brought him new friends. Among them was Henry James, the elder, father of that younger Henry who was to become the novelist and of the William who was to become the philosopher of pragmatism, in which some judges profess to see the Emersonian spirit. Little Henry remembered Emerson afterwards as " elegantly slim " and "benevolently aquiline." Among other persons whom he also met for the first time were Horace Greeley and Albert Brisbane. The former he found to be " doing the thinking for the country at a dollar a head per year," and the latter almost persuaded him to be a Fourier Socialist. But not quite.

Emerson returned to Concord with the earnings which enabled Alcott to set joyful sail for England, bearing a letter from Emerson to Carlyle imploring the Scot to permit the American to " make a new and primary impression," and another to the English admirers of Alcott informing them that in his theories he was admirable, but in matters of fact he was not to be trusted! This strange introduction Alcott carried with him without objection, while Emerson resumed his Concord walks.

Among his new companions were W. Ellery Channing and Nathaniel Hawthorne. The former amused him by suggesting that a large dollar would be an appropriate monument to be set up in the central square of each New England town; and the latter's reputation as a writer he found to be a pleasing fact, because his writing was " not good for anything," which Emerson considered a tribute to the man. On September 27, 1842, he and Hawthorne took a long walk on which, for the first time, they became really acquainted. On their way to Stow, they passed the factory where Domett cloths had been made, but it was now deserted — a sign of the depression introduced by the panic of 1837. They found that the barrooms of the old taverns, once such lively centers, were now virtually deserted — emptied by the temperance movement. A farmer gave them a ride in his wagon to the village of Harvard where they spent the night. The next morning they walked to the Shaker village, where the Brethren exchanged some humor with Emerson, Hawthorne remaining aloof and Jove-like. Thence they went to Littleton and then homeward by way of Acton, having covered, in all, about twenty miles. The trip had made them friends, but nothing could make them intimates. Hawthorne's stories always made Emerson shudder.

Meantime, Alcott had returned from England, triumphantly bringing with him his English friends, Henry G. Wright and Charles Lane, and followed by a mystical library of more than 300 books. With this equipment and very little else, the three reformers set about the purchase of an experimental farm near the village of Harvard, which they named " Fruitlands," because it possessed a half-dozen dispirited fruit trees, one of which was capable of bearing. Emerson tried hard to admire Wright and Lane, and succeeded partly; but he could never quite like them. Their notions, which forbade the use of animal manures in the soil as well as the use of animals themselves; their rejection of flour, eggs, milk, butter, and even honey for food, and wool and cotton for clothing; and their endeavor to sustain themselves and Alcott's family of little girls on unbolted wheat bread without yeast, and drinks without sugar except that from maple trees; all offended his New England common sense and provoked him almost to the point of profanity. Louisa Alcott said there was only one beast of burden on the farm — Mrs. Alcott.

When one day Charles Lane come to see him dressed entirely in linen, even to the lining of his shoes, because the Fruitlands' code forbade the use of animal products in any form, Emerson went to his wife and said it was time for something to be done. That lady sympathized with the hardships of Alcott's family, but was mirthful in regard to the Fruitlands menfolk. She thought that their food was too gross entirely, and that to be consistent they ought to live on snow. Emerson sometimes tried to induce Alcott to take occasional cognizance of actualities, but, since Alcott considered himself the only realist of the two, the conversation seldom progressed beyond a new description of Alcott's latest dream of truth and beauty.

The Fruitlands experiment was, of course, bound to fail — which it did within a few months. There was scarcely anything about it, except for the sufferings of Mrs. Alcott, that was not nonsensical and absurd. But this ridiculous farm, where the tonnage in conversation far outweighed that of the expected fruit, can now be seen for what it was — an extreme reaction from the dollar-devotion and mechanized system of life which was threatening that quality of life which the old New England, despite its man-despising creeds, had held precious. Emerson never quite recognized this fact, perhaps because he was too close to its particulars; and he continued to praise the experimenters with faint damns. So, while the wild, giddy, and occasionally lunatic projects of the Fruitlands, the Communities, and the Phalanxes went on nearby, the Emerson home in Concord, with its square front, white paint, and green blinds, remained orderly and tranquil, conducted with that quietude and seemliness which alone could have maintained Emerson, both the inner and the outer man, intact.

"Without a spice of bigot and fanatic," he wrote, " no excitement, no efficiency "; also " Be true to your own act, and congratulate yourself if you have done something strange and extravagant, and broken the monotony of a decorous age." But Emerson most admired what was strange and extravagant when it was at a little distance.

Chapter Twenty-Two

I

ALTHOUGH he had said, concerning the death of little Waldo, that he grieved that he could not grieve, and although he went about his duties with his customary cheerfulness, Emerson found himself again possessed by that apathy and indifference to life which periodically overcame him. It was necessary, however, to rouse himself to new exertions to avoid getting into debt. The expenses he had incurred by making advances to Carlyle's American publishers had made a severe drain on his resources, already low because certain bank stocks in which he had invested had failed to pay dividends. Meantime, he had been generous in his loans and gifts to friends and mendicants. Another attack upon his bank account occurred when he found it necessary, in order to protect his favorite walk to Walden Pond, to purchase additional land adjoining his own, his estate being thus expanded to fourteen acres. And so he resumed his lecture tours, to which he devoted every winter, save one, as long as he was physically able. Despite his reluctance to leave Concord and its healing pastures, and his hatred of the lacquered life of hotels, travelling from town to town was immensely beneficial to his mental circulation. New faces, new conversations, new contacts, fertilized his mind and banished the languorous dullness into which he was apt to fall in Concord.

For example, he astonished himself by finding a particular delight in the service at the Roman Catholic Cathedral in Baltimore, which gave him a sudden aversion for " Unitarians and Martin Luther and all the parliament of Barebones." He even considered it well for his Protestantism that Concord had no Catholic cathedral. He blamed the Unitarian Church for forgetting that men are poets. He admired the Catholic Church because in it an Idea seemed to be supreme over both priest and people. He saw it as in harmony with that Nature which ignores the individual and concerns itself only with processes. At that moment it seemed contemptible to him that every Protestant must have his pew, which he thought presaged the day when there would have to be a church for every individual citizen.

On the road he even enjoyed an occasional argument, and derived marked stimulation from a battle one day on the Camden ferryboat to Philadelphia with a combative Presbyterian preacher, who provided the " bear's meat " which he could not get at home. The " excessive virility " of the people he met in hotels tired him out, and yet he was pleased by the blandness of Philadelphians, in contrast to the " more selfish manners " of New Englanders. In Maine he met a judge who was full of despondency in regard to the state of the nation, and saw universal suffrage as the cause. He amazed the worthy jurist — and himself — by proclaiming that " anarchy is the form and theocracy the fact to which we and all people are tending." Prophets of evil never failed to exasperate Emerson. After listening to them, he was ready to pronounce all existing things as good — even " phrenology and mesmerism, and the old Beelzebub himself."

The frequent references to " mesmerism " and " animal

magnetism " in Emerson's writings at this time reveal how rife was the agitation over these topics in the uneasy minds of the period. Books on these subjects had a large circulation, and sensitive persons saw themselves being subjected to malign influences from every shadowed corner. Among those affected was the New England young woman who became Mrs. Mary Baker Glover Eddy, founder of Christian Science, in whose writings repeated warnings against " malicious animal magnetism," often designated as " M. A. M.," are conspicuous.

II

Emerson was a true man of his day in his determination to acquire personal pecuniary independence. He regarded it as the duty of every man to obtain his own livelihood, although in a "blameless " fashion. " Society is barbarous until every industrious man can get his living without dishonest customs." A man must " make his place good in the world," but must also " add something to the common wealth." Wealth he defined as consisting of those "tools and auxiliaries which give the greatest possible extension to our powers " — beginning in "a tight roof that keeps the rain and wind out; in a good pump that yields you plenty of sweet water; in two suits of clothes, so as to change your dress when you are wet; in dry sticks to burn; in a good double-wick lamp; in three meals; in a horse, or a locomotive to cross the land; in a boat to cross the sea; in books to read." So great was Emerson's admiration for economic independence that he was frequently silent and ill at ease in the company of affluent men; he even felt a secret sympathy with the merchant and trader who were already at work undermining the sills on which the old New England of small farms and a peasant psychology had rested. " The Saxons," he wrote, " are the merchants of the world; now, for a thousand years, the leading race, and by nothing more than their quality of personal independence and, in a special modification, pecuniary independence. No reliance for bread and games on the government, no clanship, no patriarchal style of living by the revenues of a chief, no marrying-on — no system of clientship suits them; but every man must pay his scot."

He disposed of the question of surplus wealth by saying, " They should own who can administer." Surplus capital used for ostentation and babyish indulgence, however, " would bring us to barricades, burned towns, and tomahawks presently." Although he saw that " the value of a dollar is social, is created by society," he was too convinced an individualist to view economics as other than a personal problem. In this respect he was again a genuine representative of his time, the spirit of which was in accord with the *laissez faire* doctrine prevalent during the Victorian era. " Wealth brings with it its own checks and balances. The basis of political economy is non-interference. The only safe rule is found in the self-adjusting meter of demand and supply. Do not legislate."

Emerson preached the all-sufficiency of Spirit, but kept his powder dry. In this he was at the other pole from poor Alcott, who was doubtless the " Hotspur " of the following passage: " Hotspur lives for the moment; praises himself for it; and despises Furlong, that he does not. Hotspur, of course, is poor; and Furlong a good provider." And we should perhaps be not far wrong if we surmised that it was his friend Alcott's penniless career as a peripatetic philosopher which spurred Emerson onward in the pursuit of pecuniary independence, when he would have much preferred the solitudes of Concord, with its middle-class frugality.

At the very moment Emerson was admiring the energy with which the merchants were going about their labors, he noticed the thinness which characterized the American intellectual stream. Irving, Channing, Bryant, Dana, Prescott, and Bancroft, all he found " thin." By the time the middle 'forties were reached, the nation, so long hesitant before a fork in the road, had made its choice, and the greatest volume of its energy was pouring into the arteries of trade. There was little left for letters and the arts. In 1844 Emerson noted that, even in quiet Concord, Henry Thoreau was " the only man of leisure."

III

Soon after he had entered his fortieth year the anti-slavery agitation entered an intenser phase; but at first no pressure was able to make Emerson join it. His opinion of Abolitionists remained low. He considered that the man who worked all day in his garden did more to abolish slavery than platform speakers. He asked, Do the Abolitionists consume agricultural products and are they their own servants? If not, he thought that their position was inconsistent and should be made more " symmetrical." The slave-owner, he contended, desired not so much slavery as luxury. The solution lay in the introduction of machinery. The Northerner he saw as surrounded with " churches and Sunday Schools," and thought the Southerner less hypocritical because he did not cant. He considered that only men like Webster and Andrew Jackson, or his farmer neighbor, Edward Hosmer, men who were fearless of " competition from the best whites or Saxons," should be Abolitionists. Among those existing, he found only Garrison admirable.

At this stage Emerson showed scant sympathy for the black slave, his doctrine of compensation inducing him to believe that no man's condition is pitiable for long. " It is in vain," he coolly wrote, " that you put to me any case of misfortune of calamity — the extremest, the Manchester weaver, the Carolina slave. I doubt not that the history of the individual is always an account of his condition, and he shows himself to be a party to his present estate. Put me in his condition, and I should see its outlets and reliefs though now I see them not." Emerson's early attitude toward the Abolition movement was not only cool but cold. However, in 1844, Judge Samuel Hoar went to Charleston, S. C., to obtain the release of colored men who, although they claimed Massachusetts citizenship, had been seized by the South Carolina authorities. Judge Hoar was one of the stateliest inhabitants of Concord and was regarded by Emerson with peculiar reverence. He was accompanied south by his daughter, Elizabeth Hoar, who, after the death of Charles Emerson, had been regarded by Emerson as a sister. In Charleston, Judge Hoar and his daughter were ordered out of their hotel by a committee which warned them not to return to South Carolina.

Emerson's sentiments regarding Abolition at once underwent a perceptible change. Soon afterwards he delivered an address in which he deplored any sort of retaliation, but proposed that in future South Carolinians who came to Massachusetts should be socially boycotted. For several years afterwards he advocated settlement of the slavery question by Federal purchase of the slaves and recompense to their owners. From this position he passed to one in which he urged that arms and ammunition be sent to the anti-slavery settlers in Kansas. A few years later he was counselling all good men to disobey the Fugitive Slave Law, and finally he was advocating war as the safest way of dealing with " the shooting complexion " which he thought was peculiar to the South. He even suggested that Southerners who crossed their line could be dealt with as " fanged animals." He never quite obtained his own consent, however, to become an established Abolitionist lecturer, although he believed a " course of mobs " would do him good.

IV

In 1844 the question of the annexation of Texas, which was so intimately related to the slavery problem, became acute; but here again Emerson was at first cool and detached. He considered it certain that Anglo-Saxons would eventually overrun that territory, as well as Mexico and Oregon, " and it will in the course of ages be of small import," he said, " by what particular occasions and methods it was done." However, in the following year he changed his views and took part in an anti-annexation convention in Concord. He excoriated Massachusetts for its lack of courage, saying: " If the State values the treaties with Mexico, let it not violate them." He saw the question as containing a moral issue, regarding the event of annexation as immaterial, but deeming it important that an upright community should maintain its integrity by making its opposition known. He was unable, however, to attain the heat which burned in Alcott and Thoreau, who went to jail rather than pay a tax to a government which was capable of perpetrating the Mexican iniquity and protecting slave-owners. It was at this time that Emerson went to visit Thoreau where he had been put behind the bars by good old Sam Staples, of which meeting this story is told:

"Why are you in there, Henry?" said Emerson.

"Why are you *out* there?" said Thoreau.[1]

V

The struggle going on beneath the surface life of the country was adequately summed up by Emerson in his lectures on "New England Reformers," in March, 1844. "There is observable throughout," he said, "the contest between mechanical and spiritual methods." He was not sure that the rise of mercantilism was bringing the blessings expected. "This whole fabric of trade gives me to pause and think; it constitutes false relations between men. . . . I begin to suspect myself to be a prisoner, though treated with all this courtesy and luxury. I pay a destructive tax in my conformity."

He considered that one defect lay in dead education. "We are students of words: we are shut up in schools and colleges and recitation rooms for ten or fifteen years and come out at last with a bag of wind, a memory of words, and do

[1] See Léon Bazalgette's *Henry Thoreau: Bachelor of Nature.*

not know a thing." He noted that once upon a time Latin and Greek had had a relation to science and culture, but now the study of such languages had become stereotyped and useless. He viewed the period as one devoted to the removal of rubbish, but he confessed he could not always like the rubbish-removers — he found them "partial-men." He considered it hopeless for a man, who was himself not renovated, to attempt to renovate things around him. " He has become tediously good in some particular, but negligent or narrow in the rest; hypocrisy and vanity are often the disgusting result. . . . Do not be so vain of your one objection. Do you think there is only one? Alas! my good friend, there is no part of society or of life better than any other part. All our things are right and wrong together."

He doubted whether prevalent evils could be best removed by men acting in associations; he feared that social communities might become an asylum to those who " have tried and failed, rather than a field to the strong." He thought the task of removing evils belonged to the heroic individual. " Wherever a just and heroic soul finds itself, there it will do what is next at hand, and by the new quality of character it shall put forth, it shall abrogate that old condition, law, or school in which it stands, before the law of its own mind." That Emerson was aware of the tendency of his countrymen to live a life divided into compartments is revealed by this paragraph:

" When the individual is not *individual*, but is dual; when his thoughts look one way and his actions another; when his faith is traversed by his habits; when his will, enlightened by reason, is warped by his sense; when with one hand he rows, and with the other backs water, what concert can be? "

He condemned the want of faith and hope in society, and the tendency to falter in the face of new problems. " We have cunningly hid the tragedy of limitation and inner death, which we cannot avert. Is it strange that society should be devoured by a secret melancholy which breaks through all its smiles, and all its gayety and games? " Even the scholar had become a " showman, turning his gifts to marketable use." He believed that every man was at heart a lover of truth, but " we are paralyzed with fear; we hold on to our little properties, house and land, office and money, for the bread which they have in our experience yielded us, although we confess that our being does not flow through them."

The remedy lay in the connection of the individual genius " with Power over and behind us." He saw no necessity of interfering with the onward march of the good globe. " Our own orbit is all our task, and we need not assist the administration of the universe." All men wish to be lifted up, " but few are willing to let go their weights of opinion and property. . . . We wish to escape from subjection, and a sense of inferiority — and we make self-denying ordinances, we drink water, we eat grass, we refuse the laws, we go to jail: it is all in vain; only by obedience to his genius, only by the freest activity in the way constitutional to him, does an angel seem to arise before a man, and lead him by the hand out of all the wards of the prison."

In analysis Emerson was always acute and powerful; his criticisms were founded upon actual contact with men and events obtained on his lecturing tours; but he could not make clear to his audiences his proposals in the way of a synthetic program. Indeed, he did not possess, any more than other Transcendentalists, a program which the mind of the period

EMERSON BEFORE HE BEGAN TO GROW GREY

From a portrait owned by W. L. Haskell

could grasp. The Yankee mind was not fitted to comprehend mystic goals. Emerson's solution for virtually all problems was a reliance by the individual upon the Supreme Government of the Universe, the existence of which was not perceptible by mortal organs, but in whose beneficent authority he was confident. The Yankee mind could grasp Calvin's God, because this God was recognizable in terms of ill-temper, prejudice, self-will, and stubbornness; but Emerson's God, as diffuse as the ether, lacked the body and outline which canny intellects craved. A god must be personal and palpable; Emerson caused only resentment when he referred, as he sometimes did, to the Supreme Being as " It."

VI

It was in the midst of this period that Thoreau went off to found his " community of one " on the shores of Walden Pond, where, with the help of Alcott and Hosmer, he constructed his little house out of the remains of a shack left behind by an Irish railroad laborer, on land owned by Emerson. Here he remained two years, afterwards returning to become a familiar and caretaker again in the Emerson household.

When the news came to Henry that Emerson, in company with Agassiz, the naturalist, and other friends, had gone off to the Adirondacks with rifles in their hands, he was not pleased; and when he heard that the party had been bringing down small birds and breaking ale bottles with their bullets, he snorted. " It sounds rather Cockneyish," he wrote.

" Think of Emerson shooting a peetweet (with shot) for Agassiz, and cracking an ale bottle (after emptying it) with his rifle at six rods! It is just what Mike Saunders, the merchant's clerk, did when he was there."

It afterwards transpired that Thoreau's snorting was unjustified, for though Emerson had boldly fired at an ale bottle, he had not murdered any peetweets.

Chapter Twenty-Three

I

W HEN this period of about five years, filled with labors and agitations, was over, Emerson again found himself at a solstice. His vital fund, which he himself thought had been lowered perceptibly after his thirtieth year, and which he was compelled to nurse so carefully, had been depleted by the whole chain of exhausting events dating from the death of little Waldo. He told Margaret Fuller that he feared he was getting into the " past and pluperfect tenses." He craved some stimulus to set him aglow. He thought vaguely of accepting a professorship, and even felt a momentary yearning for the quiet, routine duties of a pastorate, although he had forever cut himself off from the church. However, when Theodore Parker and other friends proposed the establishment of a magazine which should be less stupid than the *North American*, he was only faintly interested. He was induced to take part in drafting an address to the public, but when the first issue of the *Massachusetts Quarterly Review* appeared, Emerson had lost interest in it.

At this moment he was re-awakened when various friends in England, including Alexander Ireland, urged him to come over and read his lectures in the industrial districts of Lancashire and Yorkshire. Despite all he had said concerning America's cultural dependency, Emerson found himself no more free from " the tapeworm of Europe " than the rest of his uneasy countrymen, and all his denunciations of travel were forgotten when Carlyle added his voice to the invitation. Here was fresh bear's meat on which to try his saws, new and critical eyes to be met and subdued; and it was with a boyish eagerness that he packed his bags — or, rather, watched Mrs. Emerson pack them — and wrote his English friends to hold the fort.

Those mysterious reasons which yearly impel hecatombs of Americans to cross the Atlantic Ocean have never been adequately stated, but perhaps Emerson's chief motive then was the same as theirs is today — not so much the desire to see Europe as to escape from America. Emerson's instinct in going to Europe at this time was possibly sound. He had not the stamina to cope with the bawlings and the tumults which were rapidly concentrating themselves into a boiler-pressure that eventually found a roaring vent in the Civil War. It is even possible that Emerson might not have survived this gathering hurricane had he remained within its orbit. Its preliminary blasts were shocking to his nervous fibers, while his need was for the orderly and gentle stimulation of an older and more settled social system which was not less agreeable because flavored with a slight decay. Wars and war-times are for men who have purple veins in their faces; the scholar who finds himself caught in them, unless padded by physical remoteness, is either debilitated or ground to powder. Hence it was with alacrity that Emerson sailed for Liverpool in October, 1847. His ship was the *Washington Irving*.

On his previous visit Emerson had had no opportunity to do more than glide over the surface of English life. It had remained to him the subject of the greatest curiosity. He now intended to penetrate it thoroughly and to dig as far as possible into its very foundations. Being an ideal English gentleman himself, he had carried in his heart an ideal of his British counterpart, and he now wished to study this specimen at first hand. At present he could do so on something like equal terms, for he was no longer an obscure young Yankee preacher slinking bashfully about in Britain, but a master in his own sphere, and as property-owner having that passport without which a man in early Victorian England was considerably less than the dust.

II

It may be imagined with what a searching gaze Carlyle and Emerson surveyed each other, in the light of the lamp which the Scot carried in his hand when he opened his London door to Emerson one night fourteen years after the day when they had parted among the moors of Craigenputtock. These fourteen years had been kinder to the American than the Scot. His eyes of light blue, once almost prominent, had sunk far back into his head, but serving thereby to accentuate the gracious aquilinity of his face which his English audiences found similar to the Red Indian's. The expression was kindly and peaceful, his manner tranquil like that of a man at peace with himself. The Scot, by contrast, showed on his face the ravages of his ceaseless internal wars. Though his tongue was bitterer than ever, and his dyspepsia increased, he could no longer maintain an attitude of amused indulgence towards his visitor, for, although Carlyle was now the most discussed writing man in England, Emerson was now, though somewhat less celebrated, no less distinguished. The Scot had published *Sartor Resartus, The French Revolution, Chartism, Past and Present,* and *Cromwell;* but Emerson was the author of essays, poems, and lectures which had not only impressed his country, but had gained him a following abroad.

" Well," said the Scot, " here we are shovelled together again."

Carlyle afterwards remarked that Emerson " did not give us much to chew the cud upon," also " good of him I could get none, except from his friendly looks and elevated, exotic, polite ways." Emerson was seldom a free out-giver in conversation, though perhaps he would have been willing to do his share had Carlyle given him the opportunity. The Chelsea sage at once seized the conversation and ran away with it until the stroke of one o'clock halted his flood of talk. Carlyle's grouchy conversation, studded with epithets such as " windbag, donkey, bladder," etc., was painful to the Concordian, who perceived that his companion was only accidentally a scholar, and was chiefly a hard-headed Scot, although not yet, as the English used to call his kind, unspeakable. Emerson perceived, moreover, as if for the first time, that Carlyle's rancors and vituperations were the outpourings of a frustrated man, of a Romantic who could not reconcile himself to the disappointments of life which Emerson had learned to accept as a part of Nature itself.

He was relieved when the Scot proposed a walk. They went by way of Hyde Park and the Royal Palaces to the National Gallery, and thence down the Strand, Carlyle talking all the time and bespattering everything with ridicule. Emerson could not perceive that his friend was himself a disillusioned Transcendentalist. Following the destruction of Napoleon, in wars which had inflicted untold miseries upon the British population, Britain had seemed to recover itself through the sudden expansion of a young industrialism; but now this, too, had brought upon the nation a ghastly depression, during which a newly formed proletariat was trying to rescue itself through the movement of Chartism and laws for shorter hours. Carlyle, whose dyspeptic temper had been exacerbated by the social depression, had sought to find escape in the Past, while Emerson was more than ever convinced that the Present was always equal to itelf. Had Emerson not been a mild-mannered Unitarian and remained passive and polite, he and Carlyle would probably have soon been rolling in the dust, biting and kicking, for the Scot smashed every image as fast as Emerson set one up. When Emerson mentioned art, Carlyle called it a delusion, saying, "As soon as a man begins to talk of art, architecture, and antiquities, nothing good comes of it." When Emerson turned the talk to science, the Scot was even less tolerant, comparing "the savants of Somerset House," by which he possibly meant laboratory researchers and experimenters, to the boy who asked Confucius, "How many stars in the sky?" As he listened to this molasses-stream of pessimism, Emerson, who had heard similar expressions from other low-spirited Britons, consoled himself with this conclusion:

"I surely know that, as soon as I return to Massachusetts, I shall lapse into the feeling, which the geography of America inevitably inspires, that we play the game with immense advantage; that there and not here, is the seat and center of the English race; and that no skill or activity can long compete with the prodigious natural advantages of that country, in the hands of the same race; and that England, an old and exhausted country, must be contented like other parents, to be strong only in her children."

However, when a few days later the two men went down to Stonehenge, Carlyle's blacker mood had passed, and he talked reasonably and even gently. While Emerson gazed over the great expanse of Salisbury Plain, looked at the Roman fort of old Sarum, and noted the circular procession of upright stones, with a lintel laid across, Carlyle remarked that the whole suggested to him the flight of ages and the march of religions. The older Britons, he said, had been truly religious men, but " now even Puritanism is gone. London is pagan." At Salisbury Cathedral they found a service in progress, and Carlyle remarked, " the music is good; but somewhat as if a monk were panting to some fine queen of heaven." On going to Winchester they stopped at the Church of St. Cross and asked for the bread and beer which were dispensed free to all comers as provided by its founder in 1136. While Emerson was amused at the quaintness of the custom, Carlyle pronounced a malediction on the priest who received " two thousand pounds a year that were meant for the poor, and spends a pittance on this small beer and crumbs." But when the tomb of William of Wykeham was unlocked, " Carlyle took hold of the marble hands of the recumbent statue and patted them affectionately."

III

When Emerson returned from London to his lectures in the northern provinces, he had his first glimpse of industry's devouring effect on the people. The men of the upper classes, with their large bodies and red faces, pleased him; but the sight of frail prostitutes and drunken women in the streets, and the begging of dirty little girls, was inexpressibly shocking to a man fresh from the banks of the peaceful Musketaquid. He found that his little daughter Edith, at home, was costing him " many a penny," because each tiny mendicant reminded him of her. He noticed the wide disparity between Englishmen and Americans in manner and appearance. A "sauntering gait and roving eyes" were American characteristics, whereas "the axes of an Englishman's eyes are united to his backbone."

His audiences found more amusement in looking at Emerson than in listening to his discourses. His platform manner was novel and amusing. He began his lectures without preliminaries and continued them without flourishes. He spoke without gestures, except for an occasional angular movement of his forearm and a slight tremble in body and voice when he came to a moving passage. His hesitations and difficulty in bridging the gaps between paragraphs appeared to them like a man crossing a brook on stepping-stones. His voice was clear and penetrating, but did not appear to be musical until listeners had become accustomed to his slight nasal twang. His lectures as a whole, however, were like rain, or a gentle stream of electricity.

Socially he was a success from the beginning. He ceased to confine himself to hotels and accepted the hospitality of friends to whom he had introductions. They regarded his physical presence as more impressive than his lectures. His gravely smiling features were now like those of an ancient Greek, now like a Red Indian's while his whole bearing suggested something inexpressibly gracious and noble. Emerson was always a trifle self-conscious among strangers, and in his letters to his wife he constantly referred to his " porcupine manners "; but the English hosts, if they noticed such things, disregarded them and yielded readily to his benign charm. At Chesterfield he was invited to dine with George Stephenson, builder of the first locomotive. The old engineer did something that few men attempted: he put his arm around Emerson, who, in his turn, considered him " the most remarkable man I have seen in England." Stephenson tried to induce the American to come to his home and stay for days.

Emerson had occasional attacks of homesickness, and more than once might have cut his tour short, had he not been comforted by the recollection that his wife and children were safe in the care of Henry Thoreau, who wrote to him regularly all the domestic news. He gradually surrendered himself to the delight he felt in being received so generously by what he regarded as England's true aristocracy — in the original sense of the word as derived from the Greek *aristos*, the best.

" I see the best of the people," he wrote, " the merchants, the manufacturers, the scholars, the thinkers, men and women, in a very sincere and satisfactory conversation. My admiration and my love of the English rises day by day."

He wrote his wife that several English friends were proposing shortly to go to America and that she must keep " a guest chamber *with a fire* this Winter and every Winter, as last Winter we had none." Also if any Englishman should come to Concord, she should " give him bread and wine before he goes to bed."

IV

At Edinburgh he met Dr. Samuel Brown, the painter David Scott, "Christopher North," Robert Chambers, author of *Vestiges of Creation*, and Lord Jeffrey. But none interested him as much as De Quincey, then seventy years old, and free from bailiffs, from his fury of a Mrs. Macbold, and from opium. De Quincey walked ten miles through the rain to dine with Emerson at Mrs. Crowe's and sat there in his wet pantaloons, because the hostess had no dry clothes to lend him. In turn De Quincey invited Emerson to dine with him and his three daughters, which Emerson did, but failed to record the conversation, which omission must be regarded as an irreparable loss to literature. De Quincey was an agreeable surprise to Emerson, who had expected to find him " some figure like the organ of York Minster," but, instead, the author of *The Confessions of an Opium Eater* proved to be a delicate, soft-spoken little old man, with the simple manners of a child. He accepted an invitation to come to Emerson's next lecture, but came into Edinburgh trembling with terror lest his enemy, Mrs. Macbold, find him there and renew her reign of terror.

In the Lake Country, Emerson was the guest of Harriet Martineau, who took him again to see Wordsworth, then nearly eighty years old. The old poet had changed little since Emerson had seen him fifteen years before, and on being waked up from a nap was not at first particularly hospitable, but became more animated when the upheaval in France was discussed. However, he had a poor opinion of

Frenchmen, and had not raised his estimate of Scotchmen. "No Scotchman," he said, "can write English." His whole conversation was egotistical, but Emerson forgave him his want of grace because of his "real inspiration as a poet."

On returning to London, Emerson attended numerous lunches and dinners in the wake of Mr. and Mrs. George Bancroft, and, as sponsored by Carlyle, began to meet the gentry and nobility. Among the conspicuous persons he met were Macaulay, Dickens, Hallam, Thackeray, Disraeli, Kinglake, Lyell, and Buckland. He noticed that it was the habit of society to "pet Carlyle a good deal," and to amuse itself by making him talk.

Tennyson was encountered for the first time at the house of Coventry Patmore, and Emerson liked him at once, finding pleasure even in his "air of general superiority." It was plain that Tennyson was "accustomed to be petted and indulged," and Emerson, who had already deplored his lack of "wood notes," at length decided that the Englishman was best suited to garden atmospheres. Tennyson invited Emerson to his lodgings, but when the latter visited him there there was no conversation, because of the presence of a third person, a clergyman.

A curious conversation took place when Emerson dined with Carlyle and Dickens at the home of John Forster in Lincoln's Inn Fields. Emerson remarked that he felt concerned at the sight of the numerous prostitutes in London and Liverpool. Carlyle and Dickens replied that male chastity was virtually unknown in England; and the former asked if the same thing were not true of America. Emerson assured the company that this was not true, and that the better class of American young men went " virgins to their nuptual bed as truly as their brides." Dickens remarked that if his own son were " particularly chaste " he should be alarmed on his account.

Emerson, who now purposed going to France, invited Tennyson to accompany him, but the latter preferred Italy. An English friend told Emerson: " We tell him that he must go and he goes, but you will find him heavy to carry." Emerson had eventually to go to Paris without the company of the poet, who, however, promised to be in the same lodgings if the Concordian should escape the French bullets. When Emerson returned, however, Tennyson had been carried off to Ireland, where he had consented to go on three conditions: " First, that he should not hear anything about Irish distress; second, that he should not come downstairs for breakfast; third, that he might smoke in the house."

V

Despite warnings from friends, Emerson felt an irresistible craving to see France in the grip of the Revolution of 1848, and arrived in Paris in May of that year. He noticed that the boulevards were bare, the trees having been cut down for barricades. " At the end of a year," he said to himself, " we shall take account and see if the Revolution was worth the trees," which remark indicates Emerson's skeptical attitude toward all social upheavals. He noted that the population was now divided into soldiers and speakers, and an important new word had been added to the world's vocabulary — " blouse." He attended meetings at the clubs of Blanqui and

Barbes, and witnessed the defeat of the conspirators by the National Guard. Despite his distaste for many of the sights seen in the streets, he now felt more kindly toward the French than on his previous visit. " What influence the English have," he wrote, " it is by brute force of wealth; that of the French, by affinity and talent." The animation of the people and their democratic manners pleased him; and he felt reassured when he noticed that " social decorum seems to have here the same rigors as is in England."

Although he took a keen interest in the endeavor of Frenchmen " to secure a fair share of bread to every man, and to get God's justice done through the land," he was not entirely in sympathy with their " patent methods "; the whole uprising was to him little more than a spectacle; and after spending twenty-five days in Paris he was relieved to be able to escape to London. " I shall bring home," he wrote to Mrs. Emerson, " a contentedness with home, I think, for the rest of my days."

VI

In June he gave six newly written lectures before the Portman Square Literary and Scientific Institution of London. The admission fee was very high, and notabilities of the first rank attended, including social celebrities such as the Duchess of Sutherland, Lady Ashburton, and Lord Lovelace. Carlyle, Barry Cornwall, Lyell, and others represented science and literature. Emerson remarked that he liked none better than " Jane Carlyle and Mrs. Bancroft, who honestly come." Carlyle himself was a regular attendant, punctuating his friend's best passages with grunts and snorts of laudation. To offset criticism of the high fees in the West End, Emerson then gave four lower-priced lectures in other halls.

There followed a new outburst of invitations, most of which he accepted, including a special one to meet Leigh Hunt; but he told Margaret Fuller that even in London palaces he was a victim of " the old deoxygenation and asphyxia." He added that he would leave England with " an increased respect for the Englishman," and that this respect was " the more generous that I have no sympathy with him, only an admiration."

Although the London lectures were so successful socially, the monetary reward was somewhat less than he had expected, as he cleared only eighty pounds from the first six discourses. However, his visit had immensely fertilized his thought and he returned to America in July, 1848, with his horizons widened and a new store of material for his notebooks. At home he began a new series of lectures on his English experiences with this epigram as his keynote: " English history is aristocracy with the doors open."

VII

Seven years after Emerson had returned to Concord, he published his *English Traits*. The title would have been more nearly accurate if the book had been named Emerson Traits, for his treatise attributed to his hosts those virtues in which he himself most excelled. This was entirely natural; for Emerson saw the country of his ancestors under the most favorable auspices, and his contacts were with affable and cultivated persons. His book gives a glowing, but on the whole, perhaps, just, estimate of the upper-class English-man when seen at his ease; but the picture would have been more complete, and would have possessed another dimension, had it included an account of the one person in England whom Emerson seems never to have encountered — the British trade-unionist whom Chartism had just introduced to history.

Chapter Twenty-Four

I

IN September, 1848, Emerson noted that "the railroad is the only sure topic for conversation in these days. . . . The railroad is that work of art which agitates and drives mad the whole people . . . and now we have one more rival topic, California gold." He felt a little melancholy one day when Ellery Channing, in the course of a walk through the cranberry meadows, remarked that the railroad had corrupted all the farmers "like a war." Emerson replied that he feared old Saxons like Hubbard and Hosmer would not be seen in the next generation. "They have the look of pine trees and apple trees," he said, "and might be the sons got between the two."

As lecturer, Emerson now for the first time invaded the West, and almost at once a change took place in his discourses, both in style and content. Illinois and Missouri fumbled with Universals, and Absolutes left them as cold as the country hotels in which Emerson stayed. "It is necessary," he recalled, "that you should know the people's facts. If you have no place for them, the people absolutely have no place for you." And so he modified the metaphysical content of his lectures considerably and inserted more illustration and anecdote. In the West he found "a new test for the wares of a man of letters. All his thin, watery matter freezes; 'tis only the smallest portion of alcohol that remains good . . . the committees tell you that the people want a hearty laugh."

The older settlers were not particularly eager to hear lectures even with hearty laughs in them; but young committee members sent in repeated calls which Emerson was glad to obey, because he was fond of addressing young people and because of the extra earnings. This dragging out of a " decorous old gentleman," he said, amounted to this: " I'll bet you fifty dollars a day for three weeks that you will not leave your library, and wade, and freeze, and ride, and run, and suffer all manner of indignities, and stand up for an hour each night reading in a hall; and I answer, I'll bet I will. I do it and win the nine hundred dollars." And so he was drawn again and again into " these dangerous precincts of charlatanism; namely, lectures." His chief comfort was an occasional meeting with " a wise and great heart," such as W. H. Furness at Philadelphia and Henry James at New York. Emerson was baffling to James, who was kept " tasting and sipping him " without getting any nearer to his core. James thought it queer that Emerson " managed to do without conscience," and in a moment of spleen he called Emerson " an unsexed woman," saying, " I am satisfied that he never in his life had felt a temptation to bear false witness, to steal, to commit adultery, or to murder."

At this period, Emerson's bipolarity was a little baffling to himself. " I affirm melioration," he said. " I affirm also the self-equality of Nature. But I cannot reconcile these two statements. I affirm the sacredness of the individual. . . . I see also the benefits of cities, and the plausibility of phalansteries. But I cannot reconcile these oppositions."

These confessions indicate how Emerson was subconsciously affected by the two strong currents running through the life of the period; one emphasizing the individuality of man, the other contending that men are inexorably social. Emerson oscillated between one side and the other, and even tried to find a middle ground between the two poles. Failing, he endeavored to rise above the conflict, recalling that " the world is always equal to itself." He resolved to give free rein to his own doubts. " We may well give skepticism as much line as we can. The spirit will return and fill us. It drives the drivers. It counter-balances any accumulation of power." In his essay, *Worship*, he reached this conclusion: " We are not to do, but to let do; not to work, but to be worked upon." Man is to rely on " the nameless Thought, the nameless Power, the super-personal Heart."

II

In the Spring of 1851, he delivered six lectures at Pittsburgh, going there from Philadelphia after three days and nights of travelling by rail and canal boat. The third night he passed on the floor of the boat among "a wreath of legs."

In the middle of that year, Emerson was aroused to a pitch of feeling such as he had never exhibited before. It was caused by Daniel Webster's endorsement of the Fugitive Slave Law, which compelled every Massachusetts citizen to assist in the return to the South of escaped slaves. It was the first time that Emerson had ever felt the hand of the State reaching into his personal life; and on May 3rd, 1851, the mildest mannered man in Concord amazed his fellow citizens with this defiant declaration:

" This is a law which everyone of you will break on the earliest occasion."

Whenever he thought of Webster's defection, his indignation rose almost to fury. Webster had been one of his boyhood heroes. Only a few years previously he had been a guest at Emerson's home, and his host had written this of him: " It seems to me the quixotism of criticism to quarrel with Webster because he has not this or that fine evangelical property. He is no saint, but a wild olive-wood, ungrafted yet by grace, but according to his lights, a very true and admirable man." He now wrote: " The word *liberty* in the mouth of Mr. Webster sounds like the word *love* in the mouth of a courtezan." Emerson later campaigned in Middlesex County for a friend who was pledged to work for the law's repeal in Congress, and for the first time in his life heard himself hissed from the audience.

Emerson's gradual passage from a state of relative indifference to one in which he was openly attacking slavery did nothing to add to his popularity in his own state. Massachusetts in general, and Boston in particular, had a vested interest in the continuation of slavery, and it required considerable courage to take the Abolition platform; but Emerson was certain that the anti-slavery agitators, however repellent personally, were working with the currents of destiny.

" Our success is sure," he wrote. " Its roots are in our poverty, our Calvinism, our schools, our thrifty habitual industry; in our snow and East wind, and farm life." By way of contrast, he gave this curious picture of what he imagined life to be in a typical slave State: " Life is a fever, man is an animal, given to pleasure, frivolous, irritable, spending his days in hunting and practising with deadly weapons, to defend himself or his slaves and against his companions brought up in the same idle and dangerous way." At the same time he had to admit the truth in the utterance of John Randolph when the Virginian said: " We do not govern the people of the North by our black slaves, but by their own white slaves." Even at this period, although a few labor unions had won a ten-hour day, most of the " hands " in New England mills worked twelve to fourteen hours a day. Included were many women and children.

III

Almost simultaneous with the slavery question arose the agitation for political rights for women, and at first Emerson's attitude was that of the gallant gentleman: " through sound and beautiful women, men are magnetized, heaven opens and no lawyer need be called in to prepare a clause, for woman moulds the law-giver." However, he admitted that as long as women had not equal rights of property and suffrage " they were not on the right footing." When a woman's convention was held at Worcester, he permitted his name to be used as one of the patrons, but made it clear that he did not mean to attend.

In 1853, when Emerson was fifty years old, his mother died at the age of eighty-five. " It is very necessary that we should have mothers — we that read and write," he wrote Carlyle, " to keep us from becoming paper."

Her death brought his thoughts back to home, and it was with relief that he forsook the pestering questions of the day to walk in the woods and fields again with Thoreau and Ellery Channing.

IV

For several years he continued to lecture in the East and Middle West, ranging as far as Michigan and Wisconsin. His chief subject was England, but he also prepared a new lecture dealing with France, in which he made a note of the prediction of Bonaparte: " in twenty-five years, the United States will be writing the treaties of Europe." In an address before Williams College, Williamstown, Mass., he returned to one of his favorite themes and said: " It is the vulgarity of this country — it came to us with commerce, out of England — to believe that naked wealth, unrelieved by any use or design, is merit. Who is accountable for this materialism? Who but the scholars? When the poets do not believe in their own poetry, how should the bats and the swine? "

In this year of 1855, Emerson wrote a passage in his journal which has since become one of the most misquoted in literature. What he actually wrote was:

" I trust a good deal to common fame, as we all must. If man has good corn, or wood, or board, or pigs, to sell, or can make better chairs or knives, crucibles or church organs, than anybody else, you will find a broad, hard-beaten road to his house, though it be in the woods."

The common misquotation which has it, " If a man makes better mouse-traps," etc., is attributed to Elbert Hubbard, who possibly relied on a defective memory.

V

The year was not a prosperous one for Emerson. He had made considerable investments in railroad stock, particularly in the Erie and Mad River, also the Vermont and Canada lines; and when no dividends ensued for several years his income was much reduced, and he was compelled to lecture more resolutely than ever, going as far west as Iowa. In Davenport, he noted that the rules of the hotel forbade gentlemen to sit at tables without coats and that pie was eaten in quarter sections. This latter fact was of peculiar interest to Emerson, who throughout his life ate pie for breakfast every morning.

In the winter of 1856, the Mississippi was frozen so solid from Natchez northward that he was able to cross it three times on foot. However, at Beloit his landlord assured him there was no cold weather in Illinois, " only now and then Indian Summer and cool nights." The West at this time was recovering from the hard times that had begun with the panic of 1837, persisting to 1845, during which period men journeyed a hundred miles to Chicago with their wheat to sell it for twenty-six cents a bushel. Land values were rising and men were prosperous and optimistic. A citizen of Freeport, Ill., informed him that it was not the first settlers who became rich, but the second-comers. The first arrivals, he said, were usually too visionary, and the practical men reaped what they had sowed.

Contact with the hardy plainsmen of the West sometimes made Emerson blush for his own lack of practicality. " 'Tis worse than tragic that no man is fit for society who has fine traits. At a distance, he is admired; but bring him hand to hand, he is a cripple. One protects himself by solitude, and one by courtesy, and one by an acid, worldly manner — each concealing how he can, the thinness of his skin and his incapacity for strict association." In these passages, we are probably justified in detecting a portion of Emerson's defence-mechanism.

VI

When Emerson was fifty-four years old, the *Atlantic Monthly* made its first appearance with James Russell Lowell as editor, and Emerson began at once to contribute to it those poems which he had written since the publication of his first book of verse in 1847. One day all Boston was set agog by the rumor that Emerson had " gone Brahma." Proof was offered in the form of the poem entitled " Brahma," the first three verses of which were:

" If the red slayer think he slays,
   Or if the slain think he is slain,
They know not well the subtle ways
   I keep, and pass, and turn again.

Far or forgot to me is near;
   Shadow and sunlight are the same;
The vanished gods to me appear;
   And one to me are shame and fame.

They reckon ill who leave me out;
When me they fly, I am the wings;
I am the doubter and the doubt,
And I the hymn the Brahmin sings."

For the first time Boston thus learned that Emerson had been seeking consolation for the turbulence of the times in Hindoo literature. " Brahma " was derived from the *Brihadaranyaka Upanishad*, and in part paralleled passages in the *Bhagavad Gita;* but Boston thought that Emerson was becoming wilfully freakish, and a raucous outburst of ridicule followed. Rhymsters contrived so many imitations that there were few journals of the day which did not carry a parody of the " Brahma." Following is a specimen:

" If the gray tom-cat thinks these things,
And if the song thinks it be sung,
He little knows who boot-jacks flings,
How many bricks at him I've flung."

" Brahma " was simply one of the intense, cryptic utterances in verse to which Emerson resorted when he despaired of making himself clear in prose. His more mystical poems were obviously written chiefly for his own catharsis and he probably had little expectation they would be comprehended by the generality. He used the same cryptic device in " Uriel," which contains the lines:

" Line in nature is not found;
Unit and universe are round;
In vain produced, all rays return;
Evil will bless, and ice will burn."

In the " Song of Nature " Brahma may again be imagined as speaking:

> " Let war and trade and creeds and song
> Blend, ripen race on race.
> The sunburnt world a man shall breed
> Of all the zones and countless days.
>
> No ray is dimmed, no atom worn,
> My oldest force is good as new,
> And the fresh rose on yonder thorn
> Gives back the bending heavens in dew."

And again in the longer poem, " The Sphinx," the same theme is repeated with new variations:

> " Sea, earth, air, sound, silence,
> Plant, quadruped, bird,
> By one music enchanted,
> One deity stirred."

These poems are proof of Emerson's recognition of the fact that there are things which cannot be uttered by the human tongue. These things are in the possession of " The Sphinx," who gazes but does not speak. Brahma is only another name for this being. But what Emerson meant to convey was his central belief that all things emanate from a Unity, and to Unity all things return. It was a poetical rendering of a seer's conception of the conclusion at which presentday science seems about to arrive: that everything consists of one stuff, and to this stuff tends to return. Even the very material-minded scientist is at present willing to concede that all matter seems to be constituted of one primordial substance, hydrogen.[1]

However, only a few of Emerson's poems are " riddles." Those that are not intended to convey a transcendental moral, are simple and pastoral — the cheerful, thrushlike songs of a man who finds delight in the day and its scenes and events. In poetry Emerson's weakness was a defective ear, which sometimes marred his rhythms and gave some of his rhymes a flattish sound or resolved them into a mere " jingle," which, incidentally, he believed was the chief defect in Edgar Allen Poe. Emerson was at his best in the verse which is sometimes contemptuously called " free," and in which medium of expression he was the predecessor and path-breaker for young poets who arrived one, two, and three generations later.

VII

It was Emerson's own experiments in untrammelled verse which perhaps imparted to him that breadth of perception which enabled him to write to Walt Whitman on July 21, 1855, when *Leaves of Grass* had had no other approving notice except that written by Whitman himself:

" I greet you at the beginning of a great career, which yet must have had a long foreground somewhere for such a start." At the same time he said to Moncure Conway: " Americans who are abroad can now return; unto us a man is born."

[1] See T. Swann on " Recurrent Ideas " in the *Medical Journal and Record*, August 1, 1928.

A year later he wrote to Carlyle, saying that *Leaves of Grass* was " a nondescript monster which yet had terrible eyes and buffalo strength, and was indisputably American. . . . If you think it is only an auctioneer's inventory of a warehouse, you can light your pipe with it."

And yet, as Robert G. Ingersoll once said, " There was a baked bean side even to Emerson," and there were portions of this buffalo book which sorely afflicted that element in the Concordian which was Puritanic, even Calvinistic, to the last. The same year that saw the Civil War begin, found Emerson and Whitman walking up and down the Boston Common, and the leaves of grass there might have overheard the elder counselling the younger man in a father's tone. As was the case in Emerson's conversation with De Quincey, civilization is the poorer that no record was made of this conversation. Emerson argued against the inclusion by Whitman of that section of his book entitled " Children of Adam."

" Each part of Emerson's statement," wrote Whitman afterwards, " was unanswerable . . . and then I felt down in my soul the clear and unmistakable conviction to obey all, and pursue my own way."

Thus was Emerson's dictum turned back upon him: " No law can be sacred to me but that of my own nature. Good and Bad are but names very readily transferable to this or that; the only right is what is after my constitution, the only wrong is what is against it."

Whitman's debt to Emerson has often been disputed, but what seems clear is that the older man had opened a way into the stodgy mind of the period without which the younger poet would have found his subsequent progress even more difficult than it was. Here again, as in so many other cases,

Emerson was not so much the model and guide as the spark-lighter. Whitman's own words were: " I was simmering, simmering, simmering; Emerson brought me to boil," although he afterwards said he had not read Emerson before he published his first edition of *Leaves of Grass;* admitting, however, that he had had " Emerson on the brain."

Whitman's use without express permission of Emerson's salutation, " I greet you at the beginning of a great career," on the backbone of the cover of the second edition of *Leaves of Grass,* has furnished the food for many literary causeries, but there is no warrant for believing that Emerson regarded the incident as discreditable. It was Whitman's liberties in other respects that made the Concordian uneasy. The freely mixing, " Bohemian " predilections of the New Yorker were not shared by the New Englander, who admired decorum not less than power, and who could not help but be shocked when at a luncheon in the Astor House, New York, Whitman removed his coat and hung it on the back of his chair. In Emerson's journals there is no record of any disapproval of Whitman, except that he quoted with obvious amusement E. P. Whipple's remark that the author of *Leaves of Grass* " had every leaf but the fig leaf."

Edward Carpenter [2] thus reports a conversation with Emerson in 1877: " When I spoke of Whitman, and asked him what he thought of him, he laughed (a little nervously, I thought) and said, ' Well, I thought he had some merit at one time; there was a good deal of promise in his first edition — but he is a wayward, fanciful man. I saw him in New York, and asked him to dine at my hotel. He shouted for a " tin mug " for his beer. Then he had a noisy fire-engine

[2] See *Days with Walt Whitman.*

society, and he took me there, and was like a boy over it, as if there had never been such a thing before.' "

As for Whitman, he spoke of Emerson affectionately throughout his life as " Friend and Master "[3] and in 1856 wrote to him: " These shores, it is you who have discovered them. I say that it is you who have conducted the States, — that it is you who have conducted me to them." And again he said of the elder man: " From the first visit which he made at Brooklyn in 1855 and the two hours which we passed together, I experienced an affection and a singular attachment for him, by his contact, conversation, company, magnetism. . . . We probably had a dozen (perhaps twenty) of these interviews, conversations, promenades, etc. — five or six times (sometimes in New York, sometimes in Boston). We had good long dinners together. I was very happy — I do not think, nevertheless, that I was entirely at my ease with him; it was always he who did the talking. I am sure he was equally happy."

These are the only occasions on record in which Emerson is described as doing the talking. His preferred rôle was that of listener.

[3] See Horace Traubel's *With Walt Whitman in Camden.*

Chapter Twenty-Five

I

SEVERAL times during the 'fifties Emerson wrote to his friends, "We are on the brink," but he himself did not declare war until May, 1856, when Preston Brooks, of South Carolina, attacked Charles Sumner, of Massachusetts, with a cane one afternoon in Washington after the Senate had adjourned. As a matter of fact, Brooks was a quiet, obscure, reticent young man who, so far as known, had never before offered violence to any man, but in the rage and tumult of the times he was painted as a low-browed monster; Emerson called him " the meanest of mankind," and when Sumner took to his bed after the assault, Emerson said: " I think we must get rid of slavery or we must get rid of freedom."

The next year John Brown came to Concord and denounced the pacifists of the day in a speech that definitely won Emerson over to the side of Abolition. At the time he described Brown as " that new saint," but when his essay on the Kansan was published ten years later, this epithet was omitted, possibly because Emerson had meantime learned that although John Brown was an earnest man, he was no saint, new or otherwise.

Emerson's anti-slavery attitude caused the cancellation of a lecture at Philadelphia, and even Boston grew frosty and

finally abusive. In 1861 when Emerson spoke with Wendell
Phillips before the Massachusetts Anti-Slavery Society in
Tremont Temple, the mob refused to hear him and raised
such an uproar that Emerson, after several attempts to make
himself heard, left the hall.

As soon as the battle at Fort Sumter had opened the abyss,
Emerson became ardently pro-war. In his enthusiasm he even
abandoned his previously low opinion of the masses and said,
" I will never again speak lightly of a crowd." He even exclaimed, " Sometimes gun-powder smells good." He was not
eager for the preservation of the Union, proposing that a
cordon sanitaire be drawn about the slave-holding States. In
this respect he differed from President Lincoln, and on that
account misunderstood him.

In Lincoln one would have expected Emerson to recognize
the Strong Man whom in fancy he had so often worshipped
and whose arrival in some troubled time he had often predicted. But at first he saw Lincoln only as " slow and timid,"
and disliked what he had heard of the President's provincial-
ity and his rumored fondness for pleasantries of a somewhat
broad character. However, when in February, 1862, Charles
Sumner took him to call at the White House, he wrote: " The
President impressed me more favorably than I had hoped,
a frank, sincere, well-meaning man, with a lawyer's habit of
mind, good clear statement of his fact; correct enough, not vulgar, as described, but with a sort of boyish cheerfulness, or that
kind of sincerity and jolly good meaning that our class meetings on commencement days show, in telling our old stories
over. When he has made his remark, he looks up at you with
great satisfaction, and shows all his white teeth, and laughs."
But Emerson could not remain unaffected by the belief, then

prevalent in New England, that Lincoln was only an uncouth prairie clown, and in 1863 he wrote: " You cannot refine Mr. Lincoln's taste, extend his horizon, or clear his judgment; he will not walk dignifiedly through the traditional part of the President of America, but will pop out his head at each railroad station and make a little speech, and get into an argument with Squire A and Judge B. But this we must be ready for, and let the clown appear, and hug ourselves that we are well off, if we have got good nature, honest meaning, and fidelity to public interest."

It is odd to behold in Emerson a war-monger, an airer of prejudices, and an opponent of merciful peace terms; but war-fevers will buckle and warp the sanest minds, as the world has re-discovered within recent years. At other times he saw the issues with more clarity, as in this letter to Herman Grimm at Berlin in 1861:

" Sometimes I think it is a war of manners. The Southern climate and slavery generate a marked style of manners. The people are haughty, self-possessed, suave, and affect to despise Northern manners as of the shop and compting-room; whilst we find the planters picturesque, but frivolous and brutal. Northern labor encroaches on the planters daily, diminishing their political power, whilst their haughty temper makes it impossible for them to play a second part."

Here, in a paragraph, is a history which if expanded might have been fairer and juster. As we see it now, it was indeed a war of manners — those of feudalism on the one hand, and of an encroaching mercantilism on the other, And, after all, it may be true that, although men will argue heatedly over principles, their fury is aroused to fighting pitch only when they sufficiently dislike each other's manners.

II

In January, 1862, Emerson demanded, in the course of a lecture at the Smithsonian Institute, complete emancipation, saying, " There can be no safety until this step is taken." He was consequently pleased when in September Lincoln proclaimed the abolition of slavery as a war measure. In his indignation against all persons who opposed the war, he even attacked his old idol, the upper-class Englishman, and accused the skeptics among his own countrymen of aping English manners. " I think the genius of this country," he wrote, " has marked out her true policy — hospitality; a fair field and equal laws to all; a piece of land for every son of Adam who will sit down upon it; then, on easy conditions, the right of citizenship, and education for his children."

Emerson did not escape the tax which the war laid upon the country. His lectures were no longer in demand, and the income from his books, which had yielded $500 or $600 a year, dwindled to a sporadic trickle. His bank stock continued without dividends, and even his wife's property at Plymouth produced no income. However, he thought it better to endure necessary economies rather than to " be driven by any impatience into a hasty peace." He lost part of his Walden woodlots in a lawsuit over titles; and then death among his friends brought new afflictions. Theodore Parker died after a vain attempt to conquer tuberculosis — the stout-hearted Unitarian preacher who once thanked God for " three good things

— the sun, the moon, and Ralph Waldo Emerson." Did Emerson remember the story that Concordians used to tell with tinkling laughter? An Adventist was supposed to have met Parker and warned him that the world was shortly to come to an end.

" That means nothing to me, sir," said Parker. " I live in Boston."

And then the herald encountered Emerson and gave him the same warning.

" Well, let it end," said Emerson, " I think we shall do very well without it."

The war was still young when Henry Thoreau, too, took his last walk in Walden woods. Though the immediate cause of his illness was a chill brought on during an inspection of snowstorms, he, too, had been already weakened by tuberculosis. (What was wrong with New England that so many of its bravest suffered from this malady? Or was this but a symptom of some deeper sickness?) Though only forty-four years old, Henry yielded tranquilly. " Never saw a man dying," Sam Staples told Emerson, " with so much pleasure and peace." " Henry," said an aunt, " have you made your peace with God? " " No, I have never quarrelled with him."

On May Day morning, 1863, Mary Moody Emerson died in Williamsburg, New York, in her eighty-ninth year, content that her nephew had justified her kingliest hopes; for the spindling lad into whom she tried to pour some of her fierce energy was now the tallest tree on Concord plain, the veritable beauty of Israel. Her body was taken to Emerson's cemetery lot at Sleepy Hollow. " The day was cloudy and warm," he wrote, " with mist resting over the south, and the rain waited until an hour after she was laid in the ground."

III

So seriously did Emerson's income become depleted at this period that he was at length glad to accept financial help from his friend and business adviser, Abel Adams, who provided the means by which Edward Emerson was able to complete his college course. Mr. Adams told Emerson one day that out of a hundred Boston merchants known to him, he could count only three who had not failed at least once. At Mr. Adams's death, the whole Emerson family received benefactions in his will.

The war ground its way onward, and then came the peace which Lincoln hoped would show " malice toward none." But when Emerson read the terms on which Grant received Lee's surrender, he was indignant. " They look a little too easy," he said. " I fear that the high tragic historic justice which the nation, with severest consideration, should execute, will be softened and dissipated at dinner tables."

Within a few weeks, however, he was again calm, and not even the news of Lincoln's assassination produced another bitter expression. At the Lincoln memorial meeting in Concord in April, 1865, he acknowledged that New England had been wrong about the President from the beginning. " He is the true history of the American people in his time," he said. " Step by step he walked before them — slow with their slowness, quickening his march with theirs; the true representative of his continent; an entirely public man; father of his country — the pulse of twenty millions throbbing in his heart, the thought of their minds articulated by his tongue."

PART THREE
Silver Years

Chapter Twenty-Six

I

AT the war's end Emerson, then sixty-two years old, knew that in himself, as well as in the nation, a tide had ebbed which would not return. Already he had begun to write to Carlyle describing himself as an old man; and when one day his wife had found on his shoulder a spot which he feared might turn into a tumor, he had discovered he did not care. His step was no longer so elastic, in winter he craved heat more than ever before, and although Whitman, who visited him after the war, found his eyes as "clearpeering" as ever, they were no longer piercing. In reading his manuscripts he hesitated for longer periods and often lost his place among his papers. Not that this mattered greatly, for his lectures proceeded not from premise to conclusion in the Western manner, but, in the Oriental way, radiated from a center outward, and hence were as good when read backward as forward. It was then that he wrote his poem, "Terminus":

> "It is time to be old,
>   To take in sail: —
>   The god of bounds,
>   Who sets to seas a shore,
>   Came to me in his fatal rounds,
>   And said: no more!

" As the bird trims her to the gale,
I trim myself to the storm of time,
I man the rudder, reef the sail,
Obey the voice at eve obeyed at prime. . . ."

The on-creep of age had another effect on Emerson:
he no longer praised the virtues of solitude, but in his desire
for congenial company became almost gregarious. He took
particular delight in the meetings of the Saturday Club in
Boston, and rarely failed to be present at the Parker House
on the appointed day. This club, which had Emerson for its
nucleus, had grown up several years before the war, but he
seemed to derive most pleasure from it after his powers had
begun to wane. The membership was almost solidly Brahmin,
and new names were not added to the list until after due
omens had been taken. Even Charles Sumner was not admitted until a comparatively late day, perhaps owing to a
dread of his lack of humor. Among other members were
Holmes, Hawthorne, Motley, Dana, Lowell, E. P. Whipple,
Judge Hoar, Peirce the mathematician, Dwight the musical
critic, Andrew the war-governor, Dr. Howe the philanthropist, William Hunt the painter, Agassiz the scientist, and
Longfellow. Emerson usually chose to sit near Longfellow,
conversing with him quietly. At the other end of the table
there was more animation, with the hearty Agassiz as its
center. Whipple [1] records a discussion which perhaps was not
typical.

Emerson was moved one day to ask Agassiz to explain
" the genius of things." The latter, with his customary gusto,
outlined the course of the life-principle in its development

[1] *Recollections of Eminent Men.*

from the single cell up to the highest organisms; but Emerson showed his inveterate objection to considerations of life in terms of time.

" Your philosophy," he said to Agassiz, " is based on the reality of time. You must know that some of us believe with Kant that time is merely a subjective form of human thought, having no objective existence."

As Agassiz girded himself for reply, Emerson sprang up with an anxious look at his watch. He had only fifteen minutes to catch the train to Concord, and forthwith vanished from the dining-room. Whipple does not say whether the club laughed, but the Sphinx probably did.

II

As Emerson's advancing age carried him into quieter waters, his countrymen gradually became aware of his achievements, and honors began to fall upon him. Even Harvard University suddenly recognized in him a graduate of distinction. Until now his Alma Mater had regarded him as a person of doubtful tendencies. It had disliked his intellectual novelties, his Divinity School address of 1838, and his criticisms of Boston's furtive sympathy with slavery. It had, meantime, bestowed honors and degrees upon all sorts of nonentities, pretenders, and twenty-four-hour heroes. It now suddenly remembered Emerson, and in 1867 made him a Doctor of Laws (in this case a singularly appropriate title), and then asked him to be an Overseer. In an address before the Phi Beta Kappa Society Emerson spoke cheerfully, vesting his hopes for the future in the educated class. " I think their hands are strong enough to hold up the Republic," he said. " I read the promise of better times and of greater men."

When he resumed his lectures in the Middle West, he found himself much more popular than before, although it was evident that ticket-buyers came oftener to see the man rather than to be filled with wisdom, and that as an attraction he was not to be compared with John B. Gough, Frederick Douglass, Anna E. Dickinson, and Benjamin F. Taylor, who were the real lyceum heroes of the period. Nor did he fetch prices as high as those of other celebrities. At Lyons, Iowa, in 1866, Emerson was booked for a lecture at $75.00, although the committee had wanted Wendell Phillips at $110.00. At this place a ticket good for an oyster supper and Emerson's lecture as well was sold for $1.00, the committee doubtless hoping that those persons who could not be attracted by ideas would be enticed by oysters. At De-Witt, in the same state, indignation was caused when Emerson skipped part of his lecture in order to catch a train to the next point, and the local newspaper even accused him of " swindling." The fee for this lecture was twenty-five cents.[2]

Although during this tour Emerson spoke in freezing halls and endured all the hardships entailed by long buggy rides, crossings of ice-filled streams, and primitive hotels, he constantly obtained novel material for his notebooks which served to freshen his mind and relieve tedium. In Saginaw, Michigan, for instance, he noted the observation of a Mr. Brown that " men that live by their own labor are almost always moral people."

[2] H. H. Hoeltje in *Iowa Journal of History and Politics.*

III

The years between 1867 and 1872 he filled with lectures, readings, and the preparation of new poems and essays for publication. He was well aware that the habit of losing his place when delivering lectures, or skipping pages, was growing upon him, but found himself powerless to prevent such accidents. " Things that go wrong at these lectures," he said, " don't disturb me, because I know that everyone knows that I am worn-out and passed by; and that it is only my old friends come for friendship's sake to have one last season with me."

He was in reality not nearly so impaired as he thought. He had merely reached another of those lulls which often came upon him, but which, however, became longer-lasting as his years advanced. " Periodicity, reaction," he once said, " are laws of mind as well as of matter."

On the whole, he was well content that he was leaving the ocean behind and turning into a tranquil harbor. " It was strange," he wrote, in " Old Age," " if a man should turn his sixtieth year without a feeling of immense relief from the number of dangers he has escaped. . . . At every stage we lose a foe. . . . The passions have answered their purpose: that slight but dread overweight, with which, in each instance, Nature secures the execution of her aim, drops off. To keep man in the planet, she impresses the terror of death. To perfect the commissariat, she implants in each a certain rapacity to get the supply, and a little over-supply of his wants. To insure the existence of the race, she reinforces the sexual instinct, at the risk of disorder, grief, and pain. To secure strength, she plants cruel hunger and thirst, which so easily overdo their office and invite disease. But these temporary stays and shifts for the perfection of the young animal are shed as fast as they can be replaced by nobler resources. . . . I count it another capital advantage of age, this, that a success more or less signifies nothing. Little by little, it has amassed such a fund of merit, that it can very well afford to go on its credit when it will."

IV

The long solstice of this period was broken by a trip to California, in the company of his daughter Edith and a number of friends, including several lively young people, in whose society Emerson found great delight, particularly when they sang comic songs.

From Chicago they went westward in a private car, Mr. Pullman, inventor of the car bearing his name, seeing them off. Emerson's tranquillity and cheerfulness, even under tiresome conditions, at once impressed his companions; but they were awed chiefly by his unwearying devotion to pie, especially at breakfast. A noble specimen was always placed before him at the first meal of the day. Emerson once invited those sitting near him to partake of a wedge, and when they all declined Emerson was nonplussed.

" But Mr. ——, what is pie for? " [3]

He also created a sensation by smoking cigars freely, sometimes two a day, probably because the act of smoking per-

[3] James B. Thayer in *A Western Journey with Mr. Emerson.*

mitted him to listen to the conversation without taking an active part in it. From this time onward, he seemed to care less and less to do any talking himself, although finding increased pleasure in it when carried on by other persons, particularly young people.

At Salt Lake City Emerson was taken to see Brigham Young; but no exchange of views was indulged in, and neither took great notice of the other. At first the great Mormon paid no attention to the Concordian, but when he learned that his tall visitor was Emerson of the essays, he remarked casually that he had read them. Although the interview was so non-productive, those present derived some enjoyment from the contrast between the two men. The Mormon leader appeared to Professor Thayer to have the countenance of some hardy man, like a teamster recently dressed up, with his hair roached back from his forehead under some careful barber's fresh ministration; while Emerson was, as always, the scholar and gentleman. Afterwards there was some conversation about the Mormons, and it was remarked that " they impress the common people, through their imagination by Bible names and imagery."

" Yes," said Emerson, " it is an after-clap of Puritanism. But one would think that after this Father Abraham could go no further."

In the scenery of the Far West nothing impressed Emerson so much as the trees, particularly the pines and firs. He called them " those gentleman trees." In California he was invited to name a Sequoia Gigantea and selected one near Galen's Hospice which he named " Samoset," in memory of the first Indian ally of the Plymouth colony in Massachusetts. During the journey he made very few notes, but on turning to Concord seven weeks later he resumed writing with more energy. He remarked that five miracles had occurred in his lifetime — the steamboat, the railroad, the telegraph, the astronomical spectroscope, and the photograph. On reflection he thought that cheap postage, the mowing machine, and the horse rake should be added, and finally he noted that the balloon only needed a rudder " to give us the dominion of the air as well as of the sea."

He mentioned that physicists in general repelled him, but he recorded his admiration for these men because they were " poets in science ": Kepler, Hunter, Bonnet, Buffon, Geoffroy Saint-Hilaire, Linnæus, Hauy, Oken, Goethe, and Faraday.

V

In July, 1872, there occurred one of the major shocks of Emerson's life. Early in the morning he was awakened by the crackling of fire in the garret of his home, and he was compelled to run out, only partly dressed, into a rain to shout for help. Neighbors and passersby responded energetically and managed to rescue the books and manuscripts and most of the furniture. The fire spared the four walls, but consumed the roof and upper structure. As a result of the exposure, Emerson caught a cold which developed into a fever and confined him to bed. Their children being absent, Mr. and Mrs. Emerson were once more received into the Old Manse by Miss Elizabeth Ripley. A room in the courthouse was meantime given to him as a study and workroom.

Assistance and sympathy came from every direction. Francis Cabot Lowell, a classmate, arrived with a check for $5000, which he offered as the contribution of a few friends, and then Dr. Le Baron Russell opened a fund to which the subscriptions soon amounted to $11,620. This sum was presented to him by Judge Hoar, as the offering of friends who asked thus to be permitted to assist in the restoration of his home. " I am a lover of men," wrote Emerson, " but this recent wonderful experience of their tenderness surprises and occupies my thoughts day by day."

Although Emerson accepted his loss with the utmost calmness, it was soon recognized that it had inflicted upon him a grievous internal shock. His tendency to lose the track of things and to forget the names of persons and objects became daily more evident. He was no longer able to pronounce the names of common things such as an umbrella, which he defined as something that " strangers take away." He told James Elliot Cabot one day that he was going to dine with a friend, but he hoped she would not ask him her name; and Mary Hosmer Brown, in her recollections of Concord, records that, on being visited by Walt Whitman, he turned to his daughter, Ellen, and said to her in an aside, " What is the name of this poet? " He experienced pronounced difficulty in composing his thoughts, and writing was a laborious task in which he had to have assistance.

Chapter Twenty-Seven

I

IN their concern, his friends considered the advisability of diverting his thoughts by proposing a voyage to Egypt and the Nile, and perhaps Greece. He listened reluctantly, but at length consented with some eagerness, and in the autumn of 1872 sailed with his daughter Ellen for England, where his son Edward was a medical student. He had once written: " The wise man stays at home, and when his necessities, his duties, or any occasion, call him from his house, or into foreign lands, he is at home still . . . and visits cities and men like a sovereign." It was indeed like a sovereign that he now visited Europe for the third time.

Twenty years had passed since he had seen Carlyle, but now he found him again, sitting in his Chelsea study and venting what Henry James, the elder, called his " usual putrid theory of the universe." Carlyle embraced him, gazed upon his face for a long time, and then sat down with him and talked for two hours or more. The Scot showed no loss of memory, but with his well-nigh fourscore years, he was looking very old and haggard, and, having finished his work, was awaiting the end without a trace of that buoyancy which Emerson preserved to the last.

Although Emerson received friends, such as Charles Eliot Norton, William Henry Channing, Moncure D. Conway, and Charles K. Newcomb, heartily, he showed little interest in sightseeing. His appetite improved, but he arose very late in the mornings. " I love above all things to do nothing," he said. A week of London's rain and fogs was enough, and after a short visit at Canterbury, he went over to Paris where he passed a week with Mr. and Mrs. James Russell Lowell and John Holmes, his former pupil. With a Swiss servant to look after him, he and Miss Ellen went on to Pisa and Florence, and finally Rome. At all places Emerson showed small interest in passing objects, but was always pleased to stop and talk with a friend. December found the party in Egypt. The passage through the Delta of the Nile gave him moments of dismal tedium. He wondered why he had come so far " to see bareness of mud." The absence of trees afflicted him, and although the clouds were beautiful, they were merely for ornament and not for rain. The people, however, appealed to his artist's eye. He noticed that they walked and moved far more nobly than the passersby in the cities at home. " For studying the nude," he remarked, " our artists should come here and not to Paris."

When they sailed up the Nile he became more interested, rejoicing in the sight of the palms along the banks of the river, and finding poetry in the mandarin oranges, which he almost admitted were even more admirable than Concord pears. "One may call them Christianity in apples," he said. Despite the " homesick speeches " he was daily making to his daughter, his health and spirits rose, and even his hair became thicker and regained its brownish hue. But all forms of exertion were repugnant; he was unable to write, except for occasional entries in his diary, and he was quite content to dream the days away in the lotus air.

He enjoyed the joke when it was related to him that Mrs.
Helen Bell, daughter of Rufus Choate, had been asked,
" What do you think the Sphinx said to Mr. Emerson? " Her
reply was, " The Sphinx probably said to him, ' You're
another.' "

In Cairo he was taken by George Bancroft to breakfast
with the Khedive, and then sailed for Rome, going thence
to Florence. Here he was delighted to find Herman Grimm
and his wife Gisela, with whom he had corresponded for
years without ever having seen them. Grimm, who was a
biographer and essayist, had long entertained an intense
admiration for Emerson, and now found that his appearance
did not belie his works. He looked at Emerson a long time,
and remarked that his photographs did him an injustice. He
thought Emerson appeared to be " made of steel," with a
" fine, sharp, manly face, and such bright coloring."

Emerson's vigor returned so rapidly that he was soon able
to work upon a revision of his poems, and his memory so far
returned that he was once more able to find the right word
in conversation, a power which at home had sometimes failed
him. On returning to Paris, he was introduced to numerous
celebrities, including Renan, Taine, and Elie de Beaumont.
Taine sent him the next day the five volumes of his *Littéra-
ture Anglaise*. For the first time he found some enjoyment
in Paris, and rejoiced that he could awake as " master
of the bright day in a bright world," finding that to drop
the " doleful bundle of Duty " was like having a new
youth.

He and his daughter then returned to London for three
weeks, where he met a whole galaxy of stars, including
Gladstone, Mill, Huxley, Tyndall, Dean Stanley, Lecky,

Froude, Charles Reade, and Browning. He had breakfast with the last named at Lady Amberley's, and, although they were pleased with each other, Browning almost offended him by praising Shelley. Emerson had never been able to like Shelley; he found in him mere " mica glitter," although he had a faint admiration for *The Skylark*.

He readily accepted the numerous invitations to breakfast and dinner, but avoided speaking in public except when Thomas Hughes prevailed upon him to appear at the Working Men's College. Two of the students there afterwards sent him a sovereign each to be used in the restoration of his Concord home. At Oxford, he met Max Muller, Jowett, Ruskin, and Dodgson, author of *Alice in Wonderland*. After hearing Ruskin lecture, he was invited to the latter's home, where the owner depressed Emerson by a long and gloomy denunciation of the present state of society. Emerson made no attempt to conceal his displeasure, and finally " roundly rebuked him." [1]

It is possible that this episode laid the foundation for an extraordinary attack made on Emerson after his return to Concord by the poet Algernon Charles Swinburne. According to the account given by Sir Edmund Gosse in the privately printed *Catalogue of the Ashley Library*, Swinburne learned that Emerson had given to an American newspaper an interview criticizing various English writers, including Swinburne himself. Swinburne wrote to Emerson in regard to it, but received no reply. In February, 1874, Sir Edmund Gosse, on meeting Swinburne, learned that he had written a second letter to Emerson.

[1] From a note by the editors of Emerson's Journals, Edward Waldo Emerson and Waldo Emerson Forbes.

" I hope your language was quite moderate," said Sir Edmund, who gives the poet's reply as follows:

" Perfectly moderate. I merely informed him, in language of the strictest reserve, that he was a hoary-headed and toothless baboon, who, first lifted into notice on the shoulder of Carlyle, now spits and splutters from a filthier platform of his own fouling. That is all I've said."

This period is described by Sir Edmund as " the most painful portion " of Swinburne's career. It doubtless was.

II

After receiving much attention at Chester, Stratford-on-Avon, and Edinburgh, Emerson sailed for home, his seventieth birthday occurring in the course of the voyage. On landing at Boston he found that the great fire of 1873 had destroyed his birthplace there; but Concord made up for any melancholy thoughts by the heartiness of its reception at the station. A great throng was present, a band played, and school children escorted Emerson home under a triumphal arch. On reaching his own gate, Emerson was overcome to find that during his absence affectionate friends had entirely restored his home. Even his books and pictures were in their old places, and Mrs. Emerson was able to write to her friends: " If there is a lighter-hearted man in the world, I don't know where he lives."

With something like his old vigor and clarity, he was able to give several public readings and addresses, and the next year completed the compilation of *Parnassus*. But the preparation of *Letters and Social Aims*, which he had promised to a London publisher, fatigued him. His papers had become badly mixed and he at length confessed that the task was too much for him. James Elliot Cabot was then asked to assist him, and after the book was completed continued to assist him for several years.

III

The short address given by Emerson at the unveiling of the Minute Man, at the 100th anniversary of the Concord fight on April 19, 1875, was the last that he ever composed, although he continued to give short readings in public for several years. There ensued a period during which his faculties underwent a further general decline, leaving him in a state in which there was for half the time an awareness of the world about him and in the other half a soft oblivion. The shell which had for so long been growing around his inner self was now firm and opaque enough to resist all but the strongest lights and most powerful influences from external existence. He lived in an internal quietude not to be shattered even by the loudest noises. Outlines and edges were no longer perceptible, and he dwelt in a dream-like mist which hid from his vision everything that was not intimate and immediately recognizable. His mind had already signalled that it wished to be separated from his body, and, as if in preparation for total dissociation, took long flights into some remote ether, returning only occasionally and not always at the moments when its owner wished it to serve him. Persons and things ceased to have character or even body, and seemed to merge into some background on which the light shone feebly.

His love for reading continued, but words ceased to have any intrinsic meaning, and books were sought only for their general tone or flavor. Personality disappeared from all names, and when he sometimes took down from his shelves his own books they possessed a novelty for him exactly like that he would have found in the works of an unknown author. One day when his daughter entered his study, she found him reading very intently in one of his own books. His face revealed his pleasure, and looking up at her, he exclaimed, " Why, these things are really very good."

His recollection of names and labels sank lower every day, and Cabot asserts that one day when he asked him about John Sterling, the young English poet in corresponding with whom Emerson had once taken great delight, he could not remember that he had ever heard Sterling's name. He was at times quite aware of his deficiencies; but instead of permitting himself to be irritated or depressed by his shortcomings, they amused him as if they belonged to some other person. Before reading a paper at the Concord Lyceum in 1878, he remarked that it would be queer to see a lecturer who had no idea what he was lecturing about, " and an audience who didn't know what he *can* mean."

Cabot observed that, although at times he liked to talk, especially in the presence of old friends, he usually preferred to listen and smile, with the expression of a man who might have been recovering from an illness. Bodily he continued to be quite active, taking his usual walks and in warm weather often bathing in Walden Pond. He made no objection to reading an occasional paper in public, but his daughter Ellen was always present to help him keep his manuscripts in order and sometimes to supply a missing word. On one occasion

when he was asked to deliver a lecture for a charitable purpose, the hall was well filled by auditors who realized that
they might be hearing Emerson's voice for the last time.
He proceeded as usual, but half way through his manuscript
he suddenly paused. The audience waited patiently, but
Emerson continued to stand silently on the platform. He had
wholly forgotten his audience, the occasion, and his task. He
was in that other world where none could follow him, and
when it was seen that he would not be able to finish his
discourse, his daughter stepped up and quietly assisted him
from the platform.

He no longer cared to write, and letters, even to his intimates, were laboriously composed. His journals received no
more additions except for an occasional memorandum. One of
his last entries said: "The men in the street fail to interest
us, because at first view they seem thoroughly known and exhausted. . . . The best part of truth is certainly that which
hovers in gleams and suggestions unpossessed before man.
His recorded knowledge is dead and cold."

IV

The last long journey he made from home was undertaken
in 1876, when he was invited to address the literary societies
of the University of Virginia at Charlottesville. He accepted,
remembering "how admirable in my youth were to me the
Southern boys," and regarding it as an occasion on which the
sundered ties between North and South might begin a re-
knitting. The midsummer heat and long journey tired him
out; but he spoke bravely for half an hour, despite imperfect

arrangements which permitted much noise in the hall and a certain air of hostility worn by Virginians who were bitterly resenting the days of Reconstruction. His only remark afterwards was, " They are very brave people down there, and say just what they think." When returning the next day, however, fellow passengers, some of whom were on their way to the Philadelphia Centennial Exposition, showed him conspicuous attention and requested the privilege of being introduced to him.

Although rarely absent from his home, he welcomed the opportunity to meet old friends and contemporary writers, and was present on December 17, 1877, when a dinner was given to Whittier, in honor of his seventieth birthday, by the *Atlantic Monthly*, of which William Dean Howells was editor. This was an occasion made memorable by a ghastly hazing of Mark Twain, who was one of the speakers. It being a large affair, with numerous notabilities invited, Mark had exerted himself to prepare one of his broadest and most gorgeous burlesques. It was known that Twain meant to spread himself, and there was the keenest expectation of an unusually uproarious speech. The program was long. William Winter spoke briefly, and then Twain arose. He afterwards recalled the faces that his preliminary glance fell upon: " Mr. Emerson, supernaturally grave, unsmiling "; " Mr. Whittier, grave, lovely, his beautiful spirit shining out of his face "; " Mr. Longfellow, with his silken white hair and his benignant face "; " Dr. Oliver Wendell Holmes, flashing smiles and affection."

Twain, whose memories always harped back to frontier days in California, saw fit to place the setting for his story in the wild mountains of that State where dwelt a lonely miner.

One day three tramps appeared at his cabin door and invited themselves to accept his hospitality. They gave their names as Longfellow, Holmes, and Emerson. At this point, instead of the anticipating smile which Mark had expected, a slight shudder of apprehension ran across the assembly; but Mark, although detecting the chill in the atmosphere, continued in a hope of winning a warmer response. He had chosen as his device for creating laughter the wild and shaggy incongruity which previously had never failed him.

He went on to describe his three hoboes as busy with their cards and drink, meantime citing apt quotations, ingeniously altered, from the works of their namesakes. For example, a game of euchre was being played at ten cents a corner. " Mr. Emerson dealt, looked at his hand, shook his head, and said —

    ' I am the doubter and the doubt — '

and calmly bunched the hands and went to shuffling for a new lay-out. Says he:

    ' They reckon ill who leave me out,
      They know not well the subtle ways I keep,
      I pass and deal again.' "

Even at this grotesque parody of Emerson's " Brahma," not a smile broke the constraint. Longfellow looked puzzled, Holmes made tracings on his menu, and Howells, who was chairman, kept his eyes on his plate. Emerson, who was present only in body, merely looked off into the distance. Twain was well aware that he was riding headlong for a terrible failure, but kept on to the heart-breaking end. Then " fell a silence weighing many tons to the square inch — broken only by the hysterical and blood curdling laughter of a single guest." [2]

In all this assemblage there were not enough red corpuscles to create the hearty guffaw which would have relieved the common tautness, banished the constraint, and rescued Mark Twain from a miserable humiliation. Mark went home in an agony of suffering. Believing that he had committed some unnamable crime, he wrote to Howells begging him not to let his name appear again in the *Atlantic Monthly*, and asking him to return the proofs of his stories. Howells declined to accede, and although he mildly tried to cheer up Twain, he offered little consolation. To relieve his mind it was at length suggested that Twain should write to Longfellow, Holmes, and Emerson; and this he did in a spirit of abject apology.

Longfellow replied calmly, saying he did not believe " anybody was much hurt." Holmes answered that it had not occurred to him to take offence, although he " had heard some mild questioning as to whether, even in fun, it was good taste to associate the names of the authors with the absurdly unlike personalities attributed to them." He appended the consolation that two gentlemen " of the highest social standing," had even laughed freely, which news should have permitted Mark again to breathe; but he was not normal again until he had received a reply from the Emerson home written by Miss Ellen Emerson.

" Let me say," she wrote, " that no shadow of indignation has ever been in our minds. The night of the dinner, my father says he did not hear Mr. Clemens's speech. He was too far off, and my mother says that when she read it to him

[2] Albert Bigelow Paine's *Life of Mark Twain.*

the next day it amused him." She added that " to my father it is as if it had not been; he never quite heard, never quite understood it, and he forgets easily and entirely." She also mentioned that while her brother found the speech " unfortunate, still some of the quotations were very good, and he gave them with relish, and my father laughed, though never having seen a card in his life, he couldn't understand them like his children."

This episode as here outlined supplies its own commentary on the prevailing state of mind and manners among the literary Brahmins of the period. One derives the impression that they were so intent on being respectable and worthy, that they could not relax from their pose long enough even to help poor Mark Twain down from his wretched position, and in common humanity to laugh at his joke, even though it was roughly wrought and in its uncouthness unsuited to a Boston drawingroom. Their contrast with Twain was impressive. He represented not only an alien outlook on life, but a different stage of civilization. He brought in something savage, gross, and untamed, lifted directly from the coarser currents of American life, that could not be assimilated in intellectual New England, which, in its desire to be incessantly " refined," had lost touch with the bases of human existence.

Future literary history will see Mark Twain as having done himself a wrong in having during his later years, cast his portion with this anemic group. Close association with them tamed and denatured him, and a few experiences similar to that at the Whittier dinner sufficed to cow and unman him, so that in his old age he became restless, dejected, and pessimistic, no longer finding free vent for that wild, eldritch laughter, that savage, tearing mirth, which was lavishly needed in an America already grown sick of its own sins and absurdities. Among the intelligentsia it had been already forgotten that Nature comes eating, drinking, and sinning, and that her darlings do not come from Sunday Schools; nor often to Whittier dinners.

Chapter Twenty-Eight

I

EMERSON was seventy-six years old when Alcott, who had been living for several years in Boston, returned to Concord, and there in a little structure bearing curious scrolls and arabesques, near his home in the Orchard House, set up a School of Philosophy. He had hoped to induce Emerson to take an active interest in it, but the latter's infirmities prevented him from doing more than giving an occasional lecture to the students, one of which was on " Aristocracy." Emerson admired personal aristocracy no less than political democracy, and hoped it would never die out of the universe. The school had summer as well as winter sessions, and Alcott's daughter, Louisa, commemorated in verse these warmer periods as follows:

> " Philosophers sit in their sylvan hall
> And talk of the duties of man,
> Of chaos and cosmos, Hegel and Kant,
> With the Oversoul well in the van.
>
> All on their hobbies they amble away,
> And a terrible dust they make;
> Disciples devout both gaze and adore,
> As daily they listen and bake."

Emerson was meantime sitting daily for Daniel Chester French, the sculptor, who made a full-length seated figure of the seer, which was afterwards placed in the Concord Public Library. " His tall figure," writes Mr. French, " walking the village streets in a long black cloak or shawl, made me think of Dante walking the streets of Florence . . ." Emerson made no objections to long sittings, saying, " This is an easy way of sleeping," and when the statue was completed, he said, " that is the face I shave."

During this quiet but steadily declining period, he continued to read occasional papers in public, but required the constant supervision of his daughter Ellen to prevent his losing or mixing the sheets of his manuscript. Outwardly, however, he remained much the same. His stoop was accentuated, but his presence retained the aura of graciousness and benignity which caused audiences to listen to him with unfailing reverence. At moments his humor shone like the sunbeam which Hawthorne once noted that he carried in his face. At the Centennial celebration of the Boston Latin School Association, he prefaced his written paper by saying quietly, " I cannot remember anybody's name; not even my recollections of the Latin School. I have therefore guarded against absolute silence by bringing you a few reminiscences which I have written."

Mr. Cabot relates a curious adventure which Emerson had in the course of this period. In September, 1878, he was escorted by his daughter to a Unitarian convention at Saratoga, and afterwards visited Niagara Falls. He then went off alone, searching the western part of New York State for a young mechanic who had once written to him expressing his thanks for Emerson's teachings, but questioning his " com-

EMERSON IN HIS SILVER YEARS

From a photo by Joseph B. Forster

placent optimism." He learned that the young man had left the State and could not be found. This is a pity; the record of that conversation, if it had taken place, would have been worth reading.

In the following year he attended the fiftieth anniversary of the Unitarian Church at Concord, New Hampshire, where he had once preached and where he had first met the eyes of Ellen Tucker. Although her house had been moved, he found it again and walked through its rooms. In his seventy-ninth year he read papers before the Massachusetts Historical Society and the Concord School of Philosophy. After that, he was content to remain at home, excusing himself from reading or conversing in public because of his inability to recall necessary words. His hearing remained good, but his sense of personality dimmed until he could recognize only the faces of his own family and friends very close to him. His pleasure in reading books and newspapers was undiminished, but in his seventy-ninth year he took most interest in pictures. Printed words he could not always grasp, and he was wont to read the same sentences over and over, murmuring them like a child. He confined his outdoor diversions to walks of half a mile, and found his chief enjoyment in watching the children of his daughter Edith, the wife of William H. Forbes.

He had not always been a regular attendant at church — indeed, he had avoided church services for years at a time — but as the twilight thickened, he began to go more regularly, even attending twice in a day.

On March 24, 1882, Longfellow died, and although Emerson had never been intimate with the Cambridge poet he attended the funeral. He was conducted by his daughter,

Ellen, to a seat beside the coffin. In a moment he arose and stared down at Longfellow's calm face. A vagrant memory troubled him, but would not be fixed. Turning to a friend, he said, " That gentleman was a sweet, beautiful soul, but I have entirely forgotten his name." In a moment he arose again, and once more stared down into the coffin; but the faculty of recollection had fled from him, and he sat down defeated.

Almost exactly two months later, on May 25, 1882, he was expecting to celebrate his seventy-ninth birthday. In the preceding April, after one of his usual quiet Sundays, he betrayed some hoarseness and other symptoms of a cold. He found it more comfortable to be on his feet than to sit in his study chair, and took much longer walks than usual. For several days he insisted that he had no cold, and his son, Dr. Edward Emerson, saw no cause for alarm; but one morning on coming downstairs to breakfast, Emerson paused as if in distress, saying, " I hoped it would not come this way." A pain had settled in his chest, but for two days longer he went to his study as usual, and at night scattered the brands in the fireplace before going to bed, according to his habit.

On the fifth day his fever became pronounced, and his son recognized his ailment as pneumonia. Thereafter his descent was rapid, although not marked by severe pain or delirium. At moments he believed himself ill in a friend's house and that he ought to return to his own home before his friend should be inconvenienced.

At other times he was fully conscious though not always able to talk, and he gave farewell embraces to his friends with great calmness. Some of the objects in his room became strange to him, but he was able to recognize Carlyle's portrait on the wall, saying, " That is my man — my man."

At night he strove to repeat organized sentences as if reciting, and when something reminded him of his first-born, he smiled and exclaimed, " Oh, that boy — that beautiful boy."

The pain in his lungs became sharper, and ether was given to him, but he was too weak for resistance, and his breath came with difficulty, until finally it ceased altogether on April 27, 1882.

He was buried at the foot of a tall pine at the top of the highest ridge in Sleepy Hollow Cemetery, where he lies today under an unhewn boulder of native quartz. Nearby are the graves of Nathaniel and Sophia Hawthorne, and less than a hundred feet away are those of the Alcotts and the Thoreaus.

" He was just a man," wrote Walt Whitman near Emerson's new grave, " poised on himself, all-loving, all-enclosing, and sane and clear as the sun."

Chapter Twenty-Nine

I

EMERSON'S life was as transparent as glass, as clear as spring water, and nowhere in the long span which covered the major part of the nineteenth century is there evidence of any sin, either of commission or omission. In literature he was our only Olympian, and all criticisms of his precepts must appear somewhat niggardly in the light of his personal splendor. What he said or how he acted in any given circumstance appears to be of small account beside the luminous beauty of his life — the luminous beauty of the moon. The man himself was a whole. As a teacher, however, his views, which were limited to the arc of his own experience and reading, were necessarily partial; and if truth be compared to a full circle, he never attained to more than the fragments which he himself modestly called " gleams and suggestions." Emerson himself posited the problem when he said: " One man sees a sparkle or shimmer of the truth, and reports it, and his seeing becomes a legend or golden proverb for all ages. And other men see and try to say as much, but no man wholly and well."

He himself believed that each man is called into the world to carry out a task, to make his due contribution to the common wealth. He apparently conceived it to be his mission, first, to break the hold of Calvinism on his people, and to remove its claws without destroying the Puritanism which had grown up beside it as its virtual Siamese twin. He fully recognized the past usefulness of Calvinism in having held men's thoughts fast and disciplined their conduct during fierce transitions; but he was conscious that a young and expanding country could not attain a healthful stature while in the grip of a philosophy which despised and distrusted men and taught them to look to a future life for their good. He himself believed that the world, as the expression of an ineffable intelligence, was good at the core; and that whatever was temporarily evil at or near the surface could be, and would be, converted into good by intelligent men. He repeatedly observed that men are everywhere better than their religions.

In attacking Calvinism his method was not that of the Samson but of the surgeon. A limb here and a joint there, he removed so quietly and unobstrusively, meantime soothing the patient by remarking how good it used to be, that the damage was done before the victim had experienced more than a few tremors. Hardly had he blood-let the body of Calvinism, however, when he detected a disease in his own church of Unitarianism. It clung to many of the old forms which had become outworn in the older church. He therefore turned his weapons upon both churches simultaneously, and when he found them obstinate and set against change, he threw off his ministerial robes and ceased all active connection with religious institutions.

His separation was made the more easily because he had already ceased to believe in the Calvinistic and Unitarian idols, which were gods of Activity. In their stead he strove to substitute ideas on which the emphasis was on Being rather than Doing. He saw that a nervous, restless people like his countrymen were suffering because of their overweening devotion to Action. He hoped to offset this malady by inculcating something of that quietism which he had learned from the Oriental scriptures, and to which he had been already bent not only by Plato and the Neo-Platonists, but by the tendencies of his own nature. *Be* more and *Do* less, is a tenet implicit in virtually all of Emerson's writings, and is one which explains his own character. This doctrine was peculiarly suited to his disposition because of his lack of physical stamina. He had not the abounding blood-flow or the hardy frame which would have permitted him to become a fighter or even an active agitator.

Emerson's second endeavor was to substitute monism for what had been a crippling dualism in American life and philosophy. Men were distracted by the claims of a Calvinized conscience struggling with the fierce demands of external life as lived in field or counting-house. They believed in the reality of both good and evil, and tried, to their disaster, to satisfy the claims of each. Emerson sought to remedy this condition by counselling a unification which alone would enable the individual to be effective both in his life and labor. To obtain power for his message, he had to begin with himself and obtain his own integration before he could preach it to others. In so doing, he adopted the doctrine that all creation is an expression of one mind, which he identified by various names — Spirit, Power, the Universal, the Great Presence, and sometimes by the word Nature itself. He avoided, however, the use of the word Absolute, to which some of his contemporaries, influenced by the new German philosophers, were prone. Goodness, he taught, was likely to be conditional.

For himself he simplified the question of good and evil

by denying that evil had more than a temporary or privative existence. Evil was not an entity, but a temporary absence of good. This doctrine explains why his contemporaries found great difficulty in inducing Emerson to enlist in any active agitation or to give more than passive support to any cause, no matter how appealing. Emerson believed that the world was made up of tendencies, which were always proceeding in the right direction, or towards melioration, and that it were better not to interfere with these tendencies by the interposition of the human will. This is the basis of Emerson's persistent optimism.

His passivity, it is true, tended to make his life appear colorless and aloof. We cannot help wishing to see more heat and glow emanating from the heights to which he climbed; and yet when we see how unduly he was heated and upset in the events leading up to the Civil War, we are compelled to admit that his instincts regarding himself were correct and that he was right in refusing to permit himself to be carried out of his own orbit.

Having won an understanding of and agreement with himself, Emerson assumed the task, thirdly, of urging the advance of that Young America in which he ardently believed. He was confident of its inherent goodness because he identified it with himself — hopeful, idealistic, and unburdened by the sins of the Old World. Emerson has, in each generation since his essays were first printed, remained the philosopher of young men. He sees the world as freshly discovered and ever new. He describes Nature as if it were just born. All things are possible, and on no glowing picture is there any shadow of disease or pessimism or questioning. To Young America, once free of European formulas, he looked for the fresh, irresistible forces which were to cleanse the stables of history. Here and there a belief in the United States as the Little Child of nations still prevails, having assumed a curiously bland form of irritating self-righteousness.

Emerson found the free reception of his gospel interfered with by the rise of an unforeseen obstacle. This was the appearance of the acquisitive, property-owning instinct, consequent upon the sudden development of machinery and railroads, which banished the old simplicities and replaced them with a civilization far more sophisticated and complex. In the face of this new situation, Young America halted, became confused and finally despondent. Emerson tried to rouse it from this inertia by preaching a process of visionizing which should transcend mundane actualities, see them as illusions, and establish a more direct connection with universals. Mercantilism did not, as it once threatened to do, defeat Emerson; but it did worse: it took from him what it could use and ignored the rest.

II

Considering the date of his birth and his environment, Emerson is curiously modern. The passing of a century has not aged his tone or manner. He was a product of an era in which science had gradually begun to replace tradition. His tendency to mysticism did not prevent his becoming a spiritual brother of Michael Faraday and Charles Darwin. He loved the sciences because they revealed laws to him. But he followed science only as long as it concerned itself with law. When science busied itself too exclusively with facts, he lost patience, fearing pedantry, which he despised. Above knowledge he preferred wisdom. In gaining wisdom he saw Asia as superior to Europe and America. Wisdom is not synonymous with science or knowledge; he saw it as derived from a survey of the world and its doings in the light of an inward illumination, which illumination is bestowed by the eternal presence of Brahma. Considering his limited contacts with men and the lack of system in his studies, the variety and extent of Emerson's wisdom astonishes us. His more penetrating aphorisms will remain good as long as man is encompassed by a Sphinx-like Nature. They have an enduring quality, a permanent luster, not to be rusted by years. They are derived not from tuition, but from intuition; for which he compels us to have a deeper respect.

Emerson's knowledge of men was large and canny. In acquiring and distributing wisdom, he was careful not to create a " school." He saw how easily the human mind becomes content to cling to and to solidify itself around a body of opinion; and he would therefore have no following. In his desire to prevent the accretion of worshipping disciples he hid himself away too much, and so lent color to the charge of undue aloofness. He could not endure the formation of crusts. The world, in his view, is fluid; Providence works *ex tempore*; and life is distinguished by incessant change and eternal recurrence.

Scarcely any of Emerson's ideas were new. He was a philosopher in the sense that he was a lover of *sophos*, wisdom; but not in the sense that he was a founder of a system of thinking. His power lay in the novel face, the fresh turn, that he gave to very ancient wisdom. He did not wish to direct, but to instigate.

III

Emerson's personal sweetness has been unfortunate for his fame. He was almost too good. We crave more roughness in our heroes, more edge and gritty surfaces. But we forget that, although his life was so limpid, he could speak in hard words. Those quotations which appear on dainty calendars are not all that he uttered. In such essays as *Friendship*, *Love*, and *Illusions*, there are passages which are not only hard but are cold and almost unfeeling. Around Emerson's inner core there was a freezing atmosphere, and from the protection of his inner operculum the gaze that he directed upon the world was at times as devoid of human warmth as the stare of a stone Sphinx. He was no sentimentalist, but was ever canny. In this respect again, Emerson was a true citizen of his time and place. In the North America of his day, no arterial connection was visible between heart and head. The heart might say, " Take thine ease, O, my soul! " But the head always advised, "Have a care." In Emerson's case, the head was the rasher of the twain. His head was constantly tempted to jump off and run with the radicals, but his heart remained with the conservatives to whom he was bound by the very ligaments of his being. The world might boil with all manner of notions and experiment, but Emerson remained the good citizen of his own town, never by one impulse breaking a scrupulous adherence to the conventions.

He came not to destroy but to affirm. He became, at length, the bridge of rationalization between the old and the new; between the old Calvinist, agrarian, introspective era in which men made sound implements by hand and worried lest they had sinned against the Holy Ghost, and the new, jostling civilization created by the industrial revolution and dominated by banks, factories, railroads, and internal combustion engines. He accepted the new gods just as he had accepted the old, as suited to their time and place. " Do not bark against the bad . . . the world is always equal to itself." He refused to be disturbed even by the visible inequalities fostered by industrialism. " See the facts clearly and these mountainous inequalities vanish. Love reduces them, as the sun melts the iceberg in the sea. The heart and soul of all men being one, this bitterness of his and mine ceases. His is mine."

However, when the Civil War came he no longer counselled love, but gunpowder. Since that time, the whole world has engaged in a civil war whose after-effects have created doubts as to whether it is any longer equal to itself. Civilization is once more sick of the very diseases, although older grown, which he perceived were eating the heart out of his own generation. Will Emerson's doctrine — that the world is always equal to itself and hence will eventually right itself — prove to be true; or will there be a new instructor with new precepts?

IV

Emerson was born and reached his maturity in a period of transition (which is not unusual; for what period is not one of transition?). Economic and social changes came swiftly, as New England factory textiles replaced homespun, the blast furnace succeeded the blacksmith's shop, and the railroads opened the West's free acreage to settlers. As is usual in such cases, men's thoughts failed to keep pace with the process of change. When at last they awoke to the fact that the old life was falling about their ears and a new one was rushing in, they were filled with bewilderment and foreboding. The Past suddenly assumed a golden glamour; and they tried to re-seize it and hold it, thus to prolong its tenure. Emerson hastened forward reassuringly.

Let go the Past, he cried. Its things will not serve us now. A new universe is in being — is born each moment. It is that with which we must deal. With it we must establish new and original relations, or suffer stagnation and die, repeating outgrown formulas. The Past, like the rain, is over and gone. There is only the Present; there is always only the Present; which we must value to the utmost, because in it we plant the seeds that will determine the Future.

When Emerson emerged as a platform teacher, it was believed that man was the victim of an inscrutable, arbitrary, and sometimes whimsical destiny, which in their more resigned moments his countrymen called an all-wise Providence. This dreaded specter could be moved, and its designs altered, only by the prayers, fervent and, if need be, continuous, of consecrated men, the priests of the tribe. And so, if your fields were parched, you prayed for rain; and if it came in such volume as to break your neighbor's mill-dam, that only proved that you were more righteous than he.

For Providence Emerson strove to substitute Causality. I myself am Heaven and Hell. Cause and Effect, those " chancellors of God," cannot be separated. What one does today determines what one will do and be tomorrow. If I wish a harvest in the autumn, I must sow in the spring. If I wish my ship to come in, I must first send it out. There are no accidents; calamities are but the fruits of my weaknesses. If I reap good fortune, it is because I have sown well. Once a cause is set in motion, it is vain to pray Providence to substitute other than the due effect. God is on the side of the heaviest battalions, rightly disposed. The way to win battles is to get there fustest with the mostest. The prizes go to the man who can do things, and do them in season. Have done with prayers, and join thyself to the Cause of causes; *It* has already given thee the Power. Instead of vain pleadings, Self-reliance!

This was heartening doctrine. It was in accord with the spirit of the times and with the temperament of Emerson's countrymen. With it they explored and subdued a continent; reaped unprecedented riches from unprecedented resources; filled the space between two oceans with wheels, spindles, ratchets, gears; dazzled a universe with reckless activities; by dint of war, utilitarian education, and the propaganda of speech and press they made a nation united and uniform.

At the moment of writing, there has come a pause. Voices are raised, asking: Well, what of it? Is this all? There are not lacking other voices which echo disappointment and even disillusion. Somewhere a wrong turning has been taken. Another stasis has been reached; once more there is among the intellectuals tedium, monotony, satiety, morbidity, disgust; and once more there are those who are saying, with Charles Emerson: " The nap is worn off the world." Emerson's country is no longer the little child that shall lead the nations, but a plump, conservative person with a hard mouth and a pudding-like body, surrounded by time-saving or diverting inventions that are no more than toys of a larger growth. His

bank-account is full, but his life is made up of hours like dry
· gourds that rattle in the wind. Emerson's teachings were intended for Young America; we explore them in vain for an
America that has become plethoric and middle-aged.

V

Emerson was foremost in the demand for a cultural break
with Europe. It came; but it was never complete, and is not
complete yet. For the United States is not the step-daughter
of Europe, but its blood-child. What Emerson really wished
for his country was a center; a center around which it could
stabilize itself, and attain strength, stature, and confidence.
Young America was growing up in a disorderly fashion, hap-
hazardly, loose, even wild. The body was suffering from
gigantism; the brain-case remained that of a child. It was the
proper task of the New England educated class to have cor-
rected this ill-balanced condition. But this task they shirked,
or never recognized. They permitted themselves to be seduced by incomes derived, directly or indirectly, from early
investments in rising industrialism, and soon became a separate caste — comfortably aloof, patronizing, and even self-
righteous to an irritating degree. They had no arteries which
could join a common circulatory system; they had only veins.
Thoreau and Melville were the only writers among them
who retained a wholesome virtue (from *vir*, a man). Emerson had superlative gifts, but they were not always virile
ones.

Emerson desired a center of stability for the national life
because he had seen in himself the benefits of a center for the

individual's life. His own Gibraltar lay within, and its base was formed for him by the sages of the East, " who live above the beauty of the symbol to the beauty of the thing signified." He knew there was more than one bible, and found his own in the Vedas, the Upanishads, and the Bhagavad Gita, and even in the Koran, no less than in the precepts of Moses and the teachings of Jesus. As compensation for the lack of warmth, color, and limpidity in New England life and landscape, he resorted to the poetry of the Persian Saadi. For reinforcement against the stresses of quotidian life, he sought that which is beyond Brahma. " Am I not always in the Great Presence? " As a relief from overmuch Western worship of action he escaped to the calm passivity of the Oriental scriptures. Where is the new Emerson who shall declare that both Occidental activity and Oriental meditation are good, but only in their time and place; and that better than either would be a harmonious union between active Western science and an alternating Eastern capacity for being still?

VI

Emerson introduced good things into American thinking; but with them came a certain vice. It was the vice of intellectualization, or, as it is currently called, rationalization. It is the disease of fancying that a human being does things on a rational basis; of doing a necessary, natural, or instinctive thing first and producing a plausible, logical reason for it afterward — preferably a moral one. Emerson did not introduce the rationalizing process into the American mind — the vice is an old one — but he gave it an enormous impetus:

made it, as it were, fashionable among the intelligentsia. To do a thing not because it is pleasant, but because it is good for one — that is to rationalize. To act spontaneously and unconsciously, and then to become self-conscious about the action, and to defend it on high, " sensible," or lofty grounds — that, again, is to rationalize. When the French intellectuals of the middle class, at the beginning of their Revolution in the closing years of the eighteenth century, enthroned the Goddess of Reason, she was young, blooming, and charmingly dignified. They could not foresee that she would become the hag that would ride the nineteenth and twentieth centuries as well, that she would become dry and wrinkled, not through age but through excesses. " Beware," said Emerson, " when the great God lets loose a thinker on this planet." If he had said, instead, a rationalizer, the warning would have been more apt.

For Emerson to intellectualize was as habitual as to breathe. He had piercing intuitions, and by them lived and wrote; but instincts, impulses, few or none. In his mature years they were dead of repression or atrophied from disuse. The habits of his people did not permit them to endure. And yet no man has written more eloquently of the instinctive, unconscious life than he who said, " Our spontaneous action is always the best," and again, " Nobody can reflect upon an unconscious act with regret or contempt. Bard or hero cannot look down on the word or gesture of a child. It is as great as they." And we find a certain wistfulness in the words of the cool, contained citizen of Concord when he wrote: " The one thing which we seek with insatiable desire, is to forget ourselves, to be surprised out of our propriety, to lose our sempiternal memory, and to do something without knowing how or why.

. . . Nothing great was ever achieved without enthusiasm. The way of life is wonderful. It is by abandonment."

But the last thing that Emerson and the intellectual Brahmins of his period were capable of was to forget themselves, to be surprised out of their propriety, or to give way to abandonment. Consider their reception of Mark Twain's outlandish burlesque at the Whittier dinner. Poor Mark! His was the way of enthusiasm, of abandonment; but his auditors killed him on his feet without moving a muscle, even an eyebrow. To withhold abandonment to his fun was to destroy it and its maker.

Emerson's writings have at times almost every worthy attribute except unconsciousness, except spontaneity. His first published work, *Nature,* is almost alone free of self-conscious rationalization; it is almost wholly a rapturous poetry; but rarely did he recapture the divine fire.

The example which Emerson and his circle thus set up has not been good for his or their spiritual descendants. Nor was it good for the contemporaries who were swayed by him. The self-conscious, rationalizing element in Thoreau often makes the manner of his writing, despite its satisfying content, appear stiff and even tedious. He could not subdue it and cast it away, as did Whitman, who, from editorial-writing bore, became bard and " Spontaneous Me," for a civilization lock-jawed with self-consciousness.

And yet how well Emerson knew! Did he not say in *Experience* (mark the title):

" Culture with us . . . ends in a headache. . . . Do not craze yourself with thinking, but go about your business anywhere. Life is not intellectual or critical; but sturdy. . . . To fill the hour — that is happiness; to fill the hour, and leave no crevice for a repentance or an approval. . . . In the morning I awake, and find the old world, wife, babes, and mother, Concord and Boston, the dear old spiritual world, and even the dear old devil. . . . The great gifts are not got by analysis. . . . Nature hates calculators."

But knowledge does not save. A wish, an intention, a thought, however good, do not by their existence become body. To have steam in the boiler, a fire is needed. Thought is not transformed into action by going through an intellectual process, by reason, or by rationalizing, but by having an emotion. It is easy to see why Emerson was incapable of turning thought into action. His emotions lacked transforming heat. In Emerson's day emotion was discredited. Feeling was kept out of sight, as if it were legs or some distasteful thing. The only time his mother ever astonished him was her sudden and spontaneous yielding to tenderness and thanksgiving when one day in his boyhood he came home safe after being thought lost. New England's distaste for emotional spontaneity was the product, no doubt, of a reaction. But now we have turned the wheel's rim, and there is a reaction against the reaction. We have seen Nature's wrecking punishments and have put up our hands to admit unconsciousness once more to its place in the circle of life. At the moment of writing, we find in a notice concerning the attractions of the school presided over by the philosopher, Bertrand Russell, not only " large wooded grounds " and " free access to knowledge," but a declared " attempt at intellectual achievement and social behavior without damage to emotional spontaneity." This perhaps heralds a new epoch in education, which, let us recall, means " a leading-out " of healthful faculties and not a driving-in of knotted, disconnected pegs of assorted knowledge. Had little Ralph Waldo been brought up on this program, instead of Mosheim's *Church History*, we might have had, as our gift to the nineteenth century, a Jupiter instead of an Olympian with a baked bean side to him.

VII

Regard the portrait of the man as given in the last illustration in this book. In it is the face not only of all his ancestors, but the features of a civilization, a race, a climate, and an attitude — Nordic, Protestant, Anglican, quintessentially Yankee; bound to believe, despite a sympathy with worthy men everywhere, in the ultimate superiority of his kind and clan, and that they alone are God's chosen. "The hard soil and four months of snow," he wrote very solemnly, "make the inhabitant of the northern temperate zone wiser and abler than his fellow who enjoys the fixed smile of the tropics." This was written, with conviction no doubt, by a man who had drawn the inspiration for his own wisdom from, and founded his own religion upon, the Hindu Vedas and Upanishads, products of the tropics. It is a belief which has remained unaltered among Emerson's kindred to this day, manifesting itself, on the one hand, in missionaries, and, on the other, in machine guns.

The aquilinity (from *aquila*, an eagle) of the face is saved from being merely hawk-like by the benevolence of the eyes and mouth, which soften a certain bleakness with humor and serenity. It is the face, to which harsher elements have been added, often seen in the portraits of Nordic-Protestant-Anglican-Yankee generals and business men, having that ascetic spareness which might to a casual observer have made Emerson appear to be a cousin of Henry Ford and John D. Rockefeller. Despite the predacious nose, however, it is not the face of the acquisitive or predatory man so often obsequiously captioned in contemporary newspapers. It neither hides uneasy fears nor proffers bogus propitiation. It is open, heliotropic, gently fearless; in its shaved angularity it is, to use a term lovely to the Nordic imagination, clean-cut. It represents the acme of all that Puritan, Protestant, Calvinistically disciplined America had to offer to the history of man.

Afterword

I NOTICE," wrote Emerson, "that the biography of each noted individual is really at last communicated by himself." All the quotations given in this book are, unless otherwise indicated, from his writings and are in his own language: from his essays, poems, or the ten volumes of the Journals, as edited by his son, Dr. Edward W. Emerson, and Waldo Emerson Forbes. Brief excerpts have been made from the Journals by arrangement with and the permission of the publishers, Messrs. Houghton, Mifflin & Co., holders of the copyright of important works by or relating to Emerson.

Among the chief biographies or biographical studies of Emerson are those by Cabot, Holmes, Cooke, Conway, Garnett, Ireland, Woodbury, Chapman, and Firkins.

The writer is indebted to all of them.

Index

INDEX

Kent, Mrs. W. A., 72
Kinglake, 244

Ladd, [Emerson's] Uncle, 59, 108
Landor, Walter Savage, 92
Lane, Charles, 220
Laud, Archbishop, 13
Lecky, 282
Lincoln, Abraham, 264, 266, 268
Longfellow, 272, 288, 295
Lovelace, Lord, 246
Lowell, James Russell, 156, 187,
    256, 272, 281
Lowell, Francis Cabot, 278
Lyell, 244, 246

Macaulay, 244
Macbold, Mrs., 243
Martineau, Harriet, 137, 243
Melville, Herman, 14, 308
Mill, 282
Minot, George, 169
Motley, 272
Motte, 38
Muller, Max, 283
Murat, Achille, 64–67

Newcomb, Charles K., 281
Nietzsche, Friedrich, 212
"North, Christopher," 243
Norton, Charles Eliot, 280

Ossoli, Count, 146
Ossoli, Countess — See FULLER,
    MARGARET

Parker, Deacon, 170
Parker, Theodore, 133, 162, 172,
    181, 183, 235, 266
Patmore, Coventry, 244
Peabody, Elizabeth Palmer, 48, 133,
    141
Peabody, Ephraim, 133
Perkins, Jacob, 105, 114

Phillips, Wendell, 172, 264, 274
Pierce, 272
Prescott, 227

Randolph, John, 253
Reade, Charles, 283
Renan, 282
Ripley, Elizabeth, 278
Ripley, George, 133, 181, 183, 194
Ripley, Samuel, 62, 68, 117
Ripley, Mrs. Samuel, 18
Ripley, Sarah, 133
Ripley, Rev. Dr., 171
Rotch, Mary, 111
Ruskin, 283
Russell, Bertrand, 312
Russell, Dr. Le Baron, 125, 279

Scott, David, 243
Schelling, 39
Stackpole, Lewis, 91
Stanley, Dean, 282
Staples, Sam, 170, 230, 267
Sterling, John, 286
Stetson, Caleb, 133
Sumner, Charles, 263, 264, 272
Sutherland, Duchess of, 246
Swinburne, Algernon Charles, 283

Taine, 282
Tarbox, 60
Taylor, Father, 162
Tennyson, 244
Thackeray, 244
Thenard, 95
Thoreau, Henry David, 24, 33, 133,
    146–149, 171, 183, 187, 188, 202,
    227, 230, 233, 242, 254, 267, 297,
    308, 311
Thoreau, Mrs., 20
Tucker, Ellen Louisa, 71–75, 77, 78,
    295